To Holli

Pray Every Night & ask
God to keep you safe
Read Psalms 91 in your
Bible

THE
ViBe

Love
Uncle Fred, Auntie Lois
Fred Alan Alex & Rachel

12/07

RAW AND UNCUT

VIBE STREET LIT
is a division of VIBE Media Group, LLC.
215 Lexington Avenue
New York, NY 10016
Rob Kenner, Editorial Director

KENSINGTON BOOKS are published by
Kensington Publishing Corp.
850 Third Avenue
New York, NY 10022

All Kensington titles, imprints and distributed lines are available at special quantity discounts for bulk purchases for sales promotions, premiums, fundraising, educational, or institutional use.

Special book excerpts or customized printings can also be created to fit specific needs. For details, write or phone the office of the Kensington Special Sales Manager: Kensington Publishing Corp., 850 Third Avenue, New York, NY 10022. Attn. Special Sales Department. Phone: 1-800-221-2647.

Kensington Books Reg. U.S. Pat. & TM Off.

ISBN-13: 978-1-60183-002-9
ISBN-10: 1-60183-002-5

First Kensington Trade Paperback Printing: October 2007
10 9 8 7 6 5 4 3 2 1

Printed in the United States of America

CONTENTS

FOREWORD

By Quincy Jones

The first time I was interviewed for *VIBE*, back in November 1995, staff writer Scott Poulson-Bryant asked me a question that I could not answer. It wasn't too personal, or too controversial, it was just that good of a question. What he asked me was this: *What is the Quincy Jones sound?*

Now, I have a sound as a composer, as an arranger, and as an orchestrator. But my sound working with other artists is something else. In the end, I had to tell him that I didn't know, because the sound you hear is the sound of me bonding with whoever I'm working with. It's the sound of love, of creating with another person, of exploring what kinds of sounds we can make together, like a musical conversation. When musicians get together and jam, there's a communication that takes place. Call it chemistry, a creative spark, call it whatever you want—but it's real. Something spontaneous happens and suddenly you're all there together in the zone. That's when the magic happens. It's all about love.

It's the same way with *THE VIBE Q:* our name for the magazine's most significant interviews with the people who helped to shape our music and culture over the past fifteen years. *THE VIBE Q* is way too real to be a normal interview. It's less an interrogation than a conversation, a meeting of the minds. Unpredictable things happen, and sometimes the truth comes out in surprising ways.

One of the keys to having a great conversation is putting the right people together: individuals who start from a place of respect and understanding and are willing to go wherever their thoughts take them. Like when Kevin Powell challenged Tupac Shakur to sort out his differences with people he considered his enemies. Or when Greg Tate quizzed Richard Pryor about anything he would have done differently in his life. Or when Chris Rock brought out a side of Michael Jordan that we seldom see—his sense of humor. Or when Ishmael Reed got with Sonny Rollins to explore what the bebop sensibility was really about, and how it connects to today's hip hop generation.

VIBE is a hip hop magazine that doesn't segregate hip hop from all that came before it. L.L. Cool J put it all in perspective in 1985 when he asked me, "What do the singers and the musicians think about us?" It was clear that folks had placed rappers in a third category, which, whether they knew it or not, has its roots in the *mbonge* (praise-shouters) and the griots who serve as the oral historians of African civilization. Hip hop is our latest black baby. It needs to be nurtured and respected and evolved. And it's not just a musical thing. It's about a sensibility, an attitude, a lifestyle. The bebop thing was like that too: so much style and flava, from the colloquialisms to the way you walked. Lester Young was calling Basie "homeboy" at least sixty years ago.

I have always believed that the hip hop community should take matters into their own hands and police themselves to respond to all the political attacks. It should not be a situation that works from the outside in. A lot of the rappers say they don't want the responsibility of being role models, but let's face it: They are. If it's a platform for rebellion, that's one thing. If it's just brain pollution, that's something else.

My dream would be that the hip hop nation, as well as all of our music, would constantly take a shot at being a guiding light, to show people some sunshine instead of clouds. We can report the conditions as they are, but right after the diagnosis there needs to be a prescription. I can listen to diagnosis all day long, but we need to fix it. Okay, you got gangrene, we gotta amputate or whatever. But sitting around mulling about gangrene too long—it'll just fall off, you know? So the prescription, the solution, is real important.

That's the bebop sensibility—an awareness, a hipness. Hip-hoppers have it too. At *VIBE* we're always interested in what's happening *now*— but still bringing our roots out. That's why artists like Stevie Wonder and Marvin Gaye were such giants—Donny Hathaway too. They brought all the greatness of the past into what they did. It's a cliché, but it's really true: If you know where you're comin' from, you know how to get where you're goin'. Those artists know what happened before. They don't think they just invented a whole brand-new music. There's not much new out there . . . just eleven notes—most of the time, just seven. And black folks been messing with them notes a *looooong* time.

With all the music that's available to the whole planet, from Kabuki to bagpipes, string quartets, all of it—the entire planet cleared their mind to adopt the music of the Delta and New Orleans and Kansas City and the South Side of Chicago as their Esperanto, to sat- isfy the need of their soul. That's a strange social phenomenon, and that's something I wish every young person in the hood or out of the hood would remember. That's a heritage that they should be very proud of. That's the main reason I started *VIBE*, to give our music and cul- ture the respect they deserve, not just today, but for generations to come.

Fifteen years after I founded this magazine seems like a good time to stop and take stock of where we've been, just to remind us of where we need to go. *VIBE* is an extension of what I've been doing my whole career because it all starts with the battle of the blank page. The whole communication and entertainment business is just based on two things: a song or a story. Everything else is just accoutrements. You don't call the singer or the producer or anybody else until you've got the song.

VIBE is a melody. Listen up!

L.L. COOL J

By Kristine McKenna
September 1992

GOING BACK TO CALI

During a break from filming his largest movie role yet, the legendary Queens MC talks about the L.A. Riots, keeping in touch with his ancestors, and why he feels like he's still in high school, getting chocolate milk for a quarter.

East Coast rap meets L.A. Style: Long Island-born rapper L.L. Cool J is sitting on the Twentieth Century Fox lot in his super-slick black Nissan Pathfinder, playing Lionel Richie's new tape on its hurtful sound system. A cluster of cardboard pine-tree-shaped car deodorizers hangs from the rearview. Dressed in a blue-and-orange Mets cap, baggy shorts, and a dark blue sweatshirt, the 24-year-old MC, otherwise known as Ladies Love Cool James, is interrupted occasionally by calls coming in on his cellular phone. At one point, actor siblings Joan and John Cusack drop by.

This lot is L.L.'s new favorite place to hang—understandably, since he's starring in a $39 million picture that could easily transform him into the first rapper ever to achieve white man's movie-star status. The film, his fourth, is *Toys*, directed by Barry Levinson and starring Robin Williams, John Cusack, and Michael Gambon. With his B-boy/model

1

face and well-toned shanks, a lot of people think L.L is the rapper most likely to succeed in L.A.'s shifting sands. Add to this a nuclear drive and steadfast focus. and you have a young man who never seems to lose his cool.

L.L. is at the tip of a long-running trend. Rap's early years were studded with feature films like *Krush Groove* and *Disorderlies*, modest commercial successes whose rapper stars were generally whacked-out clowns (the Fat Boys performed "Wipeout" in *Disorderlies*). Then came the resurgence of black-themed films a couple of years ago, and suddenly brothers like Ice-T and Ice Cube were inhabiting fleshy roles in unfunny films such as *New Jack City* and *Boyz N the Hood*. Cube's performance as the fatalistic Dough Boy in *Boyz*, in particular, seems to have legitimized the rapper/actor in Hollywood. At long last, the club was ready to give someone like L.L. a shot.

Born in Bay Shore, Long Island and raised In St. Albans, Queens, James Todd Smith began rapping at the age of nine. Four years later, he was laying down his own demos at home and circulating them to rap labels. One of these was Def Jam, a fledgling company started in a college dorm by Rick Rubin and Russell Simmons, who decided to make L.L.'s "I Need a Beat" their first release. L.L. was 16 at the time. The single went on to sell some 50,000 copies in 1984, and his debut album, *Radio*, appeared the following year. In 1987, his second album, *Bigger & Deffer*, sold 2 million copies—a shocking feat, one unequaled in rap until the dubious Vanilla Ice Age. *Mama Said Knock You Out*, his 1990 ("don't-call-it-a") comeback after the disappointing *Walking With a Panther*, returned him to his multiplatinum status, and L.L. was accorded one of the music mainstream's most heartfelt kudos—he was asked to perform his album's title song on the Grammy Awards.

L.L.'s rendition of "I Can't Live Without My Radio" was *Krush Groove's* high point. And In 1991, he appeared opposite James Woods and Michael J. Fox in *The Hard Way*. These were making-time movies, small-fry turns in middling projects. But L.L. was steadily stepping up to the big league. *Toys* is his largest role ever. Typically, he seems to be taking it all in stride. Ask him how the film's going, and he just shrugs, saying "It's cool." All he'll say about his role is "I play the son of an eccentric warmonger."

We talked to him as shooting was winding down, a few days before he headed back to New York to work on his fifth album [*14 Shots To The Dome*]. Overall, he seemed somewhat pensive about the prospect of leaving the City of Angels.

Q: *What's your earliest memory?*

A: Learning how to ride a bike—I taught myself.

Q: *You were an only child, and your parents separated when you were young. Was that a trauma for you?*

A: No, because it wasn't my fault. There's lots of people whose parents get divorced, and they spend the rest of their lives feeling like they're missing something. They feel dependent and want intimate relationships with other human beings, but they can't find it, and that's why you have a lot of teenage pregnancy. These girls and guys can't figure out how to find that connection that's missing at home, so they use sex, and what comes out of it is a baby, and they think the baby is gonna fix 'em. But they don't really want that baby—they want what the baby symbolizes.

Q: *You're an unusually self-confident person. Were you that way as a child?*

A: Yeah, I've always been proud to be me, and I credit my family for that. I don't believe in being weak, and that doesn't mean I'm a tough guy with no heart. I can be as tender as a lamb.

Q: *Did you do well in school?*

A: I didn't do great because the curriculum they teach in school is a left side of the brain type of curriculum that values analytical thinking above creative thinking. School was cool, but I liked gym and lunch better.

Q: *What things played a role in shaping your moral views?*

A: God and my grandfather—my grandfather was always cool. He worked in a post office and played the saxophone and was into jazz and had a calm demeanor. He was very soothing.

Q: *Were you raised in the church?*

A: I was raised to have an understanding of the church, but I don't really have a religion. I just try to get connected with my higher self and try to visit my ancestors and talk to them.

Q: *What do you mean by "visit your ancestors?"*

A: Ancestral communication is just asking your ancestors—people that you love yet have never met—what do I need to do? What's the move? This is something everybody needs to know because it will make the world a more harmonious place. People have to understand this is only a transitory state. We're not here for long, and when the day comes that we have to account for our deeds, this lifetime is gonna seem like one hour in an afternoon. It's difficult to believe in the unseen with all the material things that surround us, but people gotta realize there is a higher level of life and that we're on this earth for a purpose. We not just here floating on a round ball going thousands of miles an hour, circling around a sun that's nourishing it and shining light on it. The sun is millions of miles away, and yet some points on this earth are so hot it's unbearable. People have to understand the way that nature works. The way water comes down and evaporates, and that there's fresh water and salt water, and there are creatures that live underwater, creatures that live over water, and creatures that can do both. This is a perfect world.

Q: *Thank you, Rev. Cool J . . . Did you ever have a problem with drugs?*

A: No. People have to understand what drugs represent. Some people take drugs to tap hidden energies in their subconscious; others take drugs to escape, but the only thing you need for escape is meditation. Get into your mind, and you'll escape internally. Instead of worrying about experience, people should have *in*-sperience and tap into those energies within themselves; then they won't need drugs. I meditate. It helps me tremendously.

Q: *Did you experience much racism growing up?*

A: Sure, and I still experience it every day. I experience racism when I go into a restaurant, and they treat me great, and I know that if I didn't make music they wouldn't. I see them turn people away at the door and know the only difference between me and those people is a couple of albums. A lot of times I refuse to go in places like that. Other times I do go because life is a big chess game, and you have to understand the psychology of your enemy and deal with him. I encounter all kinds of racism, but I understand it. Take Hitler—he was the worst person in the world, and a lot of people think his mentality died when he did, but the desire for genocide still exists. God bless America, because I'm here, and I'm doing what I'm doing, but to be totally honest, I think the superstructure that runs the inner workings of this country has just done a better job of camouflaging racism. For the most part, black people and white people are raised differently. White people get raised to be superior and black people get raised to be inferior. Black people aren't from here—we were brought here from Africa 400 years ago, and we can't expect the same people who enslaved our forefathers to give us a break now. This isn't to say all white people have this attitude because they don't, but in terms of who's running the government, it's obvious how they feel.

Q: *Your music has been criticized for not being political, yet you obviously have strong political views. Why haven't you made them part of your music?*

A: Because I make music to let people forget about how hard life is. I take time in between my music to speak about these things because I want people to understand I do have political views, but they don't have to be in my music. George Bush doesn't have to listen to music about campaigning, and I don't have to be political in my music to have an opinion.

Q: Were you in Los Angeles during the riots?

A: Yes, and what happened here didn't surprise me at all. Unfortunately, the riots weren't the most effective way to deal with what happened with the Rodney King case. Those people should've taken all that frustration and anger and channeled it into mind expansion instead of ripping down their own communities. Obviously, it's the government of the society that educated those people—or *failed* to educate them—and taught them to act like that. When you teach ignorance, it breeds. The only way the racial crisis will be resolved is through a change in how people raise their children. The police and the looters all have set personalities that aren't gonna be changed. The change has to come much sooner, because racism isn't bred in the street—it's bred at home and you can't stop people from what they preach at their dinner table.

Q: Do you own a gun?

A: No, I don't feel it's necessary.

Q: Were the L.A. riots just the beginning of a wave of racial unrest in the U.S., or have we seen the worst of it?

A: Things won't improve until we start to heal the black family structure. If you take any race of people in the world and deny them the opportunity to bring home the bacon for their families, then turn around and hire their women, you're gonna have conflicts at home. The men lose their dignity, the women lose respect for their men because they're unable to get jobs, and this is how the family structure is torn up. This problem is a big part of what happened in L.A. Whether or not this was a conscious conspiracy on the part of the white power elite, it was put into effect, and it's working. Look at the corporate community, and what do you see? You see white men and black women.

Q: So, you think black women are less subject to racism than black men?

A: Of course—everybody knows that. When a big corporation decides they need somebody black, they go get a black woman, and when you go up the corporate ladder all you see is black women and white men and women. Take a walk on Wall Street and you'll see this is true.

Q: *How did you rise above these limitations?*

A: The power of God allowed me to achieve what I've achieved. It's faith in God, and how you react at the crossroads. There are many crossroads in life, and they aren't always major events. You're at a crossroads when you have a tuna fish sandwich you're getting ready to throw away, and you see a homeless guy and give it to him instead.

Q: *One of the points John Singleton made in his film* Boyz N The Hood *is that one of the reasons the black community is eroding is because black men don't stay home and provide role models for their children. Do you agree?*

A: Yeah, that's true but, it isn't because black men don't want to stay—they're too proud to stay. Part of fathering your children is being able to provide for them, and if you have people slamming the door in your face and hiring your wife, it's difficult.

Q: *You have two children from a previous relationship [with longtime companion Simone Johnson.] What's the most important thing you could teach your children?*

A: Not to be racist, but also how to deal with racism.

Q: *Will the world be a better or worse place in 100 years?*

A: Worse, because we're getting closer and closer to Judgment Day. So we gotta do the right thing now so we can have some fun later. [At this point the car phone rings and L.L. takes a minute to patch up a lover's quarrel with his girlfriend.]

Q: *How many times have you been in love?*

A: Never.

Q: *Never? That'll be unpleasant news to that girl you just spoke to on the phone.*

A: She's probably my first experience or the closest thing to that, but me and her just started seeing each other recently. Before this I've never been in love.

Q: *Is it true that you plan to get married soon?*
A: No, not yet. I'm not planning on it right now.

Q: *Have you ever had your heart broken?*
A: No. People say the pain of that allows you to go further, but it's not something I'm looking forward to. If it happens, I'll just move on. Life goes on.

Q: *Physiology aside, what's the most significant difference between men and women?*
A: Women are more emotional than men. And it's not that society doesn't allow men to express their emotions either—women really are more emotional than men. The emotionality of women can be a problem if you get into a situation where you're a puppet on a string and somebody's using their emotions to bounce you up against the wall. If you don't know how to deal with it, they gonna drive you crazy.

Q: *Do you like the way you look?*
A: It's cool. I'm alright.

Q: *How do you feel about your image as a sex symbol?*
A: You kiddin' me? That's ridiculous, because somebody handsome and sexy comes along every other month. That doesn't mean anything and it doesn't give you credibility because it doesn't last. What's important to me is making good music.

Q: *What do you think is the difference between self-confidence and conceit?*
A: Self-confidence is "I can do it because God is willing. I know I have the strength, and I'm gonna work and do the right thing." Conceit is "I'm the greatest" and not doing shit to prove it.

Q: *You recently made the comment, "I don't like to be called a rapper— I'm an entertainer." Why don't you want to be called a rapper?*

A: I don't mind being called a rapper, but I don't like it that lots of people think all rappers are the same. Don't think we're all a bunch of chicken wings in one Chinese basket, because it's not like that.

Q: *How has success changed you?*

A: I don't feel successful yet because I have a lot more to accomplish—I want to have economical, political and musical power. This isn't just about partying. That's cool, and that's part of it, but that's not all there is, and there are things I'd like to do. I'd like to see L.L. Cool J shelters and cultural awareness programs and youth organizations I've sponsored, but that stuff takes time, and it isn't something you do after four albums and think you're a star. I'm working toward being credible. For now, I still feel like I'm in high school on lunch line getting chocolate milk for a quarter.

Q: *What's the best thing about money?*

A: Unfortunately, money has a lot of power on this earth, but the only good thing about it is that it shuts people up, it allows you to provide for your family, and it gives you an opportunity to show God you're not selfish. Other than that—nothing. I'm not in love with money. You can't wave a watch and a car in my face and think I'm gonna jump, 'cause it's just not like that.

Q: *Has becoming wealthy made you more suspicious of the people who approach you now?*

A: No, because you have to be able to analyze what a situation is in order to get money in the first place.

Q: *Is it easy for you to trust people?*

A: There's a fine line between trusting and being foolish. I give everybody the benefit of the doubt, but I'm not walking around like a fool either. You have to accept people and wait and see if they're your friend when times get rough. Adversity tells you who your friends are.

Q: *In the past you've said you were only interested in movies as a way of exposing people to your music. Do you still feel that way?*

A: Working with Robin Williams has changed my opinion a little. This has been a great experience, and I'd like to do it again if I can find films that don't endorse stereotypes. My first film, *Krush Groove*, was a chance for people to see me doing my thing on film, and with *The Hard Way*, James Woods and Michael J. Fox were real nice guys, but this film is much more challenging and has made me more interested in acting. Barry Levinson has given me room to move and let me interpret the script the way I want to. He doesn't breathe down your neck and is a really good director. And Robin Williams has showed me how to play with acting.

Q: *How did you prepare for the role?*
A: I had an acting coach, and she helped me a little—she taught me how to be my own psychologist.

Q: *Have you ever been in psychotherapy?*
A: No, but I'd go and wouldn't be scared to talk. There's nothing wrong with expressing yourself.

Q: *What's the biggest obstacle you've overcome in your life?*
A: Being a black man and being able to provide for your family is a hell of an obstacle. That's a big brick wall, and I got over it through sheer determination.

Q: *Do you feel lucky?*
A: I don't believe in luck. I believe in the power of God and in doing what's right. Luck is for Vegas.

CORNEL WEST

By James Ledbetter
September 1993

2

CORNEL U

Brother West is America's hottest black academic, but can he act out the role written for Malcolm X?

I first encountered Cornel West in 1986, during weekly Monday-night installments requiring frigid uphill walks to the Yale Divinity School. He was teaching a class in 20th-century Marxism and, to everyone's shock, he was spellbinding. Not before or since have I heard anyone explain so clearly some of the most opaque political writers of all time. West's gestures echoed those of a Baptist preacher (his grandfather was an ordained minister), adorning his orations with movement bordering on frenzy. Then, as now, he could become so animated that his thin frame was transformed into a blur of arm-waving, knee-bending, and righteous shouting.

Since that time, the 40-year-old West has become perhaps the country's leading black leftist intellectual. In the first half of 1993 alone, he published three books of essays and speeches on topics as diverse as jazz, the black Marxist tradition, and Sly Stone. While West—now a professor of religion at Princeton—is certainly no radical activist, he is in many ways playing out the role posthumously scripted for

Malcolm X: namely, a public intellectual who seeks to educate the American black community, to criticize it, but mostly to express its anger. West also realizes that whites and other Americans need to heed the call, and thus spends much of his time working in multiracial coalitions. The task is immense, and there are times when West needs to draw deep into his well-seasoned humanism to meet the demands of his many audiences.

We wanted to know what West thinks about the social and political questions raised by hip hop, so we caught up with him in New York while he was touring to promote *Race Matters,* his best-selling book published earlier this year by Beacon Press. Wearing a trademark dark three-piece suit, with black-and-gold cufflinks bearing a silhouette of Africa, West discussed everything from Chuck D to Michael Jackson to the future of pragmatic thought. Here are the highlights of our talk.

Q: *In some of your statements about contemporary black music, you don't deal very often with so-called hardcore rap. Artists like Paris, Kool G Rap, and Ice Cube are strongly identified with the nihilism of which you speak—police brutality, the despair of neighborhoods ravaged by crime and drugs. What's your opinion of that particular subgenre?*

A: Well, first, there's something that I like about Ice-T and Ice Cube and the so-called gangster rappers. Paris as well. They attempt to do what I attempt to do as a public intellectual. And that is, to tell the truth. Now, any time when you want to tell the truth it's based on one's own experiences. And also in the truth-telling you're gonna have certain kinds of blindnesses, certain kinds of biases. Now, I'm deeply critical of misogyny, of the homophobia, of the preoccupation with the machismo identity that is associated oftentimes with violence. I'm very critical of that. But in telling the truth they do, in fact, express these kinds of unjustified sensibilities. Because that's where they're coming from. There's no doubt that there's a very, very powerful critique of white supremacy in the work. And that, to me, is a progressive element. That doesn't justify their refusal to come to terms with male supremacy and homophobia and to talk even more so about gender and class inequality. But the critique of white supremacy and the concern about what it means to live in poverty and so forth is quite strong.

Q: *But are these artists really accessible to a critique?*

A: Well, I think interviews like this are a vehicle. They actually read. I mean, these are serious brothers and sisters, in terms of trying to process, to mature, to develop. They don't want us to remain static and stationary in any way. So you've got a course of internal dialogue going on within the hip hop culture, where you get a variety of different kinds of criticisms of each other. In Arrested Development I think you see both implicitly and explicitly critiques of the kinds of values that gangster rappers invoke in the music. I think that's very good. That's especially so out there among the women rappers, you see. So that kind of internal dialogue, as well as the dialogue of critics from the outside, can make a difference. I think the critique of black patriarchy has had some impact on Public Enemy. Their attempts to respond by singing these songs about revolutionary black women and so forth. And my brother Spike Lee. I mean, that's one of the great lessons of *Malcolm X*, right? That here's somebody who not only has, you know, the courage to act on one's convictions but the courage, also, to attack one's convictions when those convictions are viewed more and more as impediments for freedom's struggle, you see.

Malcolm grew. Painful, but he grew. And I think when one looks around and sees Spike grappling with these problems, or a Public Enemy grappling with these problems, or anybody else, you have to give them credit. But you also have to continue to push. And I don't think you can push folks by simply throwing stones. You have to affirm what they've already done that is important. You have to criticize what they have yet to do. And then you have to leave yourself open to criticism even as you criticize. In that spirit, it seems to me, we'd be able to move America. But I don't think we can move everybody.

Q: *You said in an interview that one of the reasons jazz is so appealing to large numbers of white Americans is precisely because they feel that black humanity is being asserted by artists who do not engage in self-pity or white put-down. To what extent does that active self-expression apply to non-jazz black music today?*

A: I think if you're talking about jazz from a genius like Louis Armstrong to the best that we have now with Wynton Marsalis, you're talking about levels of artistic achievement that soar. And black humanity is taken for granted. Now, I do think that black humanity is taken for granted in non-jazz musical groups [too]. Rhythm and blues, hip hop, and so forth. I think that non-black people do feel that they have access to black humanity most readily in these particular forms. Because, again, the tradition that they've refined in the black community, that the levels of self-confidence and the relative lack of self-doubt are operative. And that's rare. Because white supremacy has played such profound tricks on black people's minds that the struggle with self-doubt, the attempt to hold at bay self-confidence, is much more difficult than in other spheres. So that I do believe it's music, athletics as well. Because, in fact, we've seen, you know, from Sarah Vaughan to . . . to Michael Jordan, reaching the highest levels of achievement and accomplishment in these traditions.

Then all of a sudden the groups are younger. Hi-Five, Silk. Let alone Boyz II Men. And you say, man, these young brothers have really seriously cultivated the craftsmanship of singing again. Which is a wonderful thing. And they're some serious artists. But Gerald Levert was, I think, the one figure who towered above the others in terms of sustaining the highest artistic expressions of the deep soul singers. And you got people like Aaron Hall. He's tough. And then you got somebody like Glenn Jones, you know, I mean, those are major torchbearers of deep soul singing. I'm not just talking about the kind of stuff I do in the shower. This is some serious soul singing. In the same way, my generation, somebody like Charlie Wilson and his brothers, in the Gap Band, from Tulsa,

Oklahoma, that's some serious soul singing that you're talking about.

Q: *In "Black Music and Youth" you talked about the profit-driven need to increase the production pace and numbers of records. And, hence, the reinforcing of fashion, fad, and novelty and the overload of black popular musical talent. This is about as close an approximation as I could find in your writing to the German cultural critic T. W. Adorno's assertion that, despite its anti-establishment stance and the very real debates that it provokes about social issues, hip hop and other popular musical forms in fact serve to perpetuate and legitimize the market economy and social order it seeks to criticize. Is there any way out of that seeming paradox?*

A: The way Adorno sets it up there's no way out. That's part of the problem. You see, I don't look at it that way. I think that the market itself is a crucial terrain in the struggle for non-market values. The opposition that is always already in the market does, in fact, have impact regarding the possibilities of alternative views, of critiques, of sustaining traditions of resistance. The market for me is a terrain that, in its dominant form, is tilted to status quo. It's tilted to reproducing things as they are. But there's always, within the market itself, oppositional possibilities.

Q: *You've discussed in* Race Matters *how black popular music and athletics have Afro-Americanized white youth. Can you flesh out this concept a bit?*

A: You see, Afro-American culture has been able to generate a variety of different styles, especially stylizations of the body over time and space. You walk a certain way, you talk a certain way. You gesture a certain way. You speak rhythmically. And all of these are various forms of resistance in a society that has degraded your body because you got the wrong nose, because you got the wrong lips, you got the wrong hips, and so forth. And style, as we know, is a certain way of being in the world. And to affirm one's way of being in the world for a people whose body itself has been so thoroughly degraded and told they're nobody is to create various stylizations of the body to assert they are somebody. And so one sees these various styles manifested in the streets, in the music. And those styles have been disproportionately influential among young white girls and boys. Teenagers across the board, you see. The music goes hand-in-hand with it. But it's the styles as well that we don't want to lose track of. The question then becomes, well, what is attractive about these styles?

Q: *Good question.*

A: Yeah. Why is it associated with being cool? Why is it associated with being hip? Why is it associated with being able to feel sure of oneself? I think James Brown's category of feeling sure of oneself is a fundamental category. Because it has to do with not just self-respect, but with the ability to affirm oneself. Well, when we look at the larger society we see young people growing up who are deeply disoriented. Who are deeply dislocated. Who are rootless. Who are deracinated and who also are in quest of feeling sure of themselves as white, or brown. Or Asian. And there is not a youth culture out there that provides them with these resources of feeling sure of themselves that is separate in any way from these black cultural products. And so you find it's not a majority, but there are vast numbers of white youth who, in order to feel sure of themselves [adopt these styles]. And this is very different from skill acquisition. See, that's not associated with black folk. You can have white youth involved in so-called intellectual matters that are severed from the social and the cultural skills. And so you can see this kind of schizophrenia at work. This is also true for black kids. You see, because the skill acquisition is not cool, it can easily be translated to becoming a white thing. Which I think is silly and foolish but it is understandable.

But for white youths, they're set with skill acquisition, but when they look at various sources of feeling sure of themselves they fall back on black stylizations of body, black stylizations of time and space. And begin to imitate, begin to emulate, now, again, unfortunately, oftentimes the nerd and the square are associated with skill acquisition. A's in school, debate club, and so forth. That's something that I'm quite critical of. I like to think of the tradition of Duke Ellington or Count Basie or Billie Holiday in which cool actually embraces all of this. So that we don't have this kind of dichotomy. If you get the A's, you can play the violin and you can sing like Luther and you can still play basketball. And that's kind of the description of my own life. But it's difficult to pull off. I think, for example, of my class at Harvard that arrived and most of us had these styles but we were still able to move on, engage in skill acquisition. And, hence, end up the kind of cultural hybrids that we are.

Q: *You've mentioned the notion of role-playing and masks in the black tradition spilling over into hip hop. How significant is that in terms of setting up a model for black listeners or white listeners?*

A: LeRoi Jones pointed this out, I think, with great insight in *Blues People,* which is still such a classic. Talked about two different features. One is the sense of pageantry, the sense of the performative, the sense of the histrionic, and the sense of the theatrical. And you do have this very much in the Afro-American culture. You see it in everyday life, as well as on the stage. A sense of dramatizing one's self-presentation. Preaching is one of the great examples of this. But also, the way in which brothers are interacting in the barber shop, or the sisters interacting in the beauty salon. There is always this very dramatic dimension that goes hand in hand with how one presents oneself. I think it's no accident that once it's married with market strategies, you get a role-playing and a mask-wearing that is quite seductive, because black folk are so good at it.

Now, there is another element to keep in mind here, and that is that black people have to function in so many different worlds. You've got DuBois's notion of double consciousness; moving from one world to another; speaking different languages in the white world and the black world, in different portions of the black world, and different portions of the white world. Black people become thoroughly multicontextual, which requires mask wearing. You think of Paul Laurence Dunbar's great poem: "We wear the mask." And he talks about how you put on a certain mask in the white world, so that the white world really has no access to who you may actually be.

Now, in addition to that, though, LeRoi Jones goes on to make the point of what he calls "the deification of accident," which is this sense of wanting to go to the edge of the cliff, and then start walking on a tightrope. It's like Marvin Gaye. The whole history of black falsetto singing is, in part, an attempt to go as far as you can go, and see how high you can go. See, it ups the ante. It makes it more dramatic, you know, like the Teddy Mills of Blue Magic, or L.J. Reynolds, you know, or Ron Banks of the Dramatics. Or Eddie Kendricks of the Temptations. He's going to go as high as he can go. When is he going to break? He can't keep going. He just keeps going up there.

That's one thing I noticed about radio stations these days that's very upsetting. They're very different from when I was growing up. What distinguished black radio stations from white radio stations was that the black radio stations always played the record all the way through. And the reason was because at the very end of the record, all hell's breaking loose. They're taking all the risks, they're going off. Because in the middle of the record, they're in control, you see. And at the very end . . . *waaah!* They're going off. And black people would wait to listen to the end. But the white radio station is cutting it off two-thirds of the way through. They think the record is over, just because two-thirds of the record is over, you see? Now you've got black radio stations that cut the darn records off the way white radio stations do. So I'll call these record stations up. I say, "Play the whole damn record."

Q: *In your review of Cedric Robinson's* Black Marxism: The Making of a Black Radical Tradition, *you talked about the tension between traditional Marxist thought and the experience of Afro-Americans, which doesn't fit so neatly into the categories of European Marxist analysis. You seem to think that some kind of modified Marxist theory is the most appropriate approach. But today, most American* *black intellectuals, or black radicals even, opt instead for a nationalist or Afrocentric view, in varying degrees of sophistication. Is that a situation that you would seek to change?*

A: Well, I would definitely seek to change it. I do believe that black national traditions—as diverse as they are—do have a variety of different insights: the crucial role of culture, and the self-love and self-respect and self-esteem. And the black nationalists tightly highlight the degree to which you can't talk about being in a black body, and then at the same time not having to deal with these assaults.

But the reason why I think the Marxist tradition is still important is that you do have to deal with the fact that it's a capitalist society, and a global economy that's driven by profit-maximizing. And you've got corporate and bank elites who have a disproportionate amount of wealth and power. If you essentially talk about black freedom, let alone freedom for working people, poor people as a whole, then you have to keep track of the activities of these elites. You can have all the black nationalism you want, you can have all the black self-love you want. But we're still going to have black poverty unless you come to terms with the distribution of wealth and power in this society and in the world.

Q: *In writing about Toni Morrison, you said, in what I think is a beautiful passage: "Beloved can be construed as bringing together the loving yet critical affirmation of black humanity found in the best of black nationalist movements, the perennial hope against hope for trans-racial coalition in progressive movements, and the painful struggle for self-affirming sanity in a history in which the nihilistic threat seems insurmountable." Do you see any such unifying moments in today's hip hop?*

A: Hmm, good question. That's interesting that you picked that up, though. That's one of the few passages I'm really proud of. In hip hop . . . I don't know. My hunch is that there would be moments in Arrested Development where I find that. Because, you see, it has to be a group that has a deep organic link to the black culture and black community. It can't be simply a kind of universalistic statement that doesn't have grounding and anchoring in the black cultural tradition. And Toni has that organic grounding. Arrested Development has that organic grounding. And therefore they're able to build with the best of black nationalism, and also a whole lot of possibility for a transracial or multiracial alliance. One thing I like about Toni's work is that it's critical of religion as it affirms spirituality. And I think that's true for Speech and company too, that they're engaged with religion. They know that there is a depth of spirituality in this tradition that has gone moribund, that must be recovered if we're going to have any serious movement. Because the people who have been so thoroughly hated and haunted and degraded and despised have to fall back on spiritual resource in order to affirm themselves as human beings before we can get anything political off the ground.

Now, I must say that for me, growing up, I found it in Sly Stone. I think that it's no accident that they tend to fall back on Sly. Because Sly was one of the first who represented, for me, this kind of deep organic link with the black community, but with an explicitly open humanistic outlook. But it wasn't a kind of cheap humanistic outlook that you get from some black folk, who really hide and conceal an obsession of whiteness. And that's always a danger among a degraded people, that you get your highly assimilated elements who are talking about universalism. And that universalism really doesn't fundamentally embrace their own tradition. They're talking about chasing after somebody else's tradition. Now, I'm a thoroughgoing universalist. But like Sly, like Arrested Development, it's got to be grounded in whence I come, even though it is critical of elements of my tradition. Or there is a risk of me simply going universalist in whiteface as a black person.

I think that's part of the problem with Brother Michael Jackson. You know, here, on the one hand, we have one of the greatest entertainers in the history of entertainment. Comes out of a very undeniable black working-class background in Gary, Indiana. Who is organically linked. I mean, you hear young Michael singing "Who's Lovin' You" . . . that brother, he is as organic as James or

Aretha. But at the same time, as he goes mainstream, he begins to articulate ideals that we all share. We all want to be human beings, you know, we don't just want to be viewed as carriers of a certain kind of epidermal right? But how you articulate that can easily be severed from that same tradition that enabled you to be here. One thing about Michael that I like is that he has a level of sincerity that people don't really know about. He can get into his own kind of mask-wearing and role-playing. But deep in his heart, he's got a deep sincerity that is one of sensitivity and love. And that's real, I think.

Q: *Have you ever been to a Michael Jackson concert?*

A: I went to his concert when he was 10 years old. And it was one of the finest performances of a young person. But I went to see him out at the Meadowlands about four years ago. And I'll tell you, it is a transcendent experience. Given all of the gigantism, he still comes through. He's on for about two and a half hours, and he's got the same intensity as James, in terms of wanting to reach the audience. He's not as effective in terms of creating the connection that James Brown was able to do in the '60s. But he comes closer than anybody else. And then, at the end, when he sings "Man in the Mirror," it goes dark, and everybody's got a candle. There are tears coming down, and they're not all crocodile. Some of them are. But not all. It's a moment of transcendence. It really is.

WESLEY SNIPES 3

By Danyel Smith
October 1993

THE TROUBLE WITH WESLEY

*Hollywood's first black action hero crashes motorcycles,
packs a semiautomatic, and heats up the bad guys—
onscreen and off.*

I t's a rare, smogless L.A. day. The sun is high and bright, the
Pacific waters bluer than usual. Wesley Snipes's house overlooks a
tame stretch of Venice Beach. No musty vendors hawking dusty
Blu Blockers. No bikini'd rollerbladers or ancient pop-lockers. The
boardwalk is dotted instead with lazy, leashed dogs and their distracted
owners. Sand cops patrol in sluggish four-wheel-drive vehicles, and
freckled, sinewy young white people play two-on-two volleyball with
unrestrained glee. Today is Wesley Snipes's day off. His natural, dyed
an ugly blond, looks chemically exhausted. His hairline is shaved, cut
into an extreme recession. His mustache is gone. The new look is for
the futuristic villain he plays in the thriller *Demolition Man,* co-starring
Sylvester Stallone (for which Snipes reportedly earned $4 million).
With *New Jack City, Boiling Point, Passenger 57, Rising Sun,* and even
White Men Can't Jump, Wesley Snipes is, without question, the first
black action hero. He's striding confidently through Hollywood, an

Ebony Man demigod, firing quips ("Always bet on black"), shooting down his enemies, existentially cool.

On the other hand, with *New Jack City, Mo' Better Blues,* and an upcoming project called *Sugar Hill,* Snipes may well become, as *New Jack City* screenwriter Barry Michael Cooper puts it, "the black Pacino." Out of the Townsends, the Fishburnes, the Gooding Jr.'s, and the Espositos, Wesley Snipes—all sweat and intensity and ghettocentric melodrama—is the chosen one. He is Tupac Shakur buffed to a glow, James Earl Jones in a badass B-boy stance. He's a kente-cloth-wearing, Africa-identifying Sidney Poitier for the '90s. He fills the hole left by Eddie Murphy, elegantly and without the guffaws. And, he's more of a sex symbol than Denzel Washington.

He's been performing for as long as he can remember. Briefly attended the High School of the Performing Arts in New York City with Gina Belafonte, actress Vanessa Williams, Steve Weber, and Esai Morales. Shot a little pool for bus and pizza money. Finished high school in Florida after his mother moved the family there, and ended up going to SUNY-Purchase on a drama scholarship. He got married his senior year, got divorced last year. He's been a phone installer. He played a drag queen in *Execution of Justice* on the small stage. He's been on Broadway and *All My Children*. His son, Jelani, is four. It's been quite a ride from the Bronx to Hollywood.

His airy, nearly furniture-free domain is cool and comfortable, but fat drops of perspiration form on his nose. He smiles and the tiny gaps in his teeth show. He looks for a minute like the boy a former school-mate describes: "Skinny," she recalls. "Wesley was a very normal kid from the streets with a radio." And like the student a former drama teacher remembers: "Very vivid and energized," says Roz Shine. "Alert, bright, quick. He was willing to do anything. He had a strong desire to succeed."

Now, sitting in his home, he seems molded from strong, elastic clay. He studies martial arts, used to be a Muslim. He's a talker, a neo-griot. He has a penchant for getting into trouble—like the recent not-so-minor trouble of crashing his motorcycle and getting arrested in L.A. for carrying a concealed 9mm semiautomatic. He chugs Snapple raspberry iced tea, then easily sips wine. The bleached-wood floors are dustless, there are big, beautiful hurricane lamps, dozens of reggae and jazz CDs, a large bowl filled with coconuts, oranges, and bananas. He's wearing black Cross Colours jeans, a gray T-shirt, and white athletic socks. He wants an air-hockey table. He likes his roof. His bed is low to the ground. His closet is painstakingly organized. He's got a huge punching bag. Blue drinking glasses. Could use a few throw rugs. But then, he doesn't really live in Venice Beach, or Brooklyn, where he has a house, or Florida, where he has another.

All the rooms are a weird shape, and he likes it that way. When we speak, he is at the beginning of two weeks off. He talks of going to Egypt maybe, he thinks, or Brooklyn "for a minute." By his own account, he's been a gypsy for the last two years. Steady working. No steady girlfriend.

We talk for eight hours straight.

Q: *What do you like most about this house?*
A: It's open. I don't like anything square. I wanted triangles, ovals, and circles. A square room is negative on the body. Africans, Native Americans, and Eskimos don't have square rooms. They have angles, circles, arcs. Scientifically, a square room is a haven for positive ions. Positive ions are dust. Germs. Small particles that have a positive charge, but have a negative effect on the body. They draw on your energy. So you want a room that produces negative ions, which are positive for the body.

Q: *How do you know all that?*
A: I studied the shit.

Q: *What do you like to do in your spare time?*
A: Ride my motorcycle. I like the speed, the freedom, and the excitement.

Q: *What kind of motorcycle do you have?*

A: I have a Kawasaki Ninja ZX1100, which goes 178 miles per hour top speed. I've driven it 145. I mean, my voice caught up to me. When I stopped I heard my yell. I mean going 125 miles per hour is mind-boggling. I feel safer doing it on a bike than I do in a car. Because unless you're in a high-performance vehicle, where you can feel what's going on with the road, you're kind of removed from it. But with a motorcycle, your awareness is so heightened, you can feel every single thing. About a month ago, I had *another* motorcycle. I was gonna meet up with these people, go up on this cliff and ride motorcycles. And when I woke up that morning I felt like, "Something ain't right." This is off, you know, it's a little weird today. So I get up to wash the motorcycle. I got rags and stuff like that. I mean, it was a spankin' bike anyway, and it was like, people was riding down the street looking at me. So I go to the boulevard, where I usually eat. I had my little breakfast. Then, I'm riding home, and I'm like, "Cool. I'ma hurry up and get home, meet these people, and then we out, have a great day," the whole time thinkin', like, "All right, brother, do not get in an accident," because you know how that is, the one day you looking forward to doing something, that's the day when you do somethin' stupid. So I'm checkin' and ridin' and I'm saying, "Don't go too fast," you know, 'cause I'll ride hard, but today I was like ridin' nice and easy. Now, do you know what I did, stupid me? I left one of the rags that I was cleaning the bike with on the motorcycle some-where. And before I could get past La Brea and Slauson the bike caught on fire.

Q: *It caught on fire?*

A: Bike caught on fire, girl. And people was honkin', *honk, honk, honk,* and I'm like, "Yeah, right, honk, honk." And I look down and went, "Oh shit!" So I pulled over and I tried to smack it out. Every time I smacked it, more fire and plastic would come off on my glove. So now my glove's on fire. Then somebody came along with a fire extinguisher and put it out.

Q: *Did people know it was you?*

A: Yeah, when I took my helmet off, yeah. They was like, "Snipes, what's up with your bike?" I was like, "Hey man, joint caught on fire." And then the cops came by. They was cool. Then I'm sittin' there with two helmets in my hand and some gloves and stuff waitin' for my boys to come find me and they came past and never saw me. I'm sittin' at the bus stop and the bus comes by. The bus driver says, "Hey, Wesley, you want to get on?" I'm like, "No, no, no. I'm just fine. Thank you very much. Take care." I was playin' it off. But I never got upset.

Q: *But your bike was ruined.*

A: Well, that's why I make movies. I buy another one, you know. I don't have that type of connection with material things.

Q: *Do you only drive a bike? Do you have a car?*

A: I drive a Lexus now. I didn't want to get a Mercedes or something like that. The cops mess with you too much. All the brothers talk to Ice-T about how many times he gets stopped. He's got a big old Rolls-Royce . . . T got *everything*.

Q: *How did you get involved in martial arts?*

A: That was my mother. I was very, very short. I don't know if that was a part of her motivation, but it was when I got to class, you know, that as a short man, I would learn some techniques to be able to deal with guys who are larger than me. I was the shortest one in the whole group. Yeah, small, skinny, you know. If a good wind came blowin' by, I'd blow on down the street.

Q: *What was the worst mistake you've ever made in your career or in your personal life?*

A: I don't see a mistake as negative. Mistakes are there to teach you, and they have to be there. If you don't make any mistakes, you'll never know what good is. I look back on some situations and say, "Nah, I had to go through that." That makes up the fiber of who I am.

Q: *How does it feel to be divorced?*

A: Good. I mean, I don't feel . . .

Q: *How did it feel at the time, Wesley? I'm sure it didn't feel good at the time.*

A: At the time it was terrible. We were married about four years. The last year in college we hooked up, and decided to hang out with each other. The sadness of the divorce was the result of not seeing the dream, the ideal, become reality. Like having a wife and a family, 2.5 kids, a muthafuckin' fence, and the dog. They tell you that's what you're supposed to have. But that may not necessarily be.

Q: *What's your favorite food?*

A: Spanish food. That's probably a result of my ex-wife. She grew up in Puerto Rico. You know, I love sisters. I don't see any distinction between a sister who speaks English and a sister who speaks Spanish. There's no difference to me. It's a sister. Now, there's a big difference between a white woman and a sister. That's a whole 'nother groove, this whole thing of race and of who's seen with whom. I know I've got myself into some really interesting circumstances by saying in articles that I deal with black women.

Q: *I've read those articles.*

A: Right. Now, in sitting and talking with me, it's cool. But what would happen if you saw me walking down the street with a white woman after reading those articles?

Q: *I would think to myself, "Danyel . . . Is that Wesley Snipes? I swear to God I heard somebody say he didn't even like white women." That's what I would say.*

A: Right. Good, good, good, good.

Q: *But you're not saying that you don't like white women. You're saying you deal with black women.*

A: No, that's not what I'm saying either. What I'm saying is that you took what I said and then formulated a whole, overall opinion that suggests I can't even be seen walking with one. So if I'm seen walking with one, that means what I said in the article is bullshit. I lied about it. And that's what I've come up against now, even on the street.

Q: *So you're saying a black girl has called you out for walking down the street with a white girl?*

A: I'm just a brother who said that most cats don't say that they acknowledge black women, that they love and care for black women. Look, I'm a black actor. I was black before I was an actor. I'm gonna be black when I can't act no more, and my acting is defined by how much work I do anyway. My title can be snatched from me, depending on the work I do. But you can't take my blackness. I can only give it away. But that doesn't mean I'm not gonna be see walking down the street with a white woman. You don't know what the circumstances are. She could work for me. She could represent me in some aspect. So don't all of a sudden just paint my whole personality as being isolated and segregative to white people. I'm not segregative to white people. At some point, maybe I'll have an opportunity to sit down and really have a serious dialogue with some sisters who have open ears, and who want to understand how it happens that, maybe, a black man might end up with white women in this business.

Q: *It sounds like you have some ideas.*

A: Absolutely. For one, there's very few sisters involved behind the scenes, and even fewer in front of the camera. On a consistent basis, the judgment of the actor, of people on the actor, is if you're seen in a movie with a black person, "Well, okay, that's a black film." So you have to be in movies with white folks to be validated as an artist. Every artist wants that type of validation, that universal acceptance. That means that you predominantly end up in films where you're the only black person on the set. So, given that this is the characteristic of your life, your natural desire to be happy will begin to make you selective. You will begin to choose the best thing out of all your options to satisfy you.

So that means if you workin' 14-hour days, seven days a week, around predominantly white women, you're gonna, at some point, choose the best of the white women that either is closest to black, to you. Or that you can get along with the best. That's a natural process. The longer that goes on, the more that solidifies. The more you become comfortable with it. And you look forward to it. And then, because you're in that arena, and you're comfortable in that arena, when you move back to where the brothers and sisters are at, you're not comfortable anymore. So your rap is different. You don't know how to get your rap off. You don't know how to sit and, culturally, laugh at the right type of joke. So now you're alienated from that which you are. You understand what I'm saying?

Q: *I understand what you're saying.*

A: So now, *boom,* you go back to over here, because this is comfortable. You don't have to work as hard, which is the other reason: Sisters are gonna demand something out of you. They want you to prove that you're a brother in your taste, in your things you like, in your loyalty. Now white women come to this in a little different way. Sisters are about, "Okay, you're successful, fine. You can think you're successful. But I'ma let you know, just because you're successful don't mean that you just gonna run up in this mix. So you show me why I should give you my time and my energy. And don't even think about sex. You'll get that down the road, when I know that you are worthy of it."

Q: *Now, all sisters aren't like that.*

A: The majority.

Q: *Some sisters would be sayin', "Wesley? Is that Wesley?" Panties down.*

A: I'm tellin' you, *it ain't like that.* They say that when they're hangin' with you and all your girls. But when you step up to the plate? No. It ain't like that. First thing you hear is, "I know you got a whole bunch of women. You can get any woman you want. Why me?"

Q: *Okay. So then what do the white girls say when you "step up to the plate"?*

A: Oh—they understand. They say. "We know that you're successful, and that's why I'm here. Matter of fact, I'm gonna stroke you on your back because you're successful. And even when you suck, I'ma tell you that you're successful. The objective is for me to get you." Now, I'm not sayin' that across the board. Sometimes brothers have a little bit more flavor than the white boys, and white women like flavor. So they go, "Well, hey, he's a little bit more animated. He's nice. He's funny." And she naturally gets attracted to that. But there are others who say, "Well, yo, you know, sisters don't want him. You're successful to me. You're really *good* at what you do. I love your movies. I loved you ever since I saw your movies."

Q: *Sisters don't do that?*

A: No, not all the time. That's a part of our culture. That's a part of our inability to accept success, to give respect to success, not unless it's just so overwhelming. But you know how cats say in the 'hood, "I ain't sucking nobody else's dick." And that means that you don't give anybody too much props because, you know, that makes you look like a punk. That is purely a cultural thing. We say that's the way it is. No, that's the way we've been conditioned to be. White folks ain't like that, though. They'll give you credit. They'll suck your butt. They'll let you think that you are the baddest thing that came along. We gonna let you know that we want you at all out parties. And we want you to come with us to the yacht, and come play golf with us. They have no problems in givin' it up. Even white boys, walkin' down the street, be like, "Yo, you the man! Snipes, you the man!" I went to a fight, white boys was up in the stands like, "Snipes!" Brothers ate real cool with me, but then, the other side of it, the sisters are a little bit like, *"Okay."*

Q: *With all the movies you've been in recently, are there any actors or directors that you've learned from?*

A: I learned a lot from Stallone. He's cool. Maybe back in the day he might have been a little difficult, but, hey, this is a cat who was struggling all his life. He was beatin' the pavement and fighting against people and getting ridiculed. Take nothing away from him. His films have made more money than anybody's in this business. I mean Arnold Schwarzenegger, he got the International Star of the Decade award. But Arnold's movies have not made, worldwide, the money that Stallone's movies have made. I'm talkin' about $2 billion. That kid is really something else, you know. What he'd tapped into was a whole 'nother groove.

Q: *What did you learn from working with Sean Connery on* Rising Sun*?*

A: Consistency. I'm a little beyond the level of how to play a scene. Now I'm into the intricacies of line delivering, you know, and how to apply things that we do in our normal, everyday life, in those weird little moments, to a scene that has specific, structured boundaries.

Q: *What about Denzel?*

A: Understating. He underplays a lot of his work. *And* the subtleties of that are valuable. But at the same time, there's two sides, there's two poles to the line. So I'm always pickin' up somethin' new from somebody else. I learned a great deal from Christopher Walken on *King of New York.* I think a lot of how I act and approach work now was influenced by his work because Christopher embodies a sense of completely unpredictable freedom in creativity. I'm always impressed by how he did something. I'd say, Now, I done thought about 16 ways to do that scene, but I didn't think about that one."

Q: *This year you have about 46 movies coming out. What are you going to do to top that in '94?*

A: I'm going to do a project that's like a real offshoot of the James Bond films.

Q: *I heard you might be Miles Davis.*

A: Yeah, we're gonna do that. I went after that. It went around to a couple of different people. I was like one of the first people Miles's family approached.

Q: *Miles's life was very intense. How are you going to tell his story?*

A: We're gonna come at it from the artistic value of the man, the dynamics of the man. We ain't gon' just talk about his drug habit and how much he cursed and how he dissed women. Everybody knows that. But that's not the real makeup of the man. And that may be the result of a bigger story.

Q: *Is it going to be better than Clint Eastwood's* Bird*?*

A: I love Clint. Clint, you know you're my man, but I'm gonna tell you right now, if it ain't, I'll kill myself. We don't need to do it if it ain't. Clint is real cool to me, but . . . Hey, you ain't told me about *Bird*. You told me about a fuckin' drug addict who played saxophone.

Q: *Amen-Ra is the name of your production company, which is producing the movie. What does that name mean?*

A: The hidden sun. Amen-Ra is the combined name that deals with the Egyptian concept of a deity. Ra was the sun in one part of Egypt. And in another part of Egypt, they called it Amen. With the unification of upper and lower Egypt, they called it Amen-Ra, but it was their word for the deity who gives life to that which is unseen. And I chose that because, numerologically, it's perfect. In and of itself, it generates power.

Q: *Are you into numerology?*

A: I'm not so much into the numerology as I am into the sciences, the African philosophical way of cosmological metaphysics. That's basically why I chose the name.

Q: *Not many black actors now would have the opportunity to be involved in that type of project in a producing capacity. Do you see any other black actors who are on your level? Eddie? You and Eddie runnin' around now?*

A: No. Me and Eddie don't hang . . . but I guess that's a good question. I don't know, you know. I think Larry Fishburne is a more versatile actor than I am. Larry Fishburne is one of the most versatile actors I've ever met in my life. I saw that when we worked on *King of New York*.

Q: *What makes you angry? What makes you frustrated?*

A: The thoughts and the perceptions that white America has about black folk and the ones that we have about ourselves. I see the circumstance that happened to Rodney King as an offshoot of a bigger problem. We parrot the behavior of white folks. We believe that everything that they have done and designed in front of us is the way. We buy into this Third World bullcrap.

Q: *We're the First World.*

A: Got to be! They're the Johnny-come-lately ones. Their formative years, in the span of time we have documentation about, ain't but a eye drop. They're still a baby. This is infancy. But we still buy into that. We still have so much collective self-doubt, distaste, and distrust for one another and ourselves. That pisses me off! It's like a joke, you know? When are we going to stop saying, "All human beings are the same. All of us are together. We should love everybody." That's bullshit! Because people don't feel that way about us. When that whole thing went down in terms of the uprising, it was a waste of our time. If there was really concern, the people that should have been out there burnin' up shit was white folk. It should have been white folk right there in the courthouse. And not white folk with black people. Just white folk. No black people. No Spanish people. Nothin' but white folk.

Q: *Why?*

A: Because they hold the most weight, and what they say means something. Everybody else listens to how they respond and react and channel their discontent. But they didn't do that. So I don't want to hear none of their patronistic little sympathy. It's a bunch of garbage. You get out there and you do something. And you say you care? Nah. If they understand us and truly respect us, and feel that what happened to that brother is inhumane, they'd expose all the problems within the system. Why we got to get out there and march? Why are we wastin' our time talking to 'em?

Q: *Then is the only option for them to give us Texas and we all move there?*

A: Well, if we can really control it, it's not a bad idea. [*laughs*]. But we don't see that because our choices have been dictated to us. And we don't see that there's other choices out there. For instance, a unified front of people who collectively understand that the collective body of the European countries, the European mind, has disdain for us as African people. They do not believe in us, they do not really care for us. The first thing we do is that we come together all of us, no white folks from any white-folk countries—and talk about the problems of African people on the African soil and in the Diaspora. And we work on getting a consensus about what the problem is and how to solve it. European people have that kind of consensus. The Japanese have it too.

Q: *There's a myth that says Africans don't like African-Americans.*

A: Bullshit. It's a myth. But Africans do not like a black American coming over there acting like a white American. You also have to distinguish the people that are African and the ones that have been colonized, and now become pseudo-colonized black-a-Saxons, you know [*laughs*]. Afro-Saxons! You got to worry about them cats, because their agenda is totally different. They want to be like the white man.

Q: *They want to be like white America.*

A: I want to be an African man. I think I embody what African manhood is about. The African man is the universal man. We have always been a part of the universe. We show more compassion to everybody else in the world than we show to ourselves.

Q: *How do you feel about the whole idea of being a role model?*

A: I accept it. And it's my duty to be so. You know? I know I have a positive and powerful effect on young minds. The things that I do, the way I act, the way I talk is going to influence people, and anybody who doesn't say that is full of shit.

Q: *For a role model, you sure know bow to play those tough guy roles, Wesley.*

A: That's the evil side of me. I'm not evil, but I'm a hothead. I'll push it. If I like you I will like you. There's no middle ground. Hey, you know, I'm trying to adjust, because I mean I used to fight when I was a kid, so . . .

Q: *When was the last time you had a physical fight?*

A: '90. After I finished *Jungle Fever. Mo' Better Blues* came out, but it wasn't like you immediately associated me with it. Anyway, a guy robbed my car. I caught him and whupped his ass. The guy smashed the back of my window and took all my cassettes out. So my partner Scott told me, "Yo, man, there's this thing about criminals, they always come back to the scene of the crime. It's something psychological to see if they got away with it or not." So he suggested we just wait there.

There was an old homeless-looking man standing on the stoop with his son. So his son goes, "Yo, I'll help you out, man. He went around the corner; he always does that around here." So we went around the cornet, looked in the garbage, and, *boom,* there's about 16 of the tapes he didn't like! So we go back to the spot and, I swear, within 10 minutes we saw the son on the other side of the street pointin', like, "Right there! Right there! Right there!" Suddenly this Spanish kid comes right in the middle of me and my man. And it's the muthafucker who robbed the car!

Q: *How did you know?*

A: Because he goes, "Hey, Pops! The car is gone, right? They're gone, right?" Pops doesn't say nothing. Then Scott sees that the dude had my cassette case strapped over his back. Scott said, "Yo. That was my *man's* car," and he pulled the case off the dude's back. And that was all I needed to start swingin' and kickin'. I mean I would knife-hand him, I would ridge-hand him, hit him in his nose.

I'd sidekick him, snapped him in his knees. *Boom!* Hit him upside his head, elbowed him in the face. Blood was just goin' *every-where.* It was so violent, the women that came out on the street started screamin'. But he kept goin', "It wasn't me, bro, it wasn't me." I felt that he was disrespecting me. He was lyin'. Every time he said, "I ain't do it," I hit him dead in his face. I hit him one time, and bop! He dropped. He just fell out right on the ground.

Q: *You're a straight fool, Wesley. You're a movie actor. You're not supposed to act like this off-screen.*

A: Nah, that ain't got nothin' to do with it. This was in my act, and this is the 'hood. This some shit in the 'hood. Then cops came out of everywhere. It must have been like seven cop cars. And I saw all the cop cars and I freaked. I just froze.

Q: *So what happened?*

A: That muthafucker took off runnin'.

Q: *What did the cops do?*

A: The cops weren't even out their cars yet. I hauled off after the dude. Finally, two cops came, and he stopped. When he went to turn the other way, *boom.* I was dead on him, like WWF, with an elbow smack dab in his face. He hit the ground. I picked his head up, and I was scrubbing his face on the ground.

Q: *You're a fool. Are you serious?*

A: Yeah. And get this: the cops let me do it. They ain't stop me. I'm tellin' you, it was five cops standing around me. The person who pulled me off was my partner, Scott. He's the one that said, "Yo, the cops gonna arrest him."

Q: *Did they arrest him?*

A: Yeah, after I let him go.

Q: *Oh, God. That story is too deep for words . . .*

A: I know it is.

Q: *What do you think about the new wave of black cinema? Do you think it's in a kind of renaissance? I ask because you haven't really*

been in a whole lot of the new black films. And you probably could have been in all of them.

A: Right. All of them. Every one of them came across my desk. But it's convenient now. It is monopolizing on what the new fad is. What white folks didn't calculate was that it would be their sons and their daughters who would turn against them, that they would start bringing the music home, that their role models would become black people. They didn't gamble on that. And because the children's role models are black people, now it makes it even more difficult for them to get away with what they're doing.

Now you get an influx of all of these films that they're down with. It's like, "Show me a day of a nigga in the 'hood. Give me the life of a nigga on the block. I want to see what the niggas on the block with a gun are doing." That's fine. We done seen it, we done done it. But that's what's making the money.

Q: *Now you're sounding like Spike Lee.*

A: If you really respect the artistic contribution of black folks, then we don't want to do no more movies about a nigga in the 'hood, 'cause a nigga in the 'hood ain't no more different from a pimp on the block back in the '70s. and you see what happened to that. After they didn't have no more pimps and they told every pimp story they could tell, *boom,* end of the industry. So we gotta change the movies, start doing movies that go beyond just a nigga in the 'hood.

Q: *Tell me about your upcoming movie called* Sugar Hill.

A: Drama, drama. I play a son. I play a brother, a heroin dealer in Harlem who became very successful and was connected with the Italians, and I'm the brother who wants to get out of the business, find a better life for myself. Michael Wright plays the brother who wants to expand and kill off all rivals who threaten our business and also keep his brother with him. I find the love of a woman who exhibits misguided genius, you know, beauty. It's gonna rock everybody. It's got deep performances in there, like Clarence Williams III, Leslie Uggams, Michael Wright, Glynn Turman, and

Ernie Hudson. It's gonna be deep. It still deals with gangsters, but it's a different approach. It ain't about spinning cars in the middle of the street, bang, bang, shoot 'em up. It's about how they're surviving and their lives.

Q: *Now that you've done all these movies and gotten so much attention, do you feel famous?*

A: No.

Q: *Even though people run up to you on the street and say, "Wesley, my name is so-and-so, and I'm beautiful. And what you doin' later on tonight?"*

A: No. It doesn't compute, "famous." And for the people that it computes "famous," those are the ones that find themselves in a world of trouble. I'm famous to my son, Jelani, who looks up to me. And everything I do is wonderful. I could pull a booga out of my nose, and he's like, "Oh, daddy, you're the greatest." But I'm not famous in that sense. I'm a young cat who's doing what he feels he can do and doing the best at what he can do. Nothing more, nothing less. And the side effect of that is a couple of people like me. That's only the side effect. I don't think I'm the *best*. Like I said, I think Larry Fishburne's a better actor than I am. So I can take it. I mean, that's cool with me, you know.

Q: *So you aren't falling for this whole black renaissance thing again, right? Or are you? Do you think there's a black renaissance going right now?*

A: Yeah, but I don't think we've seen the real blossoming of it. The spring really hasn't come for it yet. I think it's gonna come, though, when we'll be able to embrace artists on all levels, not just the ones that get the "high profile," but also the ones that are lesser known, but of a greater quality. Like back in the days of Bird and Coltrane and Wayne Shorter and Thelonious Monk—all them cats. There was a period where nobody knew who they were, but they were all there. They all put their chops down. And then after they had been out chopping and choppin', they hit it. So I think that's what's happening with the whole black renaissance. It's coming. It's definitely coming, but we ain't seen spring yet.

I just want to be around when it happens. That's my prayer—to be around when it happens, when it *really* happens, when the art begins to influence the behavior and the condition of the society, not when it's just society exploiting it. Yeah, I really want to be around for that.

Q: *Me too.*

A: That's gonna be a day like a muthafucker.

GEORGE CLINTON 4

By Vernon Reid
November 1993

BROTHER FROM ANOTHER PLANET

*George Clinton freed our minds. If only our asses would
follow. Vernon Reid, guitarist for Living Colour and founder
of the Black Rock Coalition, builds with the godfather of
funk as they fearlessly explore love, sex, drugs, and the real
secrets of the Clinton Administration.*

It's in the air. Suddenly, funk is everywhere you turn. Rappers
sample it, rockers like Prince and the Red Hot Chili Peppers invoke
its muse. Several major record labels have funk reissue series in
effect. Afros and platforms proudly walk the streets once again.

And, as always, at the center of it all is George Clinton, the
Maggot Overlord himself, ruler of the Parliament-Funkadelic army for
close to 30 years now. Check the climax of Dr. Dre's "Let Me Ride"
video. Where's everybody going? To a P-Funk concert, of course, and
even Dre (who has spearheaded the resurgent Clinton madness) knows
enough to disappear from his own clip and clear the way for some
mind-blowing footage from the Mothership Connection tour—The Bomb
exploding all over your MTV.

Clinton's time has come again. After more than a decade out of print, four classic Funkadelic albums are due out any minute on Priority Records. *Tear the Roof Off,* a near-definitive 2-CD collection, recently put Parliament back on the R&B charts. The long-dormant Funkadelic—including Bootsy Collins, Bernie Worrell (who's also the newest addition to David Letterman's band), and who knows who else, the ones who first melded metal guitars, soul rhythms, and doo-wop harmonies—are in the process of signing to Dallas Austin's Rowdy Records and planning a "Mothership Reconnection" tour for next year. And, best of all, Clinton's first major-label album in three years, titled *Hey Man . . . Smell My Finger,* is a glorious return to form, a reminder to all these new jack funkers that there is only one true master.

Q: *My first concert experience was seeing Funkadelic in 1973 at Madison Square Garden, and it seemed like I was witnessing some sort of ritual. It was very powerful. What was it like to actually be onstage in the middle of all of that? It was very, very disciplined, but very loose and chaotic at the same time.*

A: Yeah, consciously that was our intention, to do chaos and order at the same time. We came from Motown. I always knew that I had been trained as a producer and a writer and there wasn't nothing else like the discipline they had at Motown. Having done that, then we saw Cream and Vanilla Fudge and all them take the music that my mother liked, flip it around and make it loud and it became cool. We realized that blues was the key to that music. We just speeded blues up and called it "funk" 'cause we knew it was a bad word to a lot of people.

See, I do hair. So cool to me ain't nothing but a style. You may be cool with this style in this city, go 50 miles to another city and be cornier than a motherfucker with your dress, your clothes, your music, and everything else. So I never worry about what's cool; I believed a long time ago that even Flagg Bros. Shoes was cool somewhere. Over here you could get your ass kicked for wearing them, but someplace they were cool to somebody.

Q: *How did funk come into being?*

A: Our show was basically R&B and we got happy and became, you know, like churchy. Still trying to keep our shirts and things but playing like we were gonna be hippies. And once we experienced what you could do to people just jumping around from soul to blues parts of our songs, we realized that nobody could even be our competition and we didn't have to worry about doing it fast—everybody in the band would tell you that I said it's gonna take 15 years for this to work, but we'll have a job. Once we realized that it was hip to be a bum, we were the only ones doing it. And it was that way for a long time. Everything was so loose on Funkadelic and so sloppy that when you hear the records in the right order, it confuses you. Did they accidentally do that right? Or did they accidentally do that wrong? But it was no accident.

Q: *You broke convention in so many ways.*

A: I did it on purpose once I realized the first album worked. We broke all the rules intentionally, and there were enough people who liked it. There were enough hardcore fans that liked me in Boston, Detroit, Toronto, Cleveland, and in all the colleges. And then the hippies and rock, that whole era to me ended with Woodstock. Most people think that's where it began.

Q: *Because that's when it turned into an industry?*

A: Yeah. Instead of sharing a tab or sharing a joint, it became "We want to buy." That whole era changed in no time. After that, if you were a hippie you was a Jesus freak. And the danger of that was Charles Manson—people who really didn't want to let go, who really loved the idea of death. They were getting really dangerous. All of a sudden people were like junkies, and all the hard hats would come up and beat up the hippies.

Q: *On records like* America Eats Its Young *you were dealing with those kinds of situations.*

A: N.W.A, Ice Cube, and all of them say it now, but I said it in a way that I tried not to blame nobody for feeling like they feel 'cause you're hip to be that way. You're hip to feel that way. But it had to be said that if you don't like the effects, don't produce the cause.

Q: *My introduction to your music was the record* Cosmic Slop. *My best friend in school at the time—he's selling insurance now—he turned me on to this record and the thing about* Cosmic Slop *is the compassion: you are talking about a mother who is a prostitute trying to shield her children. In her nightly prayers, she prays for forgiveness. She says, "Don't judge me too strong." You've always shown a tremendous amount of love and compassion for people who would normally be outcast in society and be called out by name.*

A: Like they deserve whatever they get.

Q: *Even in your strongest protest songs, there was still a sense of aspiration, of striving for transcendence. It was never just about the negativity.*

A: See, you're a damn fool if you see somebody starving and poor and you think that they should just stay starving and poor and not take care of them. Whether you're really starving or not, if you believe you're starving, you're starving. And if I got some little bit of money and I ain't making sure that you got some, I'm a damn fool if I don't expect you to come and try to take it. It's not as easy as each person is responsible for being in their predicament.

Q: *Oh yeah. "Pull yourself up by your own bootstraps."*

A: Conditions of society dictate everything. Poverty breeds privilege, straight out. So if you're just enjoying the profits of it and worrying about somebody taking it—you are responsible too. It ain't got nothing to do with goody-goody; it's self-protection.

Q: *When you listen to a lot of the younger brothers today, especially people doing gangsta rap, they say that they're reflecting reality. And there are times when I hear this and I think to myself, do these people really think that they are the only black people who've had to face hard times? Now times are bard, harsh, brutal, but you have to think about what a brother such as yourself experienced when you were young.*

A: The difference is we always experienced those things, but now the media and everybody else tells you about your experience of it. Yeah, they're reflecting the streets, but they get a lot of help. The radio stations will play that. The record companies will buy that. The kids are just trying to make some money. Now if that's what makes the money and if that's what the media is asking for, then everybody will go out and make that.

Q: *Now, I'm not nostalgic for the '70s, really, but I came up as part of that era. I was listening to your music, to Hendrix, to Sly Stone, to James Brown. And while that was going on there was a real sense of community. Those bands were doing commercial music, having hit records, but there was always a sense of . . .*

A: Something that's ours.

Q: *Something, yeah, I mean—soul. A general sense of "love your brother." We've always had gangsters, we've had pimps, and we've had criminals, but there's something different now.*

A: It was flashy then. Even pimps. Being a pimp was more of a show-biz thing, just like somebody getting a barbershop and telling lies about "my babe's got this amount of money" and "my babe's got that amount of money." These were the ways to bring the money into the barbershop. When rap came along, it was basically a news service with messages starting right out telling you what was going on in the streets. And dissin' the Sucker MC. See, the Sucker MC was a fictitious character so you could beat the shit out of him. Women and pimping has always been a part of our jokes. You know, even in blues, playing and drinking and hustling. But then rap starts talking about politics, which it's very good at. Hip hop got an Islamic influence, a certain amount of Five Percenters, and they have customs that come from another culture. We may not want to treat our women like that, but what's disrespectful here may not be like that in the Arab world. Where you get in trouble is when you get the two of them mixed up together when you are about 15 years old—a mixture of the Five Percenter philosophy and that "Bitch, Ho" mentality, which is basically just fun and games if it were by itself. If it were by itself, it would be just some-body stylin', hustling and showing off. But when you add the Five Percenters, you think you've got a legitimate reason to hate, to dis these women because they are supposed to stay behind.

Q: *I want to jump from this and talk about the funk, about the music. I always wondered what it was like to be in the studio with Parliament or Funkadelic cutting a record. Like, what was it like when y'all cut "Flash Light"?*

A: By the time we cut "Flash Light," it was just like a factory. Y'all come in and do something. You three come in and do something. First of all, the track was Bootsy's track. He didn't want it. He couldn't hear it so I took it. By then we already had done the Motown thing, harmony, scat, so with "Flash Light" I wanted to make a song like a Michael Jackson song. And then I always devi-ate from a love song just before I finish it. I try to make the love not just one-on-one, but love for all of us. Not to be goody-goody, but I think love songs get cheap. I hate songs like "we will die together." Those songs are too easy to pimp. But "Flash Light" was really about how many voices—there was like fifty voices on that one song. Okay, y'all three, five, ten, or whatever, sing five tracks. Then a whole other section would sing it. And then we started getting particular about it. First it was just the jam. Give me a crowd like you're at the baseball field. Then, okay, let's see how precise we could get that. Bernie [Worrell] taught me about motifs. You get a melody, you have every motherfucker playing it—every-body did that in "Flash Light."

Q: *Running a theme through . . .*

A: Yeah, like a movie. You get fast, you get slow. You play it on another instrument.

Q: *I love that chant in "Flash Light," 'cause it makes me think of something from opera that just showed up.*

A: It's a Jewish Bar Mitzvah chant of a friend of mine. "Da da da *dee* da da da." There was a whole lot more to it. I just took that part out of it 'cause it was a long thing.

Q: *You just took out the funky part.*

A: Aaron Myron, he went to my grade school. I never forgot it. I just played it over and over, but then you add "You turn me on." All of that was just theme on top of theme so everything kept coming around.

Q: *What about something like "Maggot Brain"?*

A: "Maggot Brain" meant how the fuck can we straighten up something if the tools that we have to use is rotten? The tool we are gonna use to straighten shit up is our brain. If that's already rotten, you startin' off fucked up. Once you admit that that's gonna kill you, you can begin to change some.

See, even when I was using drugs, I always made music so important in my life that nobody would ever be able to say "That nigger did that only because he's on dope." But paranoia is your high with crack. It's the same as driving fast, climbing a mountain, doing all those things that scare the shit out of you. My high then was I was gonna fuck up my career—all that I've done and people would be telling the truth if I fuck up right now. I don't regret having done it. It was the motherfuckin' education that I needed. Nothing happens for nothing. I don't know everything, 'cause I thought I knew everything. I done had coke all my life. Somebody gave me a 'base pipe and I took one hit. It was so unbelievable, I called everybody that I trusted right then. Said, "I don't know what the fuck this was, but I will be doing it again and anything that is this good I know that I owe some more besides that hundred dollars I paid for it."

Q: *How were you able to pull back and get out of it?*

A: "Atomic Dog." "Atomic Dog." "Atomic Dog." Once I realized that I had a hit and we've got to go on the road, I was so paranoid of fucking up. 'Cause I knew everybody was saying already we spent all this money on dope. In the '60s, we did acid to death, but I ain't never been able to do coke without shaking. I did freebasing and I always had a joint in my pocket everywhere I went. But when it came time for that motherfucker "Atomic Dog" to come out, I was so afraid of fucking up. Paranoia is the high, you just have to know that.

Then I moved south of Detroit 40 miles into the country so it would be a hassle to get back into town. And I was lucky because it worked. After about three or four months of running back and forth to town, you get halfway there and the urge wore off. 'Cause it may not be there. You know you got enough for a gram, but it'll be gone before you get back, you got one hit when you get back. I was so glad to see that I could say, I'll wait until tomorrow.

Q: *What do you think the cost of drug use has been to Sly?*

A: He's okay now. He ain't doing it now. But he done did two or three sets of drugs like that. I never could understand anybody liking Angel Dust, but he did that and cleaned up. Then when crack came in, he did that way past most of the people I know that did it. Then all of a sudden he just stopped it. There will be another one, though. There will always be something.

Q: *As a guitarist, Eddie Hazel's playing on "Maggot Brain" was really important for me. Just recently Eddie passed away. How did you feel about his passing?*

A: We had worried about Eddie so long, we just didn't know what to do anymore. He was sick, said he was sick for so long.

Q: *I played with him—jammed with him a few months before he died.*

A: And he was talking about it then—that he was gonna die.

Q: *He played really well. He played great. But he just seemed really distracted. He seemed like he was somewhere else.*

A: But he was like that all the time. He was so emotional he sang and made himself cry. He was so sensitive that consequently he rarely sang a whole song because he would get too emotional. Once I got older I couldn't talk him out of it. When I was younger we all stayed together. Whatever it took to cut a record. But after a while I got tired, you know. Just give me two minutes and I'll make a record of it. You play anything for two minutes and I'll make a record. Because somebody in the band is gonna nod off before the shit is over anyway.

Q: *One thing about P-Funk is the whole sense of community. Having fun is the bottom line, but it's not just having fun. Like "Chocolate City," that's one of those records that want so much in the 'hood, where I grew up in Brooklyn . . .*

A: But you also heard about the Vanilla Suburb in the same record.

Q: *You included everybody.*

A: If some aliens come from another planet, we are human beings. We are human beings whether we like it or not. But we still depict ourselves as black because certain people look at us that way and they'll piss you off and make you have to protect yourself because somebody is pulling the strings to make gays and straights fight blacks and whites fight, the abortion fight. To me the best way is to get out of those kinds of things. If I catch myself hating a white motherfucker, I'm wrong. One motherfucker ain't got no business hating another.

Q: *There's always been that universal, "One Nation Under A Groove" thing in your music. What do you think of the more Afrocentric, more separatist philosophies?*

A: They have to say it. Everybody has a different degree of tolerance; it's like Martin Luther King and Malcolm X. Malcolm said, "I hope you do it Martin's way. I hope we don't have to do it my way." That's when I knew Malcolm, before he went to Mecca, 'cause I watched him on the box up in Harlem long before he became Malcolm.

Q: *That's interesting; my father recently told me that he saw Malcolm X speak.*

A: He sat up on the box every day. He sat on the box up there across from the Apollo like those guys you just think are crazy today—he did that every day and you had to listen to him to know he was cool. But when the shit is right, everybody agrees with it. Ain't no different than what I would want or what, say, Ice Cube would want, just the way he says it. People are just plain pissed and can't take it no more. Most of them just try to make records. But you can't take the brother's anger away 'cause that's fear. If he could not rap then he might kill you. When you find out about it, it may be too late.

Q: *Picking up on that, the P-Funk mob grew to be a huge extended family with Parlet and the Brides and the Horny Horns . . .*

A: The older Parliament just came back with us. Grady [Thomas] and Fuzzy [Haskins—the two of whom split off and recorded as Funkadelic in 1981] will be back too. Fuzzy will be back as soon as he finishes his Jane Fonda workout tape. He weighs 300 pounds now.

Q: *Well, that's great because all the groups were working and everything, and all of a sudden it seemed like everything kind of fell apart.*

A: You know how it gets, everybody wants a little bit more money. We've been close since we were 14 years old. It ain't like I didn't understand what they were doing. Managers and people are telling them that they can get a little more, so they had to try. But I never sued them about it. I didn't sue them for using Funkadelic. Everybody tried to get me to sue them. I didn't fight [drummer] Jerome Brailey for the *Mutiny on the Mothership* record, even though that was a title of mine. See, everybody is Funkadelic. The audience is Funkadelic. There's somebody in D.C. who copyrighted the name Funkadelic. We never stopped using it so he had to stop, but he tried it. And he wants to sell it back to me for a dollar if I introduce him to Prince.

Q: *You're saying that somebody went and copyrighted . . .*

A: Copyrighted the name.

Q: *Who never played with the band or nothing?*

A: Just like samples. It's an extension of sampling. Some people like to sample part of it. Some people like to dress up like us. Some people just go out and actually start writing the name and saying,

"I'm Funkadelic." Billy Bass played with him. Eddie played with him for a minute. And I didn't raise no hell about it. Because it ain't nobody's fight. So the reason why I went back on the road is if I get visible you can't do that shit.

Q: *We're gathered today to celebrate a new George Clinton record. How do you like your new record? How do you feel about it?*

A: I really like it. I was made to wait four years to get this record out.

Q: *What was that all about?*

A: Ain't no real record people in the business no more. Ain't none—and no black folks—so soon as somebody else say, "Well I don't know," then they don't know, either. I wasn't about to put another record on the album or cut nothing out. Kerry Gordy came in, Berry Gordy's son, to work on the record. I even babysat the dude. I told him I could get Ice Cube, Dr. Dre, Yo Yo, I could get all of them on a record. I wasn't about to cut no "Paint the White House Black." I thought that was the corniest title 'cause we already did "Chocolate City." I didn't want to do that shit no more, but Cube and them, they can say that shit and it ain't so old. So he went straight back and said to the label that anybody who can't get a hit record with Yo Yo, Dre, Cube need to be fired. When I heard him say that, I'll do anything you want.

Q: *I really like the Prince cuts. What's it like for you working with Prince because you influenced him so much?*

A: He's so fucking bad. He's so bad that nothing excites him. You can play the funkiest shit, he just nods his head—like he just expects it.

Q: *You don't think he was excited working with you?*

A: He's like me, I get excited too. But I do it in the bathroom. Flush the toilet and come out and pretend it didn't bother me.

Q: *So tell me, has Prince told you how to pronounce that symbol?*

A: I told him—hermaphrodite. That's what it is. Both sex objects is a hermaphrodite. I know two of them personally.

Q: *How well?*

A: When I grew up, I knew one guy. He got a job in a carnival. You're born with it—with both sex organs and one of them don't work. A lot of animals are born like that. But one of them don't work. You can't fuck yourself [*laughter*]. You can't do that. No, see, Prince thought he was really being slick when he said that and that's all it is. Promotion.

But I told him and everybody, when it came to my title I'm not changing that, because I've been promoting an album titled *Hey Man . . . Smell My Finger* too long, and the fans pay attention.

Q: *The only band that people follow the way they do P-Funk is the Grateful Dead.*

A: We got a lot of Grateful Dead people coming to our shows now. People want to believe that somebody stayed together and lived.

Q: *It's devotion—to you as the Maggot Overlord, but also to Bernie and everybody.*

A: Bootsy, Garry [Shider], Mudbone [Cooper], some people don't do nothing but just be there. Calvin and Grady. I know goddamn well they did not expect to be here. I just come out of the clear blue. "Why don't you get your ass on back over here? It's time."

Q: *And you'll get them all back out?*

A: Fucking right. One thing we never did was fire somebody. Everybody always left and come back on their own. Sometimes they come back and we ain't got no room playing guitar so they'd end up playing bass, but they did come back. You know, when Calvin and them left I understood. I told them I was gonna buy a spaceship they thought we should buy cars and houses. I said, I swear to God a spaceship will take you farther than that car will. They got a little Seville and because I wouldn't buy a house and a Seville they figured they had to break off and thought they weren't close to me after a while. They sued me. They lost and we stayed friends at the end. Most people, I think, would not even be able to speak. I never let it get to that.

Q: *What price do you pay for being in the center of this swirling thing? What kind of toll has it taken?*

A: I get off on the funk, to tell the truth. Don't tell me I can't do that. 'Cause I know how joyful it is. I had planned to be here when the shit came back in as nostalgia, so it wasn't no big surprise to me. I had planned to be here to keep it from being like Chuck Berry and Little Richard and be more like Jimi Hendrix. So it wasn't like I wasn't gonna be here.

Q: *Do you regret anything?*

A: Yo, fuck no. That's a waste of fucking time. If I have a fight with my wife, I say that all the shit that we said, we better put in a song so at least it pays for itself. [*Laughing*] You can't stop yourself from arguing. But you ain't got to mean that shit either. My thang is, I'll be alright by Thursday. I've always said that. You're gonna rerun that picture, run that mother over and over in your mind until probably you forget it. And then you ask yourself, why the fuck did I worry and hurt so long about this shit because eventually I was gonna get over it.

So don't read me wrong; sure I regret. If you just gave somebody some pussy I might pout for three, four, five hours. But I ain't leaving and we'll be alright eventually so ain't no sense in me go runnin' about "you dirty bitch." I do understand mothers that can't look at it like that. You know, I understand that. I ain't gonna tell you 'cause I don't know, but Thursday will be here and your monkey ass will be forgotten.

Q: *What's the funniest thing that ever happened at a Funkadelic concert?*

A: I used to get naked all the time and run around onstage. My main fear was if the electric cut off and the music stopped while I was out there. I mean, if the music stopped, lights come on, you got to get up nakeder than a motherfucker. I always worried about that. And finally when that motherfucker happened, I hit the floor and was crawling through people's legs buck naked trying to get backstage. The people laughed like hell and the band laughed 'cause I had nothing to put on. Finally I just got up and walked. As long as the music is going you're cool. You're cool as a motherfucker, but when the music stops and you're out there buck naked and the lights are on—get your naked ass out of here.

Q: *I remember they used to advertise the shows, "George Clinton promises to keep his clothes on. Come out please, Earth, Wind & Fire, Funkadelic, and George promises to keep his clothes on!"*

A: The last time I did that was out of the spaceship in D.C. I was buck naked and up to one step and my shit was standing right up. They caught it sticking straight up. I left well enough alone. My mother said, "Boy, you point that chitlin' at somebody else—you never take your clothes off." Sly said, "Don't learn no better man. If you knew better you wouldn't do that shit."

But, man, fuck the hassle. It's a charge to some people—"Woe is me, woe is me." Fuck me. Now I've got room to do something. As long as I got "woe is me" in my head, I ain't got no room for nothing else. See, love is unconditional. It ain't, "If you do this, I'll do that." That ain't no love. When you love something, you'll love it whether it's there, gone, or whether it loves you. Not to say I'm not gonna be pissed for an hour or two, but, you know, only until Thursday.

ICE CUBE 5

By Joan Morgan
March 1994

THE DEVIL MADE ME DO IT

*Once he was AmeriKKKa's Most Wanted. Now Ice Cube has
a wife and family and he's embraced the Nation of Islam.
He says he's older, wiser, and true to the game, but has hip
hop's leading prophet of rage lost his edge?*

It's a beautiful day in Encino, California. A good day, if you will, in
the spanking new offices of Ice Cube's fledgling company, Lench
Mob Records. Cube's wife, Kim—a very pretty, very pregnant woman—
drift by every once in a while to tell him about an important call he
needs to take or affectionately chide him about the growing piles of
clutter on his new desk. He says it isn't messy; she says it is. Their
wedding picture occupies the one spot on the desk that is relatively
clear, a constant in a pile that seems to be ever-shifting, ever-shuffling.

It's been almost four years since Cube's debut solo album,
AmeriKKKa's Most Wanted, marked his graduation from a mere nigga
wit attitude to the nigga America loved to hate. Lookin' back, we were
ripe for it. Cube broke out at a time when hip hop was definitely on
some ol' "I feel pretty" shit. Nubians had discovered the elixir of self-
love; Afrocentria abounded—sometimes *ad nauseum.* But as Langston

Hughes once wrote, "We know we are beautiful. And ugly too. The tom-tom cries and the tom-tom laughs."

Cube came ready to serve heaping mounds of ugly. On *AmeriKKKa,* he emerged as the sonic personification of unmitigated black rage. It was violent, sexist, powerful, relentless, funny, and painful. It was also seductive as all hell. For white America, it was a voyeuristic look into the world where racism causes its equality-starved victims to feed upon themselves. For black folks, it was a long, cold, hard look in the mirror. There we were, ass out for the world to see, and all the Brooks Brothers/kente cloths, relaxers/dreadlocks, embarrassment/denial in the world were not going to change the fact that these "negative" characters were very real fixtures in the black community. In pain and insane.

On his second full-length album, 1991's *Death Certificate,* Cube stripped away the comforts of voyeurism and showed white America what *real* unmitigated black rage would look like if it ever made its way out of the ghetto. The picture was not pretty. Jews, gays, and Asians were the newest victims to get caught in the cross-fire. And many of the oh-so-liberal observers who sang Cube's praises when he was rhyming about niggas killing niggas and smackin' up bitches (read: black) were now demanding he be silenced by any means necessary. In 1992, Cube gave his critics the definitive "fuck you" when *The Predator* premiered at number one on the charts.

A lot has happened in Cube's life in the last two years. He's happily married, a follower of the beliefs of the Nation of Islam, and the father of a little namesake (O'Shea Jackson Jr.), with a baby girl on the way. Fans and detractors alike will tell you that Cube seems a lot less angry these days. His new album, *Lethal Injection*—funky, melodic, and relatively laid-back—has left some listeners grumbling, "the Nation and married life done got to Cube" and others wondering if the absence of ire means that they need to find a new vehicle for their own catharsis.

Over the course of several hours in his office, Cube spoke—full of riveting insights and maddening contradictions—about work, life, family, relationships, and how he intends to survive the pressures of being the world's most celebrated angry black man.

Q: *How conscious were you of your audience when you were making this record? On* **Death Certificate,** *for example, the concept was that side A would say one thing to your audience, and side B would say another thing.*

A: Well, from *Death Certificate* to now, my audience is totally different. From the little white kid that's nine years old to the old grandmother who likes "It Was a Good Day." That's my whole audience. So I really don't have a pinpoint idea, even though I still do my records directly for black teenagers and young adults.

But I was getting feedback, some people saying, "well, Ice Cube lost his edge." So I have to do records that you expect and records that you don't expect. With *The Predator,* I really wanted to show that Ice Cube has skills—do "Now I Gotta Wet'cha" or "Wicked," and show that I can do just a rap record with no social message. That was the main focus on *The Predator.* And one thing that's never been consistent on any of my records is the music. There's never been a certain musical feel to the whole record. So on *Lethal Injection,* I tried to keep the music consistent, and then throw the raps in for messages. My next record will be real put together, more like *Death Certificate.*

Q: *There was a time when you had to go to the 'hood to hear rap, plain and simple. There are pros and cons to its commercial success, but do you think that the expanding audience affects its ability to really be a voice of young black people?*

A: No, because the good thing is that the hardcore records are still respected more than the pop records. Once the pop records get more respect than a hardcore street group, that's when the music will hurt. But any kind of pop, bubble gum, sugar-toast group out there, the hardcore still gets more respect, and that's where it started from. So as long as we keep that base, I don't think the music is hurting at all.

Q: *What about the people who front being hardcore, but really aren't— who don't come from where they say they come from?*

A: Those records aren't pop, but they have a pop thing about them in the sense that people don't know, so they buy it and eat it up.

Q: *Do you think that waters it down at all?*

A: If you're black and live in this country, it's an experience. You got a story to tell, and you're legit in telling it. Because no matter how rich you are, how poor you are, this country sees black and white. You're going to get treated pretty much the same way. I think what matters is what a group is saying: Nobody is harder than a bullet. I don't consider myself a hard individual; I can't step through the earth, I can't stop a bullet with my bare flesh. I consider myself *real*, and that's a difference.

We have generals out there that have never shot a gun in a war, but they could *tell* you about war because they know how to look at it. I know a lot of killers, but they're in the pen now, so they can't rap. And I know people who have witnessed things and can explain it. I don't think that makes them less legit than a person who has—quote, unquote—been through it, because we *all* have been through it. Unless you're black, you don't know. Period. So no matter who you are, I don't think it waters it down.

Some people are comic books, and some people are news-papers. Comic books have a whole lot of shooting and killing, but you ain't getting nothing out of it. The newspaper maybe has less of that, but it's true, or somewhat true. I think the audience can pick out who is the comic books and who's the newspaper.

Q: *How do you think the mainstream media is handling rap right now?*

A: Well, rap is the only thing where information is distributed that don't go through these channels that information usually has to go through. Without a newspaper, Ice Cube could still sell records. Without a magazine, without a video, without the radio, Ice Cube could sell records. So there's no way to control that. That's scary to the ones who control this all. Because if you distribute information, you can teach the people.

Everybody else—movies, TV shows—has to go through certain channels, and music used to be the same way. If you didn't get played on the radio, you didn't sell. Nowadays, that's not even an issue. Radio play can damn near *hurt* you. That scares the media, so they have to attack rap and make it not so powerful. Public Enemy, Ice Cube, Ice-T, whoever is saying something, that's the main threat, and their main focus is to try to bring us down. And they use different ways, they see exactly what tempts you. Some groups they watch and try to bury from the start—let you blow up fast, then get you buried.

Q: *Is Arrested Development an example of that? They got written up in places like* **The Wall Street Journal.**

A: They saw that the group had some conscience. Let's see what happens with their next record. It's going to be like, damn, they was all over MTV last year. I didn't hear nothing about them this year. It looks like you failed, because most of the people that's watching don't know the game. You look like you're on top of the world, and next year, you ain't nothing. So it looked like you just took a nosedive. And that can kill a group, if you play into that game.

People try to play that game with me. See, I know that game; I'll take the long route. Don't give me the short route. I don't want to do that. They played "Good Day" all over the place, then they want me to play on the Rock and Jock basketball games. But, I'll play with my homeboys, you know, because those people don't love me. They don't love what I'm saying, and I know it. So before you take the gift of the devil, you've gotta see exactly what's in it for him.

Q: *Would you say that from the mid-'80s to now is the first time that young black men have had control over their public image?*

A: No. Until we can control networks, movie studios, theaters, the only image that we really control is our image through rap. We are open people, so the hell that we're going through is all in the streets. The suburbs are going though hell, too, but you don't see it in the streets. But you go in the household, and it's hell inside the household. The streets look quiet, because white people are really not open, emotional people. Their neighborhoods reflect that. But if you go inside each door, each household is going through a crisis. The tripped thing about it is, they're going through a crisis, and they got all the damn money.

Q: *What do you think of that crisis—the dissatisfaction that's affecting not just black families but white families in particular?*

A: In America, for any people to be powerful, they have to ride on the backs of the poor. How do you keep people poor? You keep them ignorant. So if you want people to be slaves, or have a slave mentality, you keep them from knowing those things that will set them free. That's the aim of the government, to keep people ignorant, and I think what you have is people fighting to gain some kind of knowledge of who they are and where they're going. It's like they're pushing down and we're pushing up. And we're going to meet somewhere in the middle, and I think that's what's tearing America up right now.

So pretty soon, it's got to change, because I can't see myself sitting on the back of nobody's bus. And my sons probably can't see themselves putting their hands up in the air when the police pull them over. If the government thinks they've got to worry about Ice Cube . . . it's that 14-, 15-year-old kid, who's buck wild and feels invincible—that's the one you've got to worry about. And the ones coming after him are going to be worse, until we have freedom, justice, and equality.

Q: *Given the realities of poverty in this country, that there are poor people who are white, who are Asian, who are Latino, do you think economic conditions could ever unify people? Do you think that there could ever be a unified movement of blacks and other oppressed people?*

A: It could be, and it should be. But when it comes to oppressed people, the black man is always at the bottom of the totem pole.

The closer you are to white, the more arrogant you are. A certain kind of arrogance is breeded into people. White folks are snotty towards black people. Orientals are snobby, all the way down the line, till you have lighter black folks more snobby than darker black folks. It comes all the way down the line to the blackest, blackest, blackest man, who everybody's an enemy of.

Once we learn how to love each other, then we can reach out for other people. But how am I going to help you build your house when mine's not finished? It don't make no sense. I think we have to stop looking for so much outside help, and start to help our-selves.

I really wish we would build a wall [laughs]—not a physical wall, but a wall around our community—till we get our thing together. It's like a football team just going straight to the line of scrimmage—no play, no huddle-up, no nothing. Just out there doing plays, running into each other. You have to huddle up, get your shit together, and then you can go and attack the other team with a play. We refuse to do that. We refuse to huddle up and get our shit together. Then we can challenge the world.

Q: *There was an article that we did in the magazine about Japan. Right now, Koreans in Japan are really treated badly. They have something that's almost the equivalent of a pass system. They make you take a Japanese name, and if you're Korean, there are certain jobs you're not eligible for. Just a lot of discrimination. And a lot of the kids are really big rap fans, because they say that they really identify with the oppression in the music. One kid said, even when you don't understand the words, you understand the feeling and the anger behind it.*

A: Do you know what I think about that? If Japan is for the Japanese, I ain't got no problem with that. At all. Japan is for Japanese. Korea is for Koreans. Now, the problem I have is, America is for Americans. But they *tell* you that America is for everybody. See, to me, that's worse. Because you're looking for something that you ain't never, ever going to get. If they said, "Look [snaps his fingers], America is for white folks. Black folks, here's yours." I ain't got no problem with that. The problem is America saying, "Oh, this is love, the melting pot." But America is for fucking white Americans. Straight up—no ifs, ands, or buts about it.

I went to Japan. And in some places, it was like, ah, you can't come in here. I had no problem with that. Because I knew that, up front. They didn't disrespect me. Japan is for Japanese. You ain't going to come over here, you ain't going to get no Japanese job. But that's honest; what you see is what you get. What I hate is the motherfuckers sitting behind a desk at the record company, with a tie on. Bigger crooks than my homeboys. To me, that's worse. Deception is worse than the truth.

So if America is for white Americans, cool. But America owes us a spot, a piece of this country that should be just for black folks. And they ain't got to worry about me ever going into that part of the airport, to where they are. I'm content.

Q: *Let's change the subject a little bit. I want to talk about you as a family man. You got married. You had a son. You have another child—a daughter this time-on the way. You moved out of South Central. How do you think being a family man has changed your life?*

A: It's made me more of a man. Not as reckless as I used to be. I thought I'd never move. Never, man this is me, right here. But when you've got a family, and you've got motherfuckers going, "We're going to kidnap your wife," and you're in Baltimore . . . damn, how do I protect my family? When you've got niggas driving by your house that you don't know: "Yo, Cube, man, come outside." So I said, let's get to a place where I'm not as popular. Or a place where nobody knows where I live. I used to think, how could you make money and then move out? But it's like having a piece of meat in the jungle. All the lions and tigers want that piece of meat, too, 'cause they don't have none. So, what you've got to do is take your meat in your den, or your tree, or wherever you are, and eat it. And then show everybody else how to get some meat too. So you won't become prey, sitting in a land of predators. I used to be a predator, and I never want to be the prey, but that's how it is. You can't fight off everything.

My family made me more cautious. I'm old and I lock my doors and all that stupid stuff that I never used to do. But, you know, you got somebody that's your blood, that's your purpose on earth, so you want to make sure your offspring survives. Some people say, "I'm never having kids"—well, fool, your history stops right there. I want to be able to sit grandkids on my lap, and tell them stories about how it was: "They burnt the city down in 1992, or was it '93?" That type of thing. I want to be able to play with my kids. You know, if my kids start running with the gangs, I'm able to relate to the things that they're going to have to go through, so I'm cool with it. I think that's my purpose, to instruct the youth—not only my own, but other youth—on how to keep out of this self-destructive cycle.

Q: *I think that people who just know your media image would be surprised that you're married. You have this image of being a raving misogynist. So I want to know what was it that you were looking for in a wife?*

A: Somebody that was strong. Just like I hate yes-men, I hate yes-women. I hate that. Because I don't know everything, so I need somebody to tell me, "Yo, you're fucking up over here."

Q: *You always knew she'd be a sister?*

A: A black woman?

Q: *Uh-huh.*

A: Oh, please. Please. Man. Nothing but. White woman took me to the store one day, during a video shoot . . . I felt so uncomfortable, just riding in the car. Just terrible. It's true: the truth is true.

Q: **You** *mentioned yes-women. Do you think black women, in particular, have problems with self-esteem?*

A: I think black *men* have problems with self esteem. I think black women know what they want. And they make no bones about it, and they hold you up to that. But for black men, there's extra, added pressure. That's why black men are more likely to die of high blood pressure and all these types of things, because of all the pressure that comes from not being the man of your house-being a man, physically, but not mentally. 1 think that's why a lot of men beat their women, feeling like, "I'm not living up to what I am, and I can't take it out on the one that's oppressing me, so I'm going to take it out on a woman."

Q: *I think you're right—I think it is about lack of power. So what do you do? I know a lot of black women who are intelligent, and beautiful, and strong. And lonely as hell. Don't really want to date white men, you know, not trying to do that. I guess I'm asking how can we heal as a community so we can come together and have positive relationships?*

A: Well, I can't answer that. Um . . . *damn*. That's a heavy one *[laughs]*. The black man is going through a plight, and we are—oh here we go: we are like children, the whole black community. Whatever the white man does, we want to do. Just like the child wants to do what the adult wants to do. And the white man disrespects his women on all levels.

So I think everything that he does, we do on a smaller level. Even killing each other. Yeah, we do Crips and Bloods, but then you look at Bosnia and Herzegovina. You take car-jacking, and then you take Panama-you know, *country*-jacking. He hates his woman, and he's been our only teacher for 437 years, so we hate our women. He erased all of our knowledge and replaced it with his own. And his own, evidently, is not good for us. We will continue to do what we've been taught, until we decide not to follow that way. Children follow their mother or father to a certain extent, and then they have to break off and do their own thing. That's what our community has to do.

Q: *So ultimately, what you're talking about is the need for us to develop a value system that's not based on the materialistic, or sexist, or patriarchal, or racist ideas.*

A: We need not just a value system, but a whole national system. We need to become a nation within a nation. We need to have our own *everything* inside this culture. That's how we survive. Because this world is the devil's world. You have to break from that, make a new reality, in your own way. And become something other than what this world is producing, which is shit, hell, destruction. And I trip off the preachers, because if this world is of the devil, you should be trying your damnedest to get away from this world. But you're trying to fit in, you want to be there with Clinton, shaking hands. What the hell is that?

Q: *A friend of mine was in this position recently, and I want to know what you think of it. She was in the car with her baby's father, and he was listening to* The Chronic, *and she was like, "I don't really care when you play it in the house; I don't like it, but you have every right to play it. But around our daughter, I don't really think she should have to hear that." And he was like. "That is my experience, my reality, this is a part of where I come from, she should hear it." So I want to know, what are you going to do when your little girl comes, and she wants to know whether it's okay to play the year 2000's version of* The Chronic *or* AmeriKKKa's Most Wanted, *for that matter?*

A: Now, why would I shield my daughter from anything that I can explain to her, inside the house? Why would I say, "No, don't listen to that," so she can go outside and hear it with no explanation, nothing behind it but what people her age know about it? I'd rather pick my child's brain, to give her the right medicine, because I can shield her from it while she's in here, until she steps out that door. And nobody's shielded from nothing when they walk out the door. I don't shut the kids out from nothing they want to look at— nothing. *Def Comedy Jam,* nothing. They don't laugh at what we laugh about, because they don't understand. But just break it down to them.

When parents are in the position to teach their kids, they don't; and then they get mad when they got rappers teaching their kids, because the rappers don't shield the kids from nothing. The rappers tell them straight up. And that's really all the kids want to know. The kids don't need to know lies, they want to know the truth. Santa Claus, the Easter Bunny . . . how are kids going to grow up with that bullshit?

Q: *There's been a movement, internally, to address a lot of these things in black music, like sex and guns in lyrics. What do you think about that?*

A: I've been saying this for years: You can't change the problem if you don't *got* a problem. If rappers didn't come out with "bitch" and "ho," we would still not be addressing that issue at all. Now, in 1994, we're starting to address that. If everybody comes to the conclusion that "bitch and "ho" aren't appropriate for the community, they won't be used. Just like "Negro" is not used no more. It's not appropriate, it doesn't fit, it has no meaning. But until somebody brings that to the table—here's what's going on, here's what's happening—you're never going to address it. It's like, if your hair is messed up and I hold a mirror in front of you long enough, you're going to use a comb. That's our whole purpose.

Q: *You said earlier that there were people who say you got married and got soft. What do you say to those detractors when they say that your music isn't as hard as it used to be, that you lost your edge, that you're not as angry as you used to be?*

A: I ain't as stupid, that's basically what it is. We hate ourselves so much that you ain't hard unless you're talking about, "I shot this nigga, I got 1,000 AKs, I killed 1,000 niggas." Motherfuckers would rather hear you say you killed 1,000 niggas than hear you say you smoked one devil. They love that more than they love themselves. So that's the only thing that's changed in my music: it's more focused. I know that killing a nigga down the street ain't going to solve none of my problems at all. And I don't put that into my records, unless I'm explaining a situation. I ain't stupid no more. And some people can't deal with that. Niggas are scared of evolution, niggas don't want to be free.

They're scared because with freedom, you have to make your own decisions. Freedom is responsibility. Shit, I live in my mama's house, cookies are there every day. Bam—you move out, ain't no more cookies in there, unless you put them in there. You're like, "Damn, I got to buy dishwasher liquid?" That's the responsibility you want to take to be free. These are scared Negroes, just like when slavery was over; yeah, you're free to go. Now what am I going to do? We sharecropped. Still a slave.

Q: *What would you say to someone who says, okay, you're married, you have two, five, maybe eight kids. You got a house, you got a car, you got a business. Cube is really living the American Dream.*

A: It ain't no dream for me. You can't compare one man's wealth to a whole nation of poverty. If they foreclose on my house, I can't go to my bank and say, "White man, let me get a loan until next month. Give me $20,000." Until I can go to my people and get help out of any financial situation I'm in, there ain't nobody rich. I'm as poor as anybody else. I know how to get some money, and my duty is to show people around me how to get it, and how we all can get it.

Q: *So might that mean taking a step like directing feature films after all these videos you've worked on?*

A: Yeah. Directing is cool, but I need to grow. I've been offered films to direct, but I'm not ready. I need to learn this game more. I'm going to be in this movie with John Singleton, *Higher Learning*. So I'll be looking over his shoulder the whole time. I never went to school, so I really want to sit and learn the game, and not just jump out there and be weak *[laughs]*. I don't want to do nothing weak. I want to make sure I win.

RICHARD PRYOR

By Greg Tate
August 1995

PRYOR LIVES

Unrepentant and reflective, the most profound and influential comedian of the late 20th century laughed in the face of divorces, drug addiction, and disease. Like all great minds, Pryor helps us appreciate how noble and absurd a creature man is. And he's still mad funny.

True confession time: When my editors first offered me the Richard Pryor assignment, I didn't exactly leap out of my seat to claim it. Neither my sense of the tragic nor the comic is so bloodless as to relish reporting how the once hyperactive Pryor copes with the ravages of multiple sclerosis. (MS is a degenerative disease that affects the central nervous system, causing uncontrollable muscle tremors and paralysis in some patients.)

Richard Pryor is, of course, the most profound and influential comedian of the late 20th century. Combine the pathos of Charlie Chaplin with the raunch of Redd Foxx, the critical insight of Dick Gregory and Lenny Bruce, and the wide-eyed wonder of Bill Cosby, and you might create a stand-up mutanoid, but not a Richard Pryor. As hilarious as these funnymen are, Pryor made comedy more than raw;

he made it ass-out, naked, and confessional. He brought the blues to American comedy—that laughing-to-keep-from-crying aspect of black life that often pushes us beyond decorum to deconstruction, or more plainly, tellin' it like it muhfukn is.

Like all great minds, Pryor's helps us appreciate how noble and absurd a creature man is. You literally have to go to Shakespeare, James Joyce, or James Baldwin to find readings of human folly as incisive as Pryor's. Yet Pryor has it one up on those masters of the word: He didn't need exclamation points—his body movement was his punctuation.

Pryor has left us some wonderful films of his standup talents (1979's *Richard Pryor—Live in Concert* is the funniest of the four) and of his dramatic acting abilities, most notably in *Lady Sings the Blues, The Mack,* and *Blue Collar.* But to his fans, there always seemed to be two Richard Pryors: the hero of his stand-up romps, and the chump of his Hollywood choices. Sometimes the twain did meet, like in Michael Schultz's Which *Way Is Up?* or his four movies with Gene Wider, but not often enough.

As Pryor's art, celebrity, and wealth increased in the '70s and '80s, so did his personal chaos: divorces, drug habits, diseases, and self-doubt. When he burned himself up in a drug-induced haze in 1980, the episode seemed more like a skit than a coke fiend's cul-de-sac.

These incidents and more are now chronicled in his autobiography, *Pryor Convictions and Other Life Sentences* (Pantheon), written with Todd Gold. Alongside them are ribald tales about Miles Davis, Pam Grier, and Billy Dee Williams; tough remembrances of growing up poor in his grandmother's whorehouse in Peoria, Ill.; and reflections about his struggle to find his own comedic style. Further documenting Pryor's work are the six Loose Cannon Records reissues of Pryor's LAFF Records comedy albums; the full catalog of 12 will soon be available.

Up until I walked into his Encino mansion and looked into his eyes, I didn't know how things were going to go. For once, I did not prepare questions. I figured I'd sit down, roll the tapes, and let the love flow. With me was Peter Harris, a fellow Howard University alum, a Pryor fanatic, poet, journalist, and family man who rolled up on me in Los Angeles the day before the interview. What neither of us counted on was the presence of Jennifer Lee, Pryor's ex-wife, now his best friend/manager/cheerleader, who complicated and enriched the session. In Pryor's bio, Lee comes off as confused, maternal, and much abused. In person, she is a centered and mature woman whose bond with Pryor seems more motherly than wifely at this point, but no less passionate and protective. (And he needs that. Lee estimates that Pryor's been bilked out of some $50 million by lawyers and hangers-on.)

Before I began the interview proper, I caught this exchange between Lee and Pryor:

"Would you prefer that I leave?" Jennifer asked. "Would that make it better?"

"No," Pryor replied. "It would probably make it worse."

Q: *When you started working on the book, did you know you were going to be as open and honest as you were with your co-writer?*
A: No.

Q: *Did you think you'd be more evasive?*
A: Yes, lots of times. It was a hard thing to do this book. 'Cause it's the truth. And the truth was something I avoided at all costs.

JENNIFER LEE: Not really. I mean, look at your work . . .

A: Oh, fuck that. That's work. That's for money, you know what I mean?

Q: *You've said that when you went to Africa, you didn't see any niggers, and so that word got excised from your vocabulary. How come bitch didn't follow?*

A: I thought a lot about that at the time. Because if I see one, I have to see the other. You're more right than wrong. My grandmother used to say that to the pimps and stuff who used the word *bitch:* "Excuse me, son, did your mother teach you how to say that?"

Q: *What did your grandmother think about the women that worked for her?*

A: Good. She was an okay boss. I didn't see it for what it was. I was a kid. I saw the house different than what it was.

JL: But how was Mama, Richard? Because I remember when she beat me over the leg with a stick like she was back in the whorehouse.

A: Listen, we're talking about Mama now. She's gone. Leave her alone. Ain't nothing we can do.

JL: But how did she treat those women?

A: I imagine she treated 'em like shit.

Q: *Did you think the way you felt about women was affected by how she treated them, or what you saw growing up in a whorehouse?*

A: I think what I saw affected me. But see, they were beautiful to me, in my mind's eye. They were like fucking fabulous. I didn't see them for what they were or nothing. I said, God, this is fucking great. But I was a kid. I really was a kid once. I really was. It's been a mystery to me how that affected me all my life, and I'm 54. I don't care.

JL: He picked women who wanted to try and fix him. I sure as heck tried to fix him.

A: Did you?

JL: Yeah, I did. It was terror, living in that scene.

A: Wasn't an ax murder?

JL: A train wreck, maybe.

Q: *An earlier version of the book has one passage that struck me as being a revelation for you. You write about women behaving like lunatics when you got ready to leave. It's like you drove them mad. You talk about how in relationships, violence can work like a hex, like a spell.*

JL: Brilliant point.

A: I'm glad you like it.

Q: *When did you realize that?*

A: Probably when I wrote it. You know, it's amazing. I'm embarrassed to say this, but I used to be a violent man, except I'd only fight women. I'd never have a fight with a man. Now listen to me: this movie company that they gave me, Indigo [Columbia Pictures gave Pryor his own production company as part of a $40 million deal], I hired Jim Brown to run it and realized I made a mistake. And I said to myself. If I don't knock this motherfucker out, or at least make the attempt, then I ain't never gonna hit nobody, ever again. And that's the truth. I said, You know, I'm so bad. I bulldoze people all over, but I ain't bulldozed this motherfucker, so there ain't shit to my stuff.

Q: *What was that moment like when you did finally tell Jim Brown that he was fired?*

A: He fucked around and turned down Prince's *Purple Rain.* That movie would have been great for us, but Jim thought it didn't have enough black people among the production assistants or whatever. I said, *"So?"* "No, see, you got to have black people. This is a black thing." I said, "What we gonna do, Jim?" I felt like I was mad. I was insane. I told Jim Brown over lunch that I didn't want this company, and Jim cried. *Jim Brown,* you dig? I was either going to die right there or live with a broken face. I didn't care because I was tired of his shit.

JL: You lost the art. You guys lost the big picture. Plus it was two big male egos in there too, right? Don't you think so?

A: I don't think so. It's just that I have the ego, and if you come with your shit, ain't nothing for me to do but hit you in the head with a hammer.

Q: *You set the stage for Spike Lee and John Singleton and the Hughes brothers. Before Indigo, who was ever thinking a black man could be in control of his career in Hollywood? There were other milestones in your career too, like getting paid $4 million for Superman III.*

A: But the *movie,* man. It wasn't my fault. They did give me the $4 million, so I did what the director said. But I didn't get to do shit in it.

Q: *You've talked about what a lot of us were thinking back in the day— that you were never as in command of your talent in a Hollywood film as you were doing stand-up. You had so much room onstage. It was your world.*

A: It was. For a minute.

   JL: You still rule, Richard.

A: Shut up.

   JL: I just want to see you work again.

Q: *You did do a tour a while back.* **You** *say it made you realize that you got more courage than stamina because of the MS.*

   JL: He's had too many martinis too. You want me to leave yet?

A: No.

Q: *Did you feel drugs gave you more energy to work night after night, or was cocaine just part of your lifestyle?*

A: Hey, listen, doing cocaine was for me like being a smart kid. I knew it was wrong. But shit, cocaine made me feel like I had something so many people liked. And since I had it, I could say, "Hey, want some?" and not even look at the roll [of bills]. I could say, "Here, have some more." I didn't understand how insane that was then. My friend Burt was the first person I saw *smoke* it, and he said, "I saw God. God is here talking to me." He sat in that chair, and I looked back at Burt, and I said, I'm gonna try some of this shit, because he's fucking gone.

Q: *When did you realize you were addicted?*

A: I was talking to Redd Foxx. I said, 'Why do I want it, Redd? I get so much and still I want more. Why?" He said, "'Cause you a junkie." That went past me like, *choo!* I'd never been called a junkie before, but it was true. And I always thought, cocaine doesn't hook nobody. I was under the impression that the Lady don't be bad to you, 'cause she's a Lady.

JL: He's still addicted to cigarettes.

A: She doesn't like my addictions.

JL: I hate the cigarettes because I think you could really help your disease if you stopped smoking. That's all.

A: That's what *you* say.

Q: *What is MS like for you on a day-to-day basis?*

A: It's not pleasant, but I look at it like this: I've seen people a lot worse with MS. I've seen people fucked up, man, and it scared me. I saw 150 people with MS when I'd never seen anybody else with it.

JL: Richard's actually walking again with a walker.

A: The other night when I was in the walker, I couldn't wait until I could get to the table and sit down. Because that's a frightening thing when you're walking and you feel your legs going, "Hey, wanna give me a break?" And there was another 50 feet and everybody wanted to show me the food. They said, "Hey, Rich, food's over here." And I didn't want to see no food and shit.

JL: Maybe MS is a way of keeping you alive.

A: Maybe, 'cause I'm alive. But where's the money? And the pussy?

Q: *You talk about being addicted to laughter too. How do you deal with not being able to access your talent?*

A: It makes me very angry. I say very angry and maybe that's pushing it, but I'm angry because I can't do shit. I can't jump up and do the things I want to do. I have to learn something else. I don't know what, but I'm learning it.

Q: *Do you still think of yourself as being an artist, an entertainer? Is that still in your definition of Richard Pryor now. Or is that part gone?*

A: No, it's not gone, but it's *fa-a-ar* away. Like it's through this veil and I can't see it. I know where it is but I can't reach it.

PETER HARRIS: *For the cats who were coming up when you were doing the work, it wasn't just comedy to us. It was like hearing your grandfather talk, or your big brother. Do you have a sense of the type of impact you had on people when you were at your peak? Or even now?*

A: I like hearing what you're saying. If you were around here before, and I had listened, I would have felt different about myself.

Q: *How much of an inspiration were people like Miles Davis to you?*

A: Miles . . . I met Miles at a bar on 86th Street in New York. A guy said, "Miles, I'd like you to meet a nice young man." Miles said, "What the fuck you know?"

Q: *Did he ever talk to you about your work?*

A: Yeah. He said, "You a funny motherfucker." I told him once, I said, "Miles, I got a script about Charlie Parker." Miles said, "Charlie Parker was greedy." I said, "What you mean. Miles?" Miles said, "He was really gonna rape everything. He fucked everything, and he played everything." It was too much. With Miles, all I ended up doing was saying, "Please stop, Miles. Stop." Because he just be talking. But I picked up on it, because I said this is real shit here. Bless his heart. But there is another side to being honest, you got to remember, because it's a very dangerous blade. It swipes and cuts off thousands of heads.

Q: *What's your relationship with your children? Do you have more time for them now?*

A: Hmmm, hmmm, hmm. It's like that. I didn't know that it was going to be forever, but they are. That's something I'm understanding now. To have kids, you got to have 'em forever. I admire their mothers. I really do. Their mothers call me up for things, and I know what they're going through because I had them for a little bit.

JL: Well, in some cases, having kids was a career choice, right?

A: No, it was never a career choice for people. You didn't do it.

JL: No, thank God, I didn't do it.

A: No, but you got two vicious dogs.

Q: *Has there ever been a time when you didn't help someone, and you should have?*

A: Please don't make me think of those things. Was there ever a time I could've helped and didn't? Well, I didn't go to 'Nam, that's the only thing I could think of. I wish I was in Vietnam. I don't know why. I really don't, but I just feel like I belonged there at the time. I should have been there.

JL: No, you shouldn't have. You were doing more important things. Why should you be over there killing people and killing yourself?

Q: *So do you think that maybe you're experiencing guilt for the young men that came up in your hometown and died in Vietnam?*

A: [*Softly*] Umm-hmm.

Q: *As hard as you worked, did you ever feel like, "Why me? Why was I the one to become successful?"*

A: Oh God, yes. I beat myself up a lot about that. And then I met Ethel [*his term for women*].

PH: *What kind of therapy do you have to do?*

A: The therapists massage my legs, and I walk on the walker. I hate that fucking walker, I hate it. She says that I'm doing great. And I say to her, *"But I'm on this fucking walker!"*

JL: If you're physically diminished, that doesn't diminish who you are . . .

A: Okay, then sit on my face . . .

JL: Oh, stop it, Richard. Oh God.

A: See, I can't make you do that, so that's diminishment.

Q: *Does poverty scare you more than death?*

A: No. I know about poverty. I know it very well. *Very* well. I just think poor people—they're not nice. I mean, they don't mean to hurt you, but they're not nice. And I don't want to be around them if I can help it. Poverty will make people come in your house and say, "Motherfucker, you in a wheelchair, what the fuck are you talking about? You had $50 million, and what did you do with it? Fuck that—lemme have a dollar."

Q: *How did success separate you from the people on the street, from the very thing that had made you successful?*

A: I never understood that having a dollar made me different or separate like you say. I never understood that the way, maybe, other people do. But them's the breaks, hey? Makes me sad . . . not remembering what I was going to say. I was going to say something. It was standing right here, and then I picked up this cigarette and it just said, "Fuck you."

Q: *Folks say success doesn't change you, but changes the people around you. Is that what happened?*

A: Yep. My Uncle Dickie.

JL: Yeah, he used to cry, "Oh, Richard, I just need $50,000 to get that damn truck out the garage."

PH: *Damn, what a paint job. Better have some sparkles.*

JL: No, he'd come back the next day with rhinestone glasses with his initials and a truckful o' pot and a new pink polyester suit and ten women on each arm. Dickie was terribly lovable to Richard, and he knew it.

A: He was what he was and I always thought, "If my father were alive, he wouldn't do this to me."

JL: No, Buck would have kicked some ass.

A: Yes, I know so. But also, the other side of that is, kicking ass was a bad habit with Buck. His leg would start kicking, and he didn't know how to control it. He'd say, "Down, leg! 'Cause your ass could go too."

PH: *We got to say, man, we're trying to get you to understand that you can take* That Nigger's Crazy, *put it on at a gathering of black folks in 1995, and you could still stop a party. With the wino and the junkie, and the cat hollering at Dracula—that's breakthrough stuff. I know you can't stand up on stage, but what do you think about in terms of storytelling now?*

A: I don't know that I think of anything. I think I'm tired. That's okay, but I'm tired.

PH: *What about a Mudbone movie? The way films are done, you could do the whole Mudbone character sitting.*

JL: Some people are interested in purchasing the rights and writing with Richard. I think Richard *is* Mudbone now.

Q: *Is it important to you that your work is remembered? That you have a legacy?*

A: Yes, very much so. And you gentlemen have impressed upon me that I'm alive. I feel like that Frankenstein movie. "It's alive!" *[We are interrupted by the sound of a helicopter overhead.]* I have dreams about a helicopter crashing in my backyard. In the dream,

I run out and help the people. Then the helicopter blows up. Only I don't know if the helicopter blew up while I was out there, or after I left. So that's a thought I have all the time. What am I going to do when this helicopter crashes for real in the yard? I don't know if I'll go out and try to help the people, or if I'll stand in the doorway and go, "It's gonna blow!"

PH: *Have you figured out any mysteries you didn't know how to answer in the early days?*

A: I'm glad I didn't go to heroin. That was a mystery.

Q: *What was the difference between that and cocaine for you?*
A: Good question. Stalling, stalling. Cocaine. I don't want to have to think about it.

JL: Coke just kept you up for five days and made you pass out for five years.

A: One thing about coke was, I used to go to sleep and wake up and didn't know that I'd been asleep.

JL: Yeah, absolutely. You didn't get REM with that.

Q: *You get slim.*
A: Hey, man, the hell I saw that time when I walked in the hall and saw a man—Jennifer said it was the devil, but I thought it was me, only skinnier than me, in black shorts. He walked through a door, then he walked *across* me and I said, "I'm going to leave this guy alone." I went into my room, looked around, and said, "I saw me, skinny, in black underwear, and in my mind it was real." Nobody believed me.

JL: I think it was you, as the devil incarnate in reverse, taking you to hell . . .

A: Oh.

JL: *[Laughing at herself]* I do.

Q: *In the book, you profess that God is now asking, "Hey, Rich, you ever heard the phrase 'delayed gratification?' Good. 'Cause you've done had a lot of gratification . . . Well, now comes the delay."*

A: See, the difference between me and other motherfuckers is I want all the pussy. If there's three or four billion women in the world, eventually I want to fuck 'em all. And I will.

JL: [*Sighs*] You've had enough, Richard, to last ten lifetimes.

A: There can never be enough to last ten lifetimes. I'm sorry.

KRS-ONE

By Joe Wood
November 1995

ACT LIKE YA KNOW

KRS-One is a teacher, philosopher, lecturer, Blastmaster, and hip hop prophet. Going toe to toe with Boogie Down Productions' legendary MC KRS-One, the late great Joe Wood asks, will the real Kris Parker please stand up?

Even among rappers, the Teacher has a reputation for arrogance. Had I not known this before we met, I would certainly have learned by watching him school the worshipful interviewer slotted ahead of me. The journalist was rapt as Kris bragged about his work ethic, his plans for a wordless rap album and a manual for MCs, his various theories about personal conduct, feminine spirituality, edutainment, and world peace. I wasn't rapt: KRS-One talked so exhaustively about himself that I found myself yawning during the wait and hoping to get away as quickly as possible.

Which would have been a mistake. When Kris and I finally talked, the bombast he dished me was leavened with the flashes of wit and insight familiar to listeners of the Blastmaster's eight albums, especially his latest salvo, simply titled *KRS-One*. He is justifiably proud of those "edutational" moments and the enviable career they have earned for him. "Having lectured at Harvard, Yale, Vassar, Columbia, NYU, and Stanford," his press bio announces, "KRS-One is rightfully nicknamed the Teacher." Though Kris now says the Teacher role originated as a marketing strategy, the persona—and its attendant bullshit—also plainly come from Kris's own strange and lucky and unlucky life.

Born Lawrence Parker in Park Slope, Brooklyn in the summer of 1965, the rapper left home at 14 to play basketball and read books free of the gaze of the authorities (his mother and the New York City public school system). He landed in a homeless shelter where he was dubbed Krishna by residents because of his interest in the Hare Krishna spirituality of some of the antipoverty workers. By the time Krishna met youth counselor Scott Sterling, he was also writing graffiti as KRS-One (Knowledge Reigns Supreme Over Nearly Everyone). Together he and Sterling, a.k.a. DJ Scott La Rock, created Boogie Down Productions, releasing their landmark debut album, *Criminal Minded*, in 1987.

After Scott's murder later that year, the Teacher's rep blossomed; KRS-One seemed fired up with a desire to bear witness to American hypocrisy. This mission—despite its didacticism—won him a great deal of hip hop respect, and money. Yet Kris never let go of his homelessness ethos or the consciousness he'd learned while living on the street. "The minute you hold on to something," he says cheerfully, "you are going to be destroyed by your attachment to it." Instead, he has privately made a point of avoiding investment in any one approach to politics or spirituality, and maintained a wide range of sincerely felt but frequently contradictory positions.

These contradictions can manifest cynicism, opportunism, confusion, and straight-up ignorance. Through the Stop the Violence movement he organized in 1989, the rapper bemoaned hip hop celebrations of violence, while 1992's *Sex and Violence* featured gun blather by mediocre MC Freddie Foxxx. During one creatively sluggish period, Kris advocated a vague humanism in the form of pet project HEAL (Human Education Against Lies); during another he and his boys beat down poor Prince Be of P.M. Dawn. And though he has spent much of his career criticizing capitalism, the Teacher's new album counsels rap novices to *sell* a consistent image—as he did—while tailoring the content of one's work to suit current trends.

Perhaps the Teacher should no longer be taken seriously. Parker's mission to edutain seems to be taking a backseat to other interests, including cheerleading for old-school artistry (in August, he headlined an "old-school throwdown" with longtime rival MC Shan), producing artists like Mad Lion and Channel Live, and running his management company, Front Page.

But at the same time, KRS-One is now making some of the best records of his career. "He's in a good mood today," said his publicist just before she ushered me in. Kris and I laughed a lot during the conversation; I enjoyed the several hours we spent discussing his life, opinions, contradictions, foolishness—maybe I *was* rapt.

Q: *On your new album, you attribute your longevity to success in marketing your image. Doesn't selling the image of being a teacher conflict with actually being a teacher?*

A: Only because the mainstream graphics in our mind say what the teacher's not supposed to be or that this is what the teacher is supposed to be.

Q: *It's not just because of mainstream graphics. It's because . . .*

A: Mainstream graphics! You have to understand that I'm living several separate lives at once. I have a black youth life, KRS, which is—to the drug dealers out here—the ultimate hardcore. They say, "KRS, keep it real!" Or "Spark mad izm!" Or "Jump P.M. Dawn!" They express their version of love toward me in the best way they know how. A drug dealer might offer me id on the kilo or a pound of herb to show how I can get down with their business. It's up to me to say, "I'm chilling," or not. In doing that you become hypocritical but at the same time you become very universal.

Q: *When the teacher jumped P.M. Dawn, he didn't seem universal. But the hypocrisy was clear.*

A: Looking back on that, it was a triumph for hip hop and a setback for KRS-One. That was the first time a believed-to-be-hardcore artist took a physical reaction to a believed-to-be-commercial artist. Half of my audience was like, "Yeah!" The other half were, like, "We thought you were an intelligent brother!" Most of the intelligentsia in my world despise violence because they don't understand it. My sales dropped considerably after that, but I became the real shit. And my intelligent audience is coming back because I'm the only one left. There's no Public Enemy—not the group who put out *It Takes a Nation of Millions to Hold Us Back*. There's no X Clan or Poor Righteous Teachers. I'm the only one left in 1995.

Q: *Your intelligent audience wants a teacher with integrity.*

A: Well, I'm on the lecture circuit. I'm a professor. I have honorary degrees. I expound on reality with other people who have studied this for 10 or 20 years. On the university circuit I am a very established and well-known lecturer on philosophy. And they detest that image of this gangsta.

Q: *So you have conflicting existences.*

A: You know what some people say? "KRS: the founder of gangsta rap. *Criminal Minded* was the first gangsta rap album." And I say no, it's not. N.W.A's *Straight Outta Compton* was. Or maybe Just-Ice's album was. The main thing is that before *Criminal Minded,* rappers were characters. After *Criminal Minded*, rappers became the everyday people on the corner. Realism. I was what Run-D.M.C., for example, was *characterizing* themselves to be—though in real life they were as real as me.

Q: *How do you plan on making your black-youth reportage and your professional teachings fit together more coherently—with less contradiction?*

A: Let me define the contradiction. I appear to be contradictory only because I look at the whole of a situation. And when you look at the whole of a thing, there's no such thing as right/wrong, good/bad, up/down, right/left. It's everything at once that you look at. You don't ground yourself in one thing. You say "I'm Buddhist" to Buddhists. And you be true to Buddhism. Study it, know it, and when you expound on it, speak. But when you're in a church, you say "I'm a Christian." And know Christianity and study it. Then when I'm on the corner with the Five Percenters, I'm God. Straight up. "The black man is God." And expound on that and study that and know it. But they're all real!

Q: *Slippery.*

A: I am whatever the moment is. So anyone who is looking to study KRS has to know who I am at this particular moment. And I'm true to that moment. As much as I debate and critique and talk about Christianity, if I was in a church I would say none of it.

Q: *But isn't that irresponsible?*

A: You cannot give the mind that which it cannot digest.

Q: *How do you know they cannot digest it?*

A: Because when the student is ready, the teacher will appear. Not the other way around.

Q: *So what are you teaching?*

A: I'm questioning the history of a God altogether, and why we call God a "Him" and not a "Her." The European invasions of Africa and the slave trades are the ways of God as a man. In Africa, the goddess was the creative force of the universe. If you live in a society that only gives power to a man, you create a society that can only analyze what's been created, rather than creating anything for itself. Human society will have to reach a balance. Put aside the concept of God as a man, and respect the concept of the earth goddess.

Q: *Is that all?*

A: KRS-One is teaching "reality." That's a very vague word. Reality in this sense: I think human beings must react to the real conditions affecting that human being's survival. If that human being does not react to the real conditions affecting its survival, it will destroy itself. In a nutshell, the KRS-One teaching is: In order to survive as a human being, you have to be nonattached to your memory and past experiences.

Q: *In the past you've said history is central.*

A: In a historical context. In a historical environment.

Q: *Everything is a historical environment.*

A: No. I would say everything is words and pictures. Because history ain't really history. History, no matter how you look at it, is a lie. Because we weren't there. Every aspect of history is someone's interpretation of it.

Q: *Right. But not necessarily a lie. Lie is a very loaded word.*

A: All human beings are liars because all human beings live in ignorance. We live in ignorance.

Q: *And always will?*

A: Some human beings are more aware than others, who are not aware. If you know that you are ignorant, silence is golden. If you decide to speak, you're a liar.

Q: *So you lie?*

A: Yup.

Q: *All the time.*

A: Yup.

Q: *Intentionally?*

A: Intentionally only because I know I speak out of ignorance. I'm not plotting to turn the minds of people in my direction by altering the truth.

Q: *I didn't think you were. But it seems to me that a lot of times your ignorance is obvious. Sometimes it's clear that you haven't tried to do any studying. I want to ask you about books.*

A: I don't do much reading anymore.

Q: *Why not?*

A: Because I realize that I'm only reading the opinions of another person. And I don't want to hear nobody. [*Laughs*] Let me clarify that statement. I'm into conversations. And I'm really getting into meditation.

Q: *Why can't you read and converse and meditate?*

A: Hmmm . . . well, you're in the middle of a working thought. So you're actually at where my thinking is actually at. Now I don't know that this thinking is right or not. It is just where I am today. I feel that if I can truly study me and know who I am and how I really feel about and react to certain things, I can turn that on to the rest of the world and define at least a portion of society.

Q: *What kind of books were you reading in the past?*

A: I've read every pro-black book I can find on the market. I've studied every philosopher from Aristotle to Martin Luther King, who I think was the last philosopher. I know what book knowledge is. Book knowledge basically just repeats itself over and over and over again.

Q: *People do too.*

A: No. People can't repeat themselves, because they must react to the present. Books are trapped. They are what they were.

Q: *But at the same time, books can be useful in the present because they can help you understand how you got here.*

A: But what if you're caught up?

Q: *So you feel that you're caught up? You've read enough?*

A: Yeah.

Q: *[Laughing] What are the things to read so that our readers can feel that they've read enough?*

A: They should read all Bibles. They should start with the reading of the Bhagavad-Gita and the Koran. If they'd like to further their study and get a little more deep, they can branch off into certain philosophers of these books. There's also a book by Will Durant, named *the Pleasures of Philosophy*—very good book for updating yourself in terms of philosophy. I would read all the pro-black stuff.

Meaning Diop, Ivan Van Sertima, Dr. Frances Cress Welsing, and Dr. Yosef Ben-Jochannan's work.

Q: *You've read Frantz Fanon?*
A: What's the title?

Q: The Wretched of the Earth. *It's a basic text.*
A: No.

Q: *How about James Baldwin?*
A: Yeah, but not from that philosophy perspective.

Q: *I meant from the "pro-black" perspective.*
A: No. I don't know, maybe I'm wrong, but James Baldwin seems like an Afro-American to me. The poetry of Marcus Garvey is more pro-black.

Q: *Frederick Douglass?*
A: House nigger. Straight up. He sent the whole fucking country to war—he tricked Africans to go fight for their freedom in the Civil War when he knew that the war wasn't about freedom. He was a fuckin' sellout.

Q: *He didn't need to trick anybody to get slaves to fight for their freedom.*
A: Only a small percentage of slaves thought they were slaves.

Q: *What do you mean by that?*
A: The reality of slavery is not the reality that we have today. The history of slavery is taught to us in blocks of revolts, lynchings, murders, laws, and wars. Then they're clouded up with who was president at certain times or who was the one who spoke out at that time. And you might get folklore in. Like the guy who busted his heart trying to outwork a coal machine and died.

Q: *John Henry.*
A: This is history. That's not real history from the perspective of how it's taught to those people on the street out that window. But if you

go to the 23rd century, and look back on 1990 to '95, it will look identical to slavery.

Q: *No.*

A: What would be the difference? The only difference between then and now is technology. Wage slavery exists today, identical to chattel slavery. Today, we don't have to do work with our hands. We direct a machine to do it. But the concept is still intact.

Q: *I think chattel slaves were dealing with circumstances that are far worse than most people have to deal with today.*

A: Most slaves were happy.

Q: *What?*

A: This is documented history. The only slaves that spoke out against society were like me. To whom people say, "Why are you so angry?" Out of 100 percent of slaves, 20 or maybe 10 percent of them were, like, "We need to free ourselves. We need to get off this shit."

Q: *That's ridiculous—the slaves knew they were living in misery. But let's look at the people you say are speaking out, the people who want to teach mind revolution. Some folks say that if people like you really can teach through rap, y'all can also make folks mindlessly violent. So that rap should be regulated.*

A: Well that's arrogance. Because they can't really censor us. The more you do to rap, the bigger it gets.

Q: *But Snoop and them are being targeted.*

A: Same thing. The way to destroy Snoop is . . . *hmmm.* Maybe I shouldn't say that. [*Laughs*] I'll say this: It's the world of opposites. Rap is created under constant oppression. The more you want to lock me up and shut me up, the stronger I get. So the more you do that to Snoop, the bigger he's going to get. You can't destroy rap. Only the people can destroy rap.

I think all of hip hop music is positive. There is no such thing as negative. I'd like to introduce a new word, *niggative.* It is the final expression of the slave mentality that Snoop and them are dealing with. They've said it themselves: They're real niggas. The nigga mentality is really the ghetto mentality.

Q: *Personally, I'm tired of the macho posturing in the music. Is rap on a creative upswing or downswing?*

A: I think rap is on an upswing. But only because I'm here.

Q: *What do you mean?*

A: I take responsibility for rap's positive image. And so, yes, rap is on an upswing. It's just where you place your perceptions. If you're looking at Snoop—Snoop could be a positive thing to people in Long Beach. Eventually Snoop is going to do a positive record. It's natural. Eventually I'm going to put out another gun-buck, "Let's kill 'em all!" Actually I'm manifesting that through Mad Lion. [KRS produced Mad Lion's "Shoot to Kill" and "Take it Easy."] But rap is on a positive swing, because I know what my influence is going to be.

Q: *Biggie Smalls seemed upset about your saying, "I am hip hop."*

A: When I say "I am rap," it's not that anybody else isn't. It's my philosophical thing: I think we are not *doing* rap, it's what we *are*. It was a big misunderstanding—Biggie mistaking my philosophy for ego. Then he said he was drunk, and he wasn't himself that day, and it just came out. I consider him a friend, so he should be able to speak his mind.

Q: *How do you expect rap to change in the next 10 years?*

A: It's realty-check time. You're going to have to be a rap artist and a break dancer. Or a rap artist and a graffiti artist. Because soon, to keep your hardcore edge, you're going to have to be able to do the other aspects of hip hop. Soon. In a few minutes, graffiti is going to be as big as rap was or is. Moneywise and famewise. Break dancing the same way.

Q: *Are you linking hardcore to financial success?*

A: Let's define *hardcore.* To me being hardcore is when you hit the core of your audience hard. To me, R. Kelly is hardcore. In the R&B world, it's all about sex, sex, sex. But some artists like to beat around the bush about it. Then you got R. Kelly, who'll take his clothes off and say, "Come suck me." In fact, the more money you make, the more hardcore you can be—the more you manipulate the videos, radios, TVs. Snoop could be on the cover of VIBE and shoot two people. That's hardcore.

Q: *So you think Snoop is going to become a graffiti artist?*

A: I think he's going to have to study that or break dancing if he wishes to survive in this game for the next 10 years.

Q: *Because the business is cyclical.*

A: Rap might have outlived its flair, its newness. It's becoming mainstream society now. Whenever Kentucky Fried Chicken or Coca-Cola openly and readily accepts you, you're no longer the underground, no matter how you slice it. I think people—especially people in America—are always looking for the underground. What is real. What is the true expression. And rap is losing its true-expression badge. There's no such thing as an underground artist anymore, especially if you put a record out. The only underground artists are unsigned. And then you don't hear about them anyway.

Q: *So what do you think constitutes a real hip hopper?*

A: A real hip hopper is a person . . . No, a real hip hopper is not even a person. It's a level of thinking. It's when you are one with inner-city youth.

Q: *In America.*

A: In America. [*Pause*] No. Wait a minute.

Q: *[Laughs] It's hard.*

A: If someone wants to learn, then he or she is being real about it.

Q: *Can someone who is not African-American be "real"?*

A: I don't think they will be accepted. That's what you get with the *really* real versus the real. I think there's levels of real. Like Kid Capri is really real. He's the father of the mix tapes. If it wasn't for him, S&S, Ron G., Doo-Wop wouldn't have jobs.

Q: *So it's not just a genetic thing.*

A: If you equate it to best, like, who's the best at it, then I think it's genetics. I think you have to be black or Latino to be the best at hip hop. No, let me take that back—you have to be oppressed.

Q: ***Then it's* not *genetics.***

A: It's not genetics. Rhythm and things like that are genetics. But you could learn that too. To be naturally hip hop is genetics. To be a hip hopper naturally, I think you have to be black or Latino, or have some African gene in you somewhere along the line.

Q: ***But what about the oppressed factor?***

A: Take Bill Clinton's daughter. If she's willing to expose herself to learning about hip hop, what she has to do is leave the White House and come live in the South Bronx or Brooklyn. If she lives there—nobody knowing that it's the president's daughter or nothing—she has to meet a guy, he has to dog her out. Dis her. Then she got to meet a guy that she really likes and dis him. Then she has to go to a party, get caught up in a fight. Maybe she's not fighting, but see it. Feel the tension of it. She has to go to a Wu Tang concert. She has to live it. She has to drive with three other black youths in a car, and they driving and the police are looking at them. She has to feel the tension *with* the black youth, and know what that shit feels like. If she can withstand that, then she too can become a hip hopper.

Q: ***The closest many rap fans come to that is through the music of people like you. And then they turn on a Supremes tape. And then after that maybe Nirvana or Soundgarden.***

A: But if they can feel oppression, for that moment they are hip hop. They are welcome to the nation. But only for the moment.

Then it was time to leave, and KRS offered me a copy of his MC's manual. He signed it with a big laugh. I didn't look at the inscription until I got home. "Everything," he had written in big graffiti-style letters, "iz a lie!"

COLIN POWELL 8

By Kevin Powell
November 1995

GENERALLY SPEAKING

Eight years before U.S. troops invaded Iraq for the second time, General Colin Powell granted an interview to VIBE scribe Kevin Powell (no relation). They spoke of race, politics, the cost of war, and the challenge of living in America.

Colin Powell, 58, the four-star general who retired in 1993 as chairman of the Joint Chiefs of Staff, marches to his own beat. Currently on a national book tour pumping his memoir, *My American Journey*, Powell is also, in his own words, the first black to be seriously considered as a presidential candidate who is not simply a "protest vote." Unlike most politicians, Powell isn't afraid to speak his mind, as evidenced by this, his first print interview in two years.

Q: *The first question I'm going to ask is rather obvious. Are you going to run for president?*
A: And you really think I'm going to answer? [*Laughs*]

Q: *I was hoping . . . Powell to Powell.*

A: [*Laughs*] Just between me and you, huh? I have spent the last two years traveling around the country learning about issues, and after my book tour is over—October, November—I will sit down with some close friends and with my family, and see how best I can serve the nation. It might be in politics, it might be in charitable or educational work, it might be an appointed office. Unlike most other candidates, politics is not my passion or profession. My thing was the army. But so many people are encouraging me that I will think about it very hard and pray on it with my family.

Q: *But you've been a White House Fellow. You rose through the Carter, Reagan, and Bush administrations. You've been around politics for the last 23 years at least.*

A: I've been around politics for a long time. And I've seen it at the very highest level. That does not make me a politician. In fact, even though I worked in the West Wing of the Reagan White House for two years in a very sensitive position, not one person in the Reagan White House will tell you today whether they think I'm a Republican or a Democrat.

Q: *Why is that?*

A: I was an active duty military officer who lived by a code that says you never do anything that reflects a partisan political view. So I never registered either as a Republican or a Democrat. I always voted for the best man. It was a tricky act, but I pulled it off.

Q: *Could it be said then that you were a true politician?*

A: I'm pretty good at solving problems. I'm pretty good at presenting cases. I'm pretty good at fighting with adversaries but not creating enemies. And I'm pretty good at fighting with friends without converting them into enemies. If that is what you mean by politics, yeah, I'm pretty good at that.

Q: *Where did you learn these negotiating skills?*

A: I get the question from lots of young people: "What's the secret to success? What was the most important thing that ever happened in your life? What was your greatest failure? Who was your role model?" Life isn't like that. Everyone I ever ran into influenced me in some way—some more good than others, some very, very much worse than others. I watched people I admired and people I didn't admire to see what they were doing right and doing wrong. So I had hundreds of role models. Don't think that there is some star that you can suddenly hitch your wagon to that's going to pull you up.

Q: *How did your roots form who you are?*

A: My family and my roots meant a great deal to me. A warm, close, typically West Indian family with cousins running in and out. A series of expectations were conveyed to their children: You will get an education. You will get a job. You will do better than we did. And you will not shame the family. Now, you got any questions? All the things that you hear people talk about in terms of family values—even though we were poor in the South Bronx, we were all there.

Q: *You were just an average student in college, correct?*

A: Yeah. I was smarter than I realized, and I also learned more than I ever displayed to the teachers at the City College of New York. I was a youngster without a great deal of direction through high school, and it was only when I hit ROTC in college that I found something I really loved and did well. I wasn't a great athlete. As a matter of fact, I was a pretty bad athlete. I flunked math, calculus, and physics. But thank heavens they counted ROTC toward your passing grade, so I was able to graduate. Every young person should always be searching for something to do in life that they enjoy and they can do well. Money is always a concern, but it's not everything.

Q: *Whenever someone becomes a potential candidate for president, people start picking apart their character.*

A: People have said, "Well, he worked for Reagan, so he's one of *them*. He's some kind of Tom." But the next day they find I'm down at some black school, speaking.

Q: *How do you react when you hear someone say things like that about you?*

A: Their problem, not mine. I have always been proud of my Caribbean and African roots. I have never tried to suggest that I wasn't part of the black experience or the black community. I manifested it through mostly talking about the black military experience in the United States, which is a unique kind of experience. It's the only profession that we've been able to participate in continuously for 250 years.

I have never shied away from my origins, but I have also told youngsters, "We're Americans. We're not Africans and we're not Jamaicans. We have to live in this world in this time." While I am proud of being a West Indian and West African and Irish, Scottish, and every other thing, and while I want to know about those things also want to know about the roots of our democratic system.

Q: *A read a survey recently that said fewer African-Americans knew who you are than white Americans.*

A: That doesn't trouble me particularly. I work in an environment that is not that well known to all Africans. There's limited penetration of the media in the African-American community. I wish that were not the case, but it is.

Q: *Do you ever feel like you're performing a balancing act?*

A: I simply refuse to believe I have to perform a balancing act. Ask me what I am and I'll tell you. Ask me where I'm from, I'll tell you. Ask me to deny that background and I won't. But any job you give me, I will do to the best of my ability. Let others judge as to whether I'm too white, I'm too black, I'm too European in my thinking, or I'm not traditional Afrocentric. I can't spend time thinking about that. I just gotta do what I think is right, and go with my instincts and training.

Q: *Hypothetically, if you became president, what could you bring to this country?*

A: One of the reasons I am this political unknown is that both parties appeal to me in some ways. I am Republican in my economic thinking. I am an absolute believer in free market economics. So I would do anything to keep businesses growing, to allow people to make as much money as their talents and hard work will let them. The government should do little more than make sure it's all being done honestly so that, in case greed starts to take over, workers are not being exploited. But after that, I think the government should keep its hands off.

Having said that, I also realize that government does have an important role to play in taking care of citizens who are very needy—those who are losing faith, losing hope. Government has to play a role when the rights of citizens are being abused and there's nobody to stand up for those citizens. I certainly have been a beneficiary of that. So, with respect to social issues, I start to sound like a Kennedy Democrat.

Q: *You come from an immigrant family. What's your position on immigration?*

A: If immigration is illegal, it ought to be stopped. I think the nation has benefited over the years by having a flow of new blood, new citizens, new culture, new color, come into the country. But there are practical limits to what we can absorb. And if we have laws, they should be obeyed. So I think we should do whatever is necessary to seal our borders to illegal immigration so that we can give all the advantages necessary to legal immigrants.

Q: *What about affirmative action?*

A: My view, and I think the view of most Americans, is that affirmative action has been good for the country. It's easy to talk about, "Hey, climb up by your own bootstraps." But if you got no boots, what's the point? All you're doing is handing people rhetoric. Affirmative action was designed to put in place certain preferences to do away with preferences that existed for 200 years. It's not as if we invented preferences. Preferences for white people caused affirmative action to come in after the great civil rights legislation in the '60s.

But if some of these programs have gotten out of whack and

are nothing but pure quotas that serve no social purpose, then I think we ought to get rid of them. The American people are willing to support affirmative action to make sure there's a level playing field. But we're not there yet. It was only two years ago that six Secret Service agents, dressed in nice suits, all college graduates, preparing to spend the day guarding the president of the United States, went into a Denny's restaurant in Maryland and weren't served. Don't tell me that we're color blind. It isn't there yet.

Q: *Why do you think so many people want you to run for president?*

A: Because they're unhappy with the current political scene. People have a deep sense of anxiety. They don't like what they see in Washington, they don't like the screaming and shouting. The president has some serious character problems that he hasn't been able to shake—Whitewater and other things. I'm not making a judgment. I'm just saying they're there.

Q: *You were decorated in Vietnam, and you directed Operation Desert Storm as well as the U.S. invasions of Panama and Somalia. Do you ever sometimes think to yourself, "My God, war is horrible?"*

A: War is horrible. People ask, "Are you a hawk or a dove?" I don't get paid to be a hawk or a dove. I get paid to provide the best military advice I can to my civilian leaders, and to accomplish their political objectives in a way that minimizes the loss of American lives in combat. We know how to die in combat, but we don't like to die for unclear purposes. We don't like to die 'cause some columnist is excited. We don't send our young people in to die because Congress has been screaming up on the Hill. We send them in for clear purposes, because they've got parents.

Q: *Have you been back to your old neighborhood recently?*

A: I was in the South Bronx two weeks ago with Barbara Walters. I walked right on my street and the years just peeled back. I felt like I was a kid again. I even bought Barbara Walters a *biaqua*. Do you know what a *biaqua* is?

Q: Those icies?

A: Yeah. Scraped ice with syrup. Then I took all the cops from Fort Apache to White Castle for hamburgers. But there are pockets of despair. There are youngsters there who do not have the kind of family I had. They are parented by a woman with no husband. Either there never was a husband or the husband's in Rikers Island, or the husband can't get a job.

Q: Could you have imagined finding yourself in this position 30 years ago?

A: Not at all. Along with the role model question, I get this question: "Did you ever dream that you'd be chairman of the Joint Chiefs of Staff as a kid?" There I was in the South Bronx, I didn't even know what the Joint Chiefs of Staff was. All I knew was I always tried to do the very best I could. Always getting myself ready for tomorrow, thinking about the day after, dreaming about the future.

The unique thing about this situation I find myself in—no matter what I do, whether I go into politics or not—an epochal event has occurred. That America would seriously consider a black man as the president of the United States. Not as sort of a protest vote that comes out of the civil rights community—you know, not like Jesse or Shirley Chisholm. To think that we have reached a point where it's possible for an American who is also a black American to be on the cover of magazines, to be interviewed and taken seriously—that, in and of itself, should tell every young person in America that there is nothing you cannot set your sights on.

And don't forget, there is no other place on the face of this earth—no country, no political system, no economic system, no social system, where these kind of achievements are possible than in the United States of America. So get mad sometimes, but it don't get no better than this. Is it perfect? No. Does it have some rough spots? Yeah. And what is our challenge? To fix it. But don't give up. It's the best there is.

TUPAC SHAKUR

By Kevin Powell
February 1996

During his career as a VIBE staff writer, Kevin Powell conducted three major interviews with Tupac Shakur. The first was the basis for Powell's April 1994 cover story, "This Thug's Life." The second interview, conducted behind bars on Rikers Island, was published as a Q&A in April 1995. Their third and final interview was a phone conversation that took place shortly after Shakur signed to Death Row Records. Excerpts from this interview ran as a sidebar to Powell's February 1996 cover story "Live From Death Row." Seven months later, Shakur was fatally shot while riding down the Las Vegas strip with Suge Knight at the wheel. After more than a decade, the murder has yet to be solved. The full transcript of this revealing interview has never been published before.

ALL EYES ON ME

When this interview took place, I hadn't spoken with or seen Tupac Shakur since our Rikers Island interview in

January 1995. In that story, published in *VIBE*'s April '95 issue, Shakur declared the death of Thug Life and swore off smoking weed. He spoke of devoting his life to a higher calling, "something extremely extraordinary," as he put it. He also suggested that Bad Boy CEO Sean "Puffy" Combs, the Notorious B.I.G., Shakur's longtime friend Randy "Stretch" Walker, and others had behaved suspiciously after Shakur's shooting in a New York recording studio on November 30, 1994. Since then rumors of beef were running wild throughout the hip hop industry. The drama only intensified after Suge Knight picked Shakur up from prison in a limo, flew him to L.A. in a private jet, and signed him to Death Row Records. When Randy "Stretch" Walker was killed the following month—on the one-year anniversary of Pac's shooting—I felt the need to contact Shakur. I reached him by telephone in a California recording studio where he was working on his Death Row Records debut. He was, as usual, very candid.

Q: *How you doing brother?*
A: Strugglin'. Hold on, lemme get my cigarettes.

Q: *Did you hear Stretch died?*
A: I don't got no comment.

Q: *Do you remember it was one year ago to the day since that whole situation at the studio?*
A: Yeah I remember. I don't really wanna talk about that.

Q: *So how does it feel to be on Death Row?*
A: I feel right at home.

Q: *I notice that everybody talks about Death Row being a "family."*
A: It's not like I'm gonna be corny and be like, *Everybody love each*

other. It's not like that. Nobody has beef internally. And if we do, then we handle it internally. The family part to me . . . it's like a business, an organization more than like a family. It's like a machine, that's what it is. Death Row to me is like a machine, it's like a vehicle.

Q: *Why did you decide to switch?*
A: Because I wanna go to the next level. The strategy of moving to the next level entails me moving over to Death Row. The biggest, strongest superpower in the hip hop world. In order to do the things that I got to do, we gotta have that superpower. Now that we got that superpower, we gotta expand and show exactly what a superpower really is.

Q: *How is Death Row different from other labels you've worked with?*
A: I loved DU for what they gave me. I loved Interscope for what they done for me. At Death Row I don't have to worry about embarrassing nobody or standing out or doing something they don't want me to do. I'm still Tupac. At Death Row, I got my own shit. Y'know what I'm sayin'? I'm independent. But this is the machine that I roll with, this is the car that I ride with . . . Death Row.

Q: *Suge is now your manager as well?*
A: Basically, my whole move to Death Row was basically a move with Suge.

Q: *Did you get with him for some sort of protection?*
A: Aw, hell no. Nigga I thought you knew—print this. My only fear of death is coming back reincarnated. I thought I put that in the last interview. Don't nothing scare me. Nobody. There's nobody in the business strong enough to scare me. I'm with Death Row cause they ain't scared *either*.

Q: *What is the next level for you? Movies?*
A: Movies, not just acting in the movie but writing. Some control over it production-wise.

Q: *Directing as well?*

A: I already wrote a script. I'm writing a book with Sister Souljah. It's going to be about sex between black people, all the problems, all the questions, all the myths.

Q: *Were you at the Million Man March?*

A: No.

Q: *But you did support it?*

A: Yeah I supported it, but I only been out for three days.

Q: *And you're still facing an appeal. Is it possible you could go back to jail?*

A: This is America. I can go back any day.

Q: *What about your marriage? I heard that was annulled.*

A: Yeah, I moved too fast. I can only be committed to my work or my wife. Seeing that I couldn't be committed to my wife, I didn't want to hurt her. She's a good person. So just take it back to where we were before.

Q: *But y'all are cool?*

A: No doubt.

Q: *I want to put a rumor to rest. Did something happen to you in prison?*

A: Kill that rumor. Now that rumor either got started by some guards or by some jealous niggas. Me being Tupac, you can print this, I don't have to talk about whether or not I got raped in jail. You tell muthafuckas if I wouldn't lay down on the floor for two niggas with pistols, what the fuck make you think I would bend over for some niggas without weapons? Answer that one for me. That's all these niggas, laying down to let somebody go up in *they* ass. *They* getting fucked. That don't even fit my character. They couldn't blow my nuts off, Kevin, so they just gonna take my nuts off.

Q: *That is an ugly rumor.*

A: They can't get at me. A nigga taking shots to the nuts, to the dome. They can't get at me. These punk coward niggas are talking in the VIBE magazine, about they only found one bullet. So what are they now? *Police* officers now? It was a conspiracy. The police is lying. They're lying. The police left the evidence for these niggas to find.

Q: *Do you or Death Row have any beef with Puffy or Biggie?*

A: [*laughs*] I don't got no beef with nobody, man. I just be talking my shit. I let the music speak for itself. I let the people that do know, they know. People that don't know, they don't know. If you know, you know, if you don't, you don't. Ain't no mystery . . . It ain't nothing to be pumpin' up, it ain't nothing to sell. Niggas know what time it is.

Q: *So is this an east coast / west coast thing?*

A: It's not like I got a beef with New York or nothing, but I do have problems. And I'm representing the west side now. Because I was the type of artist, though I had all this love for the west coast, and I was from New York, I never made it an issue. When niggas from New York came to the west coast, I looked out for them. You can ask any of them niggas how many muthafuckas I done gave passes to. I pointed out this is this gang or that gang. You gotta be careful with this. Niggas who lie about us getting hits on their ass. For them now to be gangbanging, first of all to be disrespecting the west coast. *We don't have talent. It ain't this, it ain't that. It's only gangsta shit. It ain't creative enough. It's fucking up the art form.* Even though we made more money for this art form than all those other muthafuckas. We corrupting the art. All the artists now who selling records stole our style. Listen to 'em—Biggie is a Brooklyn nigga's dream of being west coast.

Q: *You wanna say that on the record?*

A: I say that . . . Nigga, did you hear me? And all those other niggas, too. I don't have respect for a lot of niggas. Not because you're from New York. But because how could you do something that you stealing something? Look at all these niggas throwing up west coast gang signs. That's a violation. I was in jail out here. I was listening to the radio. [*Angrily*] They was dissing the west coast and they thought no one was *listening.*

Q: *Let's just be real for a second. We talking about black folks. How can we stop this before someone else gets killed?*

A: I don't want it to be about violence. I want it to be about money. My idea that I had, I told Suge about it: Bad Boy make a record with all the east coast niggas, Death Row make a record with all the west coast niggas. We drop on the same day. Whoever sell the most records, that's who the bombest. And then we stop battling. No more beef. Everybody just do it up. Every year we could do it again. We could do pay per views for charity, and for the community. I'm not about just being out here like a rabble rouser, but I'm not gonna be a coward for nobody.

Q: *What about getting together as black men?*

A: We *are* together as black men, they over there, we over here. If we really gonna live in peace, we all can't be in the same room, man. Because yellow M&Ms don't move with green M&Ms. I mean, you don't put M&M peanuts with M&M plain. You hear me?

Q: *But we all black, brother.*

A: We all black and everything, but I'm not talking about division. I'm talking about realism. You don't hang with us. You live different than we live. We all brothers, but we don't all live the same. Even in a real family. I don't live with my mother. I don't live with my brother. We all come together for Thanksgiving, we all get together for Christmas. If any of them call, I don't wish nothing bad to the nigga. They call and say why don't we do a celebrity this this this in my neighborhood, I'm wit' it.

Q: *What about if they say they're concerned about this hostility out there that people are feeding into. Can you and Suge and Puffy and Biggie sit down?*

A: But that's corny. That's just for everybody else to be calm. So everybody else could understand what's going on. They just want to hear what the conversation is about. I know my life's not in danger. Suge know his life not in danger. I don't feel as if I gotta worry about them. They shouldn't feel like they gotta worry about me.

Puffy wrote me while I was in jail. I wrote him back. I told him I don't got no problems with him.

Q: *Even if there is no beef, don't you think it would be better to be clarified?*

A: What's that gonna stop if we sit down and have a talk? They know they can sit down. Niggas can start some shit and say whatever they want. Cause at some point the Nation of Islam or somebody is gonna sit them down and we can make peace. That's why niggas is not being held responsible for things that they do wrong. I don't want no problems. I don't want to be fighting. I don't want no arguing. I just wanna make my money. You can't tell me I'm gonna sit down and hug and kiss niggas to make everybody else feel good. Straight up, there is no beef. If there was a beef, niggas would know. They know it ain't no beef. Puffy was at the fight [in Vegas, where Suge has a club].

Q: *We in the hip hop generation represent leadership, and in the absence of people like you or Puffy or Suge saying "there is no beef," then regular people who don't understand that are gonna continue to think that there is beef.*

A: I believe in fate.

Q: *In Faith?*

A: Fate. Fate. I know niggas didn't want to sit down and have no conversation unil Puffy started fearing for his life. I was in jail, nigga. Living in jail when everybody was having this beef. One west coast nigga in New York, maximum security prison. Nobody want to have no sit downs then.

Q: *What did you learn from your experience in prison? It was eleven and a half months.*

A: I learned that fear is stronger than love. And no matter how much love I got for my peoples, man, if somebody else making them scared, my people gonna do me in. And i learned that a lot of people support me for just being me. And I have to give back. And a lot of people look up to me to give back. So I have to be able to give back, but I can't give back if I'm broke. So I have to be about my business and my money now. Before I wanted to talk and explain what I'm doing. I'm not doing that no more. Nobody's gonna understand me. I just came up with that after reading what people was writing in VIBE. Ain't no need for me to make people try to understand me. I'm gonna be out here and do my music, do some movies. Try to give back to the hood any way I can. I'ma give out food every Christmas, I'ma give out turkeys every Thanksgiving. I'ma have a Mothers Day program.

Q: *I think you're oversimplifying. Most of the letters from readers support you. A lot of people dissed the people who responded to you in the magazine.*

A: I seen it. I read every VIBE. I had a subscription, man. Every article you did, I read every VIBE that came out. Then I started seeing this shit, I was like, *Goddamn.* They can just say that? Puffy started talking about "If you a thug you need to be a thug forever." Stretch is straight snitchin', talking about I had a pistol, and *whap de whoo.* That's just like sending me to jail. But I don't care about them. It's because of them that I'm invigorated and I'm rejuvenated to do what I got to do.

Q: *You said you were giving up smoking weed.*

A: I'm striving for that. Every day I'm striving for that. Every day. You won't see me all up on TV getting high. I'm not making it where the kids . . . I'm not making it like I'm glorifying getting high. That's a hell of a muthafuckin' thing, to shake an addiction like that. But shit, I gotta do what I gotta do.

Q: *When I talked to you before, you said "It's gonna get deep." What did you mean by that?*

A: It's gonna get deep, man, because . . . um, what the east is doing. They think it's . . . I understand it. I'm from there. It's really like unifying the east coast. Because it was really like, in a slump. But they're doing it wrong. Cause they're using the west coast as a rallying cry. And they making it look like *we* are the perpetrators of this big east coast / west coast thing. They never had no problems.

They could come out here and perform and we clap. We go out there and niggas is booing. That Source Awards, that's what start it. Not start it, but that Source Awards is what put it to a new level. They was booing. Me personally being from both coasts, but I represent the west coast, I think that's disrespectful.

Q: *What about Suge making that comment about Puffy at the Source Awards. Wasn't that kinda disrespectful?*

A: No that's not disrespectful. That's his opinion and that's real. All he was doing was saying if they tired of having a manager shake his ass in their *video*. We don't do like that on the *Row*. That's real.

Q: *But can't that contribute to the whole east / west thing?*

A: Not as much as it does when y'all niggas goin' on the radio: *It ain't about west coat, it's all about N.Y. Boo hoo hoo. Fuck the west, we the best. We started it. All them other niggas . . .* I be *listening!* Suge has got the heart to say it in front of you. All these other muthafuckas been saying it behind our backs.

Q: *By getting deep, to you, does that mean violence or death?*

A: I told you what I want. I want it to go on records. Let's make some money for the 'hood. The 'hood is what need us now. Fuck a nigga ego. I don't care, I could put all that shit aside and we could make records and give money to the 'hood. Build some community centers with this. We can make it where we have block parties, where Death Row and Bad Boy have rapping contests all over the 'hood and *boom boom boom*. We could do whatever.

Q: *Tell me about your new album.*

A: *All Eyez On Me.* The first single is "California Love," with me and Dre and Roger Troutman. And then I got a single coming out in two weeks after that with me and Snoop called "Two of America's Most Wanted." That's about me and Suge and our cases and our problems.

Q: *You mean you and Snoop?*

A: Yeah. We two of America's most wanted. But "California Love" is just me giving it up for California. You got *Crooklyn*, you got *Crooklyn* 1 and 2. You know, this is our *Crooklyn*.

Q: *Why'd you call the album* **All Eyez on Me***?*

A: Everybody lookin' at me right now. The police lookin' at me, the females, my enemies, reporters, people that want me to fall, people that want me to make it. My mama. In jail the guards. Everybody looking at me. All eyes on me.

Q: *How does that make you feel?*

A: It make me feel good. I like the challenge. I know I gotta get out here and put some good work out. I'm really into this album cause I want it to sell. I'm really trying to break some records with this. Cause no rapper's ever put out a double album. It's never been done before.

Q: *How many songs did you say are on it?*

A: It's 28 songs. All brand new songs. None of it was written in jail. All of it happened soon as I got out.

Q: *You once said you were gonna go in a different direction. Is there any introspection on this album? Like you mentioned Marvin Gaye in the last interview . . .*

A: No. This album is like, *hey*. I never did an album like this before.

Q: *Can you describe it in a phrase?*

A: Relentless. It's like so uncensored. Aw *maaaan*. All my albums to me be sad. When I was in jail in New York, niggas was like, *Man, come out with an album that's not like you're dying.* The reason I did an album *Me Against the World* is so I could do an album like this. This is an upbeat album. It's about celebrating my life. Celebrating being alive. Then I got this Outlaw Immortalz project. That's the new Thug Life project.

Q: *So Thug Life is not dead?*

A: It's not dead. It's Syke and Mopreme and some other homies from Thug Life. The project I'm involved with is called Outlaw Immortalz. That's what happens when you pass Thug Life.

Q: *And you have a single with Faith, I understand.*

A: [*laughter*] Yeah, sure do.

Q: *What's that called?*

A: "Wonder Why They Call You Bitch?"

Q: *What's the song about?*

A: Exactly what it sound like. Everybody's wondering why we call females bitches. We don't call *all* females bitches. It's just certain things—and we give examples. Leaving the kids with her mother and she's just out. She's just a tramp.

Q: *How did you hook up with Biggie's wife, given all this stuff that's going on?*

A: We met in the club and bumped it. Me and Faith don't have no problems.

Q: *What about the rumors about you and Faith spending time outside the studio?*

A: You mean the rumor that I fucked her? *Heh heh heh*

Q: *I'd rather turn the tape recorder off if you gonna say that, bro.*

A: [*Laughing hysterically*] I ain't gonna answer that shit, man. You know I don't kiss and tell.

Q: *Is there anything you wanna add? Cause this is getting real deep.*

A: I wanna add that, man . . . I want niggas in New York to not feed into this shit.

Q: *What about niggas on the west coast?*

A: They not feedin' in, they about their money and shit. I'm talking about the east coast. Cause I love a lot of niggas out there. I love a lot of people out there. I got a lot of support from New York when I was in jail. That's really important to me that New York don't think I'm trippin' on *you.* This is just something that's been in me for a long time. They just dissing us. I can't take it no more. But I love all my fans, all the people that supported me and everybody that's down for me. People like Freddie Foxx stayed down for me. And people like Latifah and Treach. And I heard that Smif-N-

Wessun gave me some love on they album. I got nothing but love for them. But see people like Mobb Deep? Stupid "Thug Life we still living it." That's what gonna start this whole new . . . When you see this Outlaw Immortalz shit, that's what started it. Biggie and them being in VIBE talking all that shit. Stretch . . . All them people. That's what started all this.

This Outlaw Immortalz is off the hook, kid. Off the hook. There's a song on there called "Hit em Up" that's gonna be one of the most talked about . . . You remember like Ice Cube's "No Vaseline"? "Hit em Up"'s gonna be like that. It's coming out a couple months after my album. On my record label and Death Row.

Q: *What's your label called?*
A: Euthanasia Records.

Q: *Why that title?*
A: I fell in love with that word. I feel like that's me. I'm gonna die, I just wanna die without pain. I don't wanna die, but if I gotta go I wanna go without pain.

Want me to tell you my verse to that? It go. *Awww maaaaan . . .*

[rapping a capella]

Niggas talk plenty shit
So many tricks
I fucked your bitch
Cause I'm true to this

Witness the heat
You talk bad about a nigga
When I get blasted
Hope you made a little money
While the fun lasted

Heard they call you Big Poppa
Nigga, how you figure?
Cause to me you'll always be
A phony fat nigga

I can't be copied
You can wear the Versace
Nigga you runnin' or what?
Scared as fuck
For the gun to bust

Now niggas duck
I got a list of player haters to fade
You bitch niggas getting blowed away . . .

You cross-eyed down syndrome crack baby
Now you and Puffy is toughies?
Now that's crazy
I got your ass in my sights
Niggas dying tonight
We screaming "West side for life"

I can't wait to see you niggas in traffic
Cause we gonna hit 'em up
When you see me you better bust
Nigga I hit 'em up

[to the melody of Junior M.A.F.I.A. "Players' Anthem"]
Grab your Glocks when you see Tupac
Call the cops when you call Tupac
Who shot me but you punks didn't finish
Now you about to feel the wrath of a menace
Nigga I hit 'em up

Q: *Don't you think that's gonna make it worse?*

A: That's hip hop. Niggas been talking shit all while I was in jail. "Who Shot Ya?" L.L. got a song "I Shot Ya." Even if it ain't about me, nigga, you should be like, I'm not putting it out cause he might *think* it's about him.

Q: *So you think Biggie's song "Who Shot Ya" was about you?*

A: It came out too quick. It was just tasteless. So if he think "Hit Em Up" is about him, hey, whatever.

Q: *You mention their names in there. They didn't mention your name in "Who Shot Ya?"*

A: I ain't no punk. I ain't gonna hide behind the facts.

Q: *Who do you think shot you a year ago?*

A: I know, but it ain't nothing to speak on.

Q: *But you know who did it?*

A: They know who did it.

Q: *They who?*

A: The people who shot me. The people who had me shot. Everybody that know, know. But I ain't worried about that. Peace on earth. I got a whole new clique, those niggas in Jersey. So I'm not gang-banging against the east side. I got niggas from the east side in my clique dissin' Biggie just as hard as me. It's niggas out there that he done wrong. As far as Da Brat, she's opening her mouth getting into some shit she don't want to be involved with. I wanna be the peacemaker, Kev. I wanna tell everybody to just stop.

Q: *Do you think this shooting in Atlanta where Suge's friend died . . .*

A: I don't have no comment about that. I don't know nothing about that. I'm just saying people want peace. I want peace. So let's just stop. I'm talking that shit. Just stop. STOP. Don't.

Q: *It's 1995. Where's Tupac gonna be in the year 2000?*

A: Hopefully, I'll be managing. I'll be producing some movies. And I'll be much calmer than I am now.

Q: *Why aren't you calm right now?*

A: You know, how you would feel if someone break in your house and didn't get arrested? They like staying right across the street. They can break in your house again. How can I be peaceful and leave my door open and be calm and be relaxed when I know the niggas that broke in my house are right across the street?

Q: *What do you mean broke in your house?*

A: Violated me. Stabbed me through my heart. You know, set me up. Violated me.

Q: *This is something you're never gonna forget, obviously.*

A: I'll forgive but not forget. I would rather have been shot straight up in cold blood. Niggas that got me caught me slippin' and shot me. But to be set up? By people you trusted? That's bad.

Q: *You used the word jealousy before. What do you mean?*

A: Let's be real. Be real. Be *real* Kev. Doesn't Biggie sound like me?

Q: *Hey man . . .*

A: Is that my style coming out of his mouth? Just New York-tized. That big player shit. *He's* not no player—*I'm* the player.

Q: *And you want all this on the record?*

A: I don't give a *fuck*. Whatever you hear. *He's* no player. How you the player? I'm the player.

Q: *What about all the young kids around the country who look up to you and Biggie who don't understand all this? And all they hear is what's going on on wax and in interviews.*

A: Regardless of all this stuff, or no matter what he say, what I say, Biggie still my brother. He's black. He's my brother. We have a conflict of interest. We have a difference of opinion.

Q: *About what?*

A: Things that occurred. Um, what should have been done. Who's who. You know, where we stand. Principles.

Q: *You talking about as far as being shot? That's what you have a difference of opinion about?*

A: It doesn't matter. Nobody needs to know but me and him. He knows.

Q: *So you and him need to sit down.*

A: No we don't need to sit down. This is when you sit down: If niggas talk shit and there's a misunderstanding. Then if I was quiet and he's quiet, then we sit down and talk about it. But we talked about it already. It's like when Stretch—God bless the dead—I didn't hear from Stretch the whole time I was locked down.

Q: *When's the last time you spoke to Stretch?*

A: After I got shot. That was it.

Q: *You mean since a year ago?*

A: And that was my closest comrade. I had no idea about Stretch being deceased. In my heart, I'm sad. And I have no comment about it out of respect for his family.

I read in the paper that Ed Lover said I got shot and that I turned on everybody. See Ed Lover's starting some shit. And he's asking me how can we talk to them niggas? Don't even say that type of shit. The old Tupac would get mad and would mash on Ed Lover. The new Tupac is not doing that. The new Tupac says, well, he made a mistake. He didn't know what he was saying. I'm not going to trip off that. But I just wanna make a comment on something while we talking. I'm gonna be real. I didn't appreciate everybody dissing my lyrics and saying this and saying that. None of my lyrics do you hear me putting a gun to a pregnant woman's belly.

Q: *You talking about Biggie?*

A: Bitches is *loving* that shit. Bitches is dancing! You can't be no player killing babies, nigga. Robbing pregnant women—that ain't no player shit. I don't be into that.

Q: *I just hope everything works out on every level.*

A: I want everybody to have peace. Print that. I want peace for everybody, man. I don't want no problems. And I wanna print that I got nothing but love for all the brothers that was down with me when I was down in Clinton. Cause they *do* read VIBE and they will be reading this issue. So, just let 'em know that I got nothing but love, and I remember everything they did.

Q: *You've been all over, from New York to Baltimore to the Bay Area to Atlanta and L.A. What is this journey that Tupac is on?*

A: To find a home.

Q: *Is that a permanent home, or are you still searching?*

A: It'll be permanent as long as there's loyalty, respect, and honor.

Everything a soldier needs. I'm a soldier. You know what that means?

Q: *Why do you think so many young black men around the country identify with you?*

A: Cause we all soldiers, unfortunately. Everybody's at war. Some of us are at war with different things. With ourselves. Some of us are at war with the establishment. Some of us are at war with our own communities.

Q: *What are you at war with?*

A: Different things at different times.

Q: *Like what?*

A: My own heart sometimes. There's two niggas inside me. One who wants to live in peace, and the other won't die unless he's free.

Q: *What about the Tupac who's the son of a Black Panther and Tupac the rapper?*

A: Tupac the son of the Black Panther and Tupac the rider. Those are the two people that's inside of me. Like, my mom and them envisioned this world for us to live in, and they strove to make that world. So I was raised off those ideals, to want those. And in my own life, I saw that that world was impossible to have. It's a world in our head. It's a world that we think about on Christmas and at Thanksgiving. And it's a world that we pass on to our children to make. So I had to live in this world like it is today. She taught me how to live in that world that we have to strive for. And for that, I'm forever grateful. She put heaven in my heart.

Q: *Do you feel like you're walking a balance between those two worlds?*

A: I follow my heart every time I pray to God. I feel like I'm doing what God wants me to do. I asked God when I got shot, *What you want me to do? Just guide me.* And I told him this time when I get out, I said, *Whatever you put in my heart, God, is what I'm gonna do—100 percent.* Whatever my heart tells me is what I'm gonna do. So please control my heart. And if I do anything you don't like me doin', say anything you don't want me to say, *please* help me to stop it. That's the only thing I can do in order to live. Or else I'll be phony or I'll be faking. I won't know what to do.

Q: *Do you feel that you're a leader?*

A: I think so, I think I'm a natural born leader. But I think I'm a leader because I'm a good soldier. If Colin Powell was president, I'd follow him. You know what I'm saying? I know how to bow down to authority, if it was authority that I respect. You know what I mean?

Q: *What if Colin Powell would have run for president?*

A: I would have supported him. I was talking to Al Sharpton about how he should run. And I would help him. I wanna get into politics.

Q: *Why?*

A: Because that's the way for us to overcome a lot of our obstacles, is to have political power. Nothing can stop power or recognize power but power. Everything you telling me to do, *Let's sit down and talk.* If Bosnia disrespects America, or Saddam Hussein disrespects America, they gonna go to war. Cause America wants its respect. And they gonna sit down *after* Saddam Hussein recognizes that they should respect America. We have to have respect before we can have communication. Before we can communicate, there has to be a mutual respect. And we don't have that.

I respect the east coast. The east coast know I respect them. I used to beat niggas up for Queen Latifah. You can ask Chuck D. When they robbed P.E., I was there. When Treach was out there and niggas wanted . . . It's not as bad as everybody think. It's not like everybody fighting. We get along with the south. We get along with Miami. The West Coast get along with Texas. New Yorkers . . . Strong hip hoppers.

Q: *What about the attacks from politicians?*

A: It made me go in the studio and just think about being more relentless. I do not suggest that children buy this album.

Q: Why not?

A: There's a lot of cursing. There's a lot of raw game that needs to be discussed in a family moment before you let them listen to this.

Q: What would you suggest parents tell their kids before they listen to your new album?

A: Most of them already know the things that I'm talking about. Explain to them that because I'm talking about it doesn't mean that it's okay. That this comes from someone who just spent eleven and a half months in a maximum security jail, got shot five times, and was wrongly convicted of a crime he didn't commit. This is not from a normal person.

Q: How do you feel about what's going on with Snoop's trial?

A: I can't make any comment on that. He's my brother and everything. I'm there with him every day. I got a song with the Dogg Pound on the album, Method Man and Redman.

Q: So you do work with people from the east coast.

A: It's not the east coast I'm mad at. I'm mad at niggas that ridin' against the west coast. I'm not against the east coast. I'm against anybody against the west coast.

Q: You said Suge covered your bail?

A: If it didn't go through, he covered my bail. Interscope gave up my money, but he said if anything goes wrong, I'll pay for it. We didn't know I was getting out. He's just looking out for me. *I'm gonna put 10,000 in your books. I handle this, handle that, everything is handled.* When I got out of jail, he had a private plane for me. He had a limo for me. He got me where I had to go. He had security. He had five police officers. Got me in the studio. I said I needed a car, I got a car. I need a house for my moms. She's taken care of. Hell no, I ain't gonna say where my mom lives. Everything's okay.

Q: When did you decide to sign to Death Row?

A: In jail. I said Suge, I need this and this and this. And for me to get where I gotta go, I gotta mash through this shit. I can't have all these people trippin' off me getting shot. What made me go to Death Row was when I was hearing on the radio I got fucked in the ass. And none of my people wasn't fighting it. My managers didn't care. And they're killing my character. And Suge was just saying, *Nigga you better ride on these muthafuckas.*

Q: What does Suge represent to you?

A: Me and Suge—right now? As of today? We're the perfect couple. I can see this is what I've been looking for, management-wise. He rides like I ride. He makes it easier for me, cause before I had to ride extra hard cause I'm smaller, and niggas be underestimating me. So I gotta bust a muthafucka in the mouth, or do this or do that just to get my respect. Now with Suge as my manager, I gotta do less. Cause before niggas wasn't scared of me. So I brought fear to them. Now I don't have to do all that to get that. Cause muthafuckas is shared shitless of Suge. I don't know why, cause Suge's cool.

Q: So all this talk about Suge isn't true?

A: He's a rider. That's all. He's a rider.

Q: So it's all just a lot of hype or myth?

A: It's a lot of cowards who's jealous. They don't have the heart to face Suge in a business situation or a one on one situation. They wanna make him look like the devil. So everybody could hate him. That's what Hitler did with the Jews. He couldn't take 'em out, just because they was a righteous people. To make everybody hate 'em, he had to make them like the scourge. That's what people doing with Suge, making him like he's the scourge of the industry. He's the reason why they fighting at concerts, he's the reason why rappers going to jail. They trying to make it like it's his fault. All Suge's doing is riding. Making it so rappers can get what they due. When I was in jail, Suge is the only one who used to see me. Nigga used to *fly* a private plane, all the way to New York, and spend time with me. He used to get his lawyer, that I wasn't paying nobody for . . .

Q: *David Kenner?*

A: Yeah. To look into all of my cases to find out how I could get out. He understood where I was coming from. I didn't have no money when I was locked down. I can't make no money. Interscope was giving me money but I was running out. Suge supported me—whatever I needed. I said I needed money, he brought me money. I said fly the person, he flew the person. Get me this, got me that. I said this is what I *needed.* But I promised him when I get out, I said Suge, I'm gonna make Death Row the biggest label in the whole world. I'm gonna make it bigger than Snoop even made it. Not stepping on Snoop's toes, he did a lot of work. Him, Dogg Pound, Nate Dogg, Dre, all of them—they made Death Row what it is today. I'm gonna take it to the next level. I'm gonna put us in films. I'm gonna blow us up soundtracks. I'm gonna put records out at an alarming speed. I'm gonna put us out there.

Q: *What about the movie Bullet with you and Mickey Rourke? Is that ever gonna come out?*

A: I think they squashing it. That's okay—because I don't want no more movies coming out with me as a drug dealer.

Q: *What kind of characters do you wanna play in the future?*

A: I wanna be a hero. I wanna be an action adventure star. I wanna show the heros outta my peer group. Like Wesley Snipes is a hero for our fathers. Stallone is a hero for our grandfathers. I wanna show the heros for my age group right now.

Q: *You told me about Higher Learning before. Do you wish you had a chance to play a role like that?*

A: No. No. I got no beef with John Singleton, I got no beef with the Hughes Brothers. I thought it was his loss that he caved in under my pressure. And it was his loss that he stole one of my ideas. I didn't push the issue that John Singleton stole my idea.

Q: *What about if you go back to jail? Then what?*

A: I'm ready for whatever has to come. I'm ready for whatever. I've got enough songs done right *now* to go to jail for five years, and have a record come out every year.

Q: *You've been working hard since you got out.*

A: Every day since I've been free, I've been doing music. I've got 45 songs done.

Q: *So you're focused?*

A: Very focused. Forty-five brand new songs. I've got everybody on this album. I'm about to do a song with D'Angelo that's just gonna sew everything up. If I don't get it on my new album it's gonnna be like a remix or something on my Outlaw Immortalz shit.

Q: *Were you surprised that* Me Against The World *went to number one?*

A: I wasn't surprised. Not to be cocky, but I thought that was the best album I ever did up to that point. I felt like it was what hip hop was about at that moment. It didn't glorify the game, it talked about the stress of the game. In one album I blessed mothers, I talked about spousal abuse, I talked about the little niggas going too wild, I talked about the temptations every man feels for other women, I talked about being against the world, talked about my rape case, talked about dying. This was all before I got shot, and everything was prophesized.

Q: *Your strongest songs are autobiographical.*

A: I got a song called "Letter To a Homeboy." I got the idea from my mother when she wrote *Briar Patch.* She had some shit on there for me before I wasn't even born yet. It's like a song to my unborn child. Life goes on. E-40 and the click. Michelle. Everything, man.

Q: *You told me in our first interview about the male figure in your life, your father, etc. Do you think about that now as you're getting older?*

A: Naw . . . They just like O.G.s to me. I don't feel them as father figures. They like O.G.s. I mean I give all my props to Mtulu Shakur, and Geronimo Pratt, and Mumia—and all the people that was down with my moms. All of them.

Q: *What is Suge like to you? Is he a big brother?*

A: He's like a big brother, you know. He's like a big brother, but he's still . . . he's more a peer that he is over me. He's just got more game now. So you know, He a homie though. He's that homie that I think I always wanted.

WYNTON MARSALIS 10

By Greg Tate
February 1996

JAZZ CRUSADER

Wynton Marsalis is on a holy mission to change the way you think about jazz, soul, hip hop—anything you've got. Greg Tate goes head to head with the sultan of swing.

You might not know it, but Wynton Marsalis is one funny brother. The man has got jokes for days, even when he's being deadly serious. Hailing from New Orleans, Marsalis embodies the many virtues of the educated southern black man. He's earthy, respectful of his elders, and sarcastically analytical of all that smacks of sham, pretense, and fakery. One of the things African-Americans lost in the migration from the South to the North was our grassroots artisan tradition, the knowledge of and skill in building things by hand. Marsalis's reverence for and militant advocacy of technique and learning—as evident in his lecturing as it is in his trumpet playing—may owe as much to the presence of such craftsmen in his immediate family tree (his father, Ellis, is a renowned jazz pianist; his brothers include sax star Branford and pianist Delfeayo) as to his musical forefathers Louis Armstrong, Duke Ellington, and John

Coltrane. His sheer productivity in so many areas is nothing short of astounding.

In the past year Marsalis, 34, has recorded his 30th album, *Standard Time, Vol. 4,* due out in March, and completed the writing and hosting of two distinctly different series on jazz for PBS and National Public Radio. The PBS *Marsalis on Music* series, derived from his Jazz for Young People program at New York's Lincoln Center (he is also artistic director of Jazz at Lincoln Center) is something all parents interested in their children's cultural development should own. The series for NPR invites musicians from many schools of contemporary black music to present their work and to analyze the improvisations of artists like Charlie Parker. Participants have included those often considered—simply because they represent a differing or opposing conception of jazz—as Marsalis's personal enemies, people such as Cecil Taylor, Steve Coleman, and Marcus Miller. But Marsalis isn't out to pick fights as much as he is interested in stirring up healthy intellectual debate: Jazz musicians are often a taciturn, cultish, and enigmatic lot when it comes to sharing trade secrets.

Marsalis loves to share what he knows with as many people as will listen—and sometimes even with those who won't. His opinions on hip hop have almost led him to duking it out in public with some well-known rappers. He's hands-down the most illuminating essayist and speaker on jazz musicology to emerge in some time. And we all know he's no joke on that horn. Nor are his talents as a bandleader, composer, and arranger anything to laugh off. All the same, Marsalis has yet to join the ranks of the jazz geniuses. No fault in that and no surprise, either: Anyone attempting monumental jazz behind what Ellington, Monk, Coltrane, and Miles laid down has their work cut out for them. What's important to consider with Marsalis is that he's even trying to rise to that challenge. Our conversation took place in my hometown of Washington, D.C., where Marsalis was burning the midnight oil for his NPR project.

Q: *How did growing up in the South impact on your development?*

A: It was tremendous, 'cause you know I love the South. When I was in it, I didn't love it as much—I learned to after I left. When I was living there, I couldn't wait to leave. I left when I was 17, because I felt the rest of the world was going to be very different. When you're in the South, you hear that it's so backward and prejudiced. But once you get out in the world you realize, *whew!*

Q: *You got a rude awakening?*

A: Very rude. *[Laughs]* It's like New Orleans music, man. My whole life I heard it and I loved it, but I wouldn't *let* myself love it because I thought it was Tomming. So when I heard it, I'd be, like, *Damn, I like this shit.* But I had so little respect for it, I wouldn't even learn it. I'd be in parades playing and wouldn't know the songs. No respect. My daddy used to tell me, "You need to learn some tunes," and I'd be, like, "Aw, man, that's old music."

Q: *I'm curious about the funk band you and Branford were in when you were teenagers, the Creators. Apparently, from things I've read, y'all worked a lot.*

A: We were a popular band. We played proms, talent shows, lounges—we worked. We worked more than my daddy, man. We had one of those big old bands like Cameo. Took us an hour to set up our equipment. We had timbales, lead vocalist, two guitars, keyboards. We had our little dance steps and uniforms and all kinds of lights that would be blowing up. It was funny.

Q: *You sang too.*

A: Yeah, that style. A few background vocals, like *[breaks into a falsetto voice]* "Oooh, *baaa*-bay." *[Laughs]* That was the gig, man. It was fun. We'd play whatever was popular, bruh. "Brick House," "Tear the Roof Off the Sucker," "What's Going On," all of Earth, Wind & Fire's and Parliament's music. If you'd see us in rehearsal, we'd be arguing and fighting with each other for an hour over who was playing what part from the records. We were New Orleans musicians, man—just vamp and solo. Matter of fact, we had to cut back on the soloing because people started saying, "The Creators, they play jazz." Playing talent shows was the best, because when cats would lose, they'd want to fight the band. One time, some cats came up singing "Kung Fu Fighting" and they were messing up bad—then they wanted to fight us. We'd say, "Boy, we got so many people in this band you making a big mistake, you don't want to come up in there."

Q: *Did you always know you were going to be a musician?*

A: Not until I got to high school. That's when I started practicing. And developing a certain curiosity. Man, all those years I lived with my father, he had all those jazz albums and I never was curious enough to put one on. But when I was 12, I put on this record of Trane's *Giant Steps.* And the only reason was because I was looking at album covers. The albums we listened to always had somebody doing something wild on the cover, like wearing some strange outfit or big glasses or wings or a wig or something. Then I looked at my albums, and cats had some vines on, and were clean, and I said, *Damn, let me see what they're dealing with.* So I put *Giant Steps* on, and I said, *Huh, this shit don't sound bad.* Every day after, I put Trane on. I didn't try to play along. This was when I was transcribing this little jazz tune Earth, Wind & Fire had on the *Open Our Eyes* album—writing it out with letters because I couldn't read music. But hearing Trane got me asking my daddy questions about "What is this?" and "Can you play along with me?"

Q: *He must have been in shock.*

A: Yeah, he was, like, "What is this?" But I had been hanging around gigs since I was a little boy, and I always liked the way jazz musicians talked. All the nasty shit they were saying. You could feel that hurt in them because the people didn't like their music, but you could also hear a lot of pride. And they were smart. They'd go in the barbershop and be winning all the arguments. They'd get respect. Cats would be, like, "Hey, man, Ellis is a jazz musician, he been all over the world."

My daddy was smart at all kinds of stuff. Once he coached our little league football team, and that's the only game we almost won. But they struggled, man. They had a hard time, my daddy and all of them. I remember that period very well. When the '70s started, we had a certain momentum and pride. And then that broke down. I remember that feeling in the street when Muhammad Ali won his legal battles and Marvin Gaye came on. Everybody was playing "What's Going On"—that was the anthem when cats were washing their cars or playing street football, whatever. I remember the feeling of that, man.

Q: *So what's your analysis of what happened to that feeling?*

A: Unreality. You take something unreal and you make it real. Chaos is always in the world. The question is always, How we can order it? And once them black exploitation movies came in—and I went and saw every one of them—that was a tremendous blow. That blow has never been assessed. Everything was "bitch this" and "ho that" and "motherfucker"—that's the beginning of that shit. And the riots hurt a lot too; the downtown areas that never got rebuilt. Then there was the lack of a transferal of information from one generation to another. Toni Morrison and I went out talking one night, and she said, "You know, it seems one generation just forgot to talk." It's like a gap. All that information is still here, but what happened to the humility? What happened to the soul? Because soul don't matter about how bad your condition is. Seems like the more struggles people had, the more soulful they were. Whose people had money, man? My grandfather started out a sharecropper in Mississippi. My grandmother was a domestic worker. My father struggled. He wasn't making no money playing modem jazz in New Orleans. But no matter if we had to pick out clothes from the Sears catalog, we had respect. Respect, that's not an economic condition.

Q: *What's your definition of soul?*

A: Soul is somebody that's bringing a feeling to you regardless of your race, your sex, or your age. That feeling that everything is gonna be all right. It has a spiritual quality to it. It's a matter of having understanding and empathy when somebody wants to fight you over nothing, and you say, "Hey, man, it's all right." It's not a weak thing, though, like, "I'm just gonna go along with whatever y'all say." Because soul sometimes means you gotta pick up a sword.

Q: *Is that why you decided to hold public debate with James Lincoln Collier [author of three controversial tomes on jazz]?*

A: Collier made me mad with some of the things he wrote. Because he writes thing like "Louis Armstrong was being treated like a nigger in the real sense of the word." Well, what is the real sense of the word *nigger?* Or "Duke Ellington couldn't write long-form music." Just a bunch of assumptions. And the technical things he got wrong just shows a level of not caring about these people. Usually you *can* never get guys like that in a forum. But with Collier I wrote a letter in rebuttal—which Collier at first said that I didn't write because he thought I'm too illiterate to write a letter, so [black author and critic] Stanley Crouch had to have written the letter. But when we started debating, I wasn't even proud of it, bruh, because he wasn't really prepared to debate. After 20 minutes I was ready to stop. I like to argue, man. I like it to go back and forth. It's like a game: If we gonna play some ball or something, I like to have to hustle. I was looking forward to him being smoking on something, where I'd have to say, *Damn, didn't think about that.* But he didn't take it seriously enough to prepare for it. Now the question is, Why won't Oxford University retract and change those things that are factually wrong in those books?

Q: *In your book* Sweet Swing Blues on the Road *[W.W. Norton], you wrote about a fellow approaching you and saying how he thought European concert music was better equipped than jazz to express the emotional complexities of the age, and you respond, "What jazz are you talking about?" and he says, "All of it." And you go, "Uh-huh." I could imagine a similar exchange between you and someone asking you about hip hop.*

A: First of all, you have to have a lot of different views of a thing out in the public so people *can* weigh them—and make their *own* decision. Music is music: melody, harmony, rhythm, and texture. Those elements combine to do a certain thing. Now music also interprets mythology. And there is a history of Afro-American music in this country where everything on that time line reflects something about America. And just like you can look around our community and say, "What happened?" you *can* also do that same thing with our music. My whole thing is—after being a veteran of thousands of schools, black and white—where are the music programs? Who's teaching our kids music? We don't need to be taught? Even Louis Armstrong got music lessons in the waifs' home.

Q: *Isn't there a way of looking at hip hop as not necessarily the next stage in evolution or devolution, but as something that is valid because of its innate ingenuity and resolution of certain musical problems?*

A: Well, first of all, it is valid because it exists. It's valid in reference to African-American musical tradition. But once something is a part of a tradition, it has to be viewed and dissected for what it is. There's a whole tradition of talking and rhyming, Rudy Ray Moore, Slim Gaillard, *ad infinitum*. Some of what hip hoppers do is creative. There's creativity in everything, man. And when you get a lot of people working on something, you're bound to come up with something.

Now one interesting thing is, a lot of times . . . *[chuckling]* the songs aren't really in a key. That's interesting to hear, because their relationship to sound is sonic, so they'll put all these elements together, and it's not in a key. So that's interesting. For a tune or two. But given the history of Afro-American music, for me the question becomes, How can you get everything in your art? How can you have music that will inspire boudoir activities with music that is spiritual *and* that has a high musical content *and* that's reflective of the real true grandeur of human life regardless of your economic status? How can you get some music that's terrible in terms of its depiction of tragedy and put that in three-minute form? Because we had forms that existed that led us to that point. Then suddenly—*boom!* It's like, okay, none of that existed, now we have this.

Q: *Yeah, but in some cases you can say that in a redemptive sense as well as a destructive sense.*

A: Well, there's always a range. You can't say all of something is bad. But if you said to me, "I want you to name 15 hip hop albums," you think I'd be able to do that?

Q: *You haven't been pulling too much off that shelf, huh?*

A: Whatever *I* think about that is coming from a limited point of reference. Now—as a musician—if you play some music for me, I can tell you what they're playing. Because I'm around kids all the time, I *can* tell you what *they* think about it. I've had this discussion about rap music *ad infinitum.* When I go out to eat, I got to damn near have bodyguards. Cats are, like, "You said you didn't like our music." It's become an absurd situation, where I have to say, "First, I'm not afraid of you. You're entitled to your right to speak, and I'm entitled to mine. We could talk about this all night if you want." And we can put the documents themselves on. We can read the lyrics. They're gonna speak much clearer than what I could say. If I had 15 CDs stacked up right here, it would speak much louder than what I could say about it.

Q: *You might be surprised too, B.*

A: Believe me, I've checked out a lot of their music, because people bring it to me and say, "Listen to this." I mean, c'mon, I speak in high schools, man. It's like, I go in there and they say, "Oh, jazz . . ." *[Laughs]* You know what I'm saying? You know that group with the song "Jazz"? A Tribe Called Quest? Man, about 20 people played that one for me. Like, "Hey, what you think about this? This is jazz."

For me, it's not so much a question of hip hop as it is, What happened to Afro-American popular music once the church tradition faded out in that music? Once you let go of the blues and the instrumental tradition of improvisation, that's when a lot of things got lost. The question is not, Why don't you like hip hop? Or, Do you not like the younger people? I love young people, and I'm always around them. When I walk into schools and principals tell me they don't have any PTA because parents don't have any concern for their kids at all, or when I go into schools and see kids not being educated . . . you can't compete in this world like that. The world does not care about your personal situation. It's a lot of human potential being wasted. And the question becomes, How *can* we develop all of that human potential? Maybe the final conclusion will be hip hop or whatever the next thing is. Hey, fine, you know. The question is, What forms promote it more?

When Afro-American music loses its sonic connection to the blues and the church and to the whole give-and-take of improvisation, it loses the most important things. It's not so much that what is created is not good or creative, because if you got 2 million people beating on steel, 40 or 50 thousand of them are gonna figure out *something*. So if you listen to the way all these people are combining sound and all the different ways they play with language, there's bound to be a lot of things in there that are interesting. But what are they doing with the things that are the core and the backbone of Afro-American music? When this fad is gone, it's gonna be back to the blues—always been and always will be.

Q: *Some would say it's an extension of the blues.*

A: How would they say that? See, that's when I iced the discussion. How is it an extension of the blues as music?

Q: *Well certainly the orality of hip hop is from the blues. Just the raw sound of the voices themselves. The tone and texture of those voices are not that far from somebody like a Howlin' Wolf.*

A: All right, I'll give them that—there's one. But what about from the standpoint of the form itself? The blues has many aspects that manifest themselves in the artifact of music. Where is the folk essence?

Q: *The properties of sound that hip hop producers are looking for when they sample are soulful properties. They're looking for bits of soul they can build upon. Because what they're sampling is the history of* *black music. And I think you could make a case for the folk essence of the blues still being in their music.*

A: What they're doing is what they do. And that's okay. Fine. I agree with you that it's part of an ongoing cycle. But after a while we got to have some music. You *can* go on forever riffing, but if you say, "Man, you got your instrument, why don't you come up here and play what you're talking about?" What I'm saying is not something speculative. It's what I know. But I have to have the music to show you where the form is coming from. Remember, we're not talking about re-creating the old folk blues. We're in the '90s so we're talking about the 60- or 70-year extension of that concept. It's not that there's an element of blues in hip hop, but how does that element reflect 60 or 70 years of musical development?

Q: *Stanley Crouch told me each successive generation was able to summarize and codify the entire contribution of the previous generation in one succinct phrase. He referenced Marvin Gaye as a sublime example of that. Hip hop could be read as a codified reading of our history and tradition too.*

A: You can argue music forever without the music, because you're using words that are not connected to anything, because the sound is not there. If you and me start talking about rocks on Mars and I say, "Well, I've seen blue ones that look better than the green ones," what does that mean? But once you get to a piano and a record player, that discussion gets cut down by about three hours.

SONNY ROLLINS

By Ishmael Reed
October 1996

11

THE COLOSSUS

*Called the world's greatest living saxophonist, Sonny Rollins
is one of bop's few survivors. He spoke with acclaimed
novelist and jazz columnist Ishmael Reed about jazz past
and future, and about stayin' alive.*

Bebop was my generation's hip-hop. It was more than a pas-
time; it was an obsession. I used to play trombone with
bebop groups. When I turned sixty, I enrolled in The Jazz-
school in Berkeley, where I studied with jazz pianist Susan
Muscarella for nearly five years. I've continued with jazz pianist Mary
Watkins. When I met Max Roach, I thanked him for keeping me out of
reform school; we were too busy listening to bop to get into trouble.
We'd spend hours at each other's homes listening to the latest recordings. We dressed like the beboppers. We were clean. We went around
looking like Gregory Peck in *The Man In The Gray Flannel Suit*. Our
idea of a party was where they'd play "Moody's Mood For Love." We
knew all of the words.

Bebop musicians didn't walk. They came at you, dancing. When
Sonny Rollins descended from his studio after our interview, he was

wearing this great greenish raincoat that hit him near the ankles. Rollins, who had turned sixty-six in the September of 1996, when the first VIBE interview took place, said that when he was a teenager, he was impressed with the way that an older trumpet player shined his shoes. Beboppers were sharp, and we were their acolytes.

Theodore Walter "Sonny" Rollins first picked up the sax in 1944 while only a sophomore in high school. By the 1950s he had come into his own, playing tenor with a variety of jazz's all-time greats, including Art Blakey, Bud Powell, Thelonious Monk, and Miles Davis. When he left the Max Roach Quintet in 1957, he created his own unique trio (sax, bass, and drums) that spotlighted the versatility of his solos and Hard Bop style. Several years later, in an attempt to regain inspiration in his playing, he stopped recording and began practicing regularly while walking along New York's Williamsburg Bridge; his triumphant return took place in 1962 with an album titled simply *The Bridge.*

Rollins' early recordings show him developing what would become the Rollins style: a broad repertoire that included blues, standards, and even spirituals; and an intense devotion to melody, so that no matter how abstract his solos might become, one is always mindful of the tune with which he started out—a trait he shares with Thelonious Monk. Though many jazz solos sound as though they're spontaneous, often they are rehearsed and memorized. Some musicians are still recycling solos originated by Charlie "Bird" Parker. Rollins, on the other hand, is known for pure improvisation. He has a dedicated following but his fame in the United States has been slow to come. For some of the white critics, who form the largest segment of the fraternity of jazz critics, Rollins has an attitude. He is recognized as being among the first artists to make reference to the growing militancy of the '60s with his "Freedom Suite."

Both the Yoruba and Biblical traditions hold that sometimes your worst adversary is inside your family—in this case, American fans and critics. The prophet is not honored in his own country. Abroad, though, it's different. Rollins' *Saxophone Colossus* is a best-seller in Japan, which he has visited 19 times, and where he has appeared in computer commercials. Since I first interviewed Rollins for *VIBE*, Rollins has been the subject of interviews in *The New York Times* and a profile in *The New Yorker*. At seventy-six, he still continues his vigorous touring.

But Rollins doesn't have to go anywhere if he doesn't want to. He's come a long way since his mother bought him that first Zephyr tenor. He can kick around his Germantown, New York farm and continue to evolve his music.

Rollins has accumulated a catalog of close to 50 albums. More importantly, he's one of the only surviving icons left from an era in jazz when genius was the norm and musicians like Miles Davis, John Coltrane, and Thelonious Monk were not only changing music but also affecting black culture and American society. When members of my generation tried to break away from the linear forms of novel writing, we did so because we were trying to keep up with the musicians and painters. How would it look if I did some refried Faulkner and Hemmingway, when I lived in a community on the Lower East Side that included Joe Overstreet, Sun Ra, and Cecil Taylor? Kenny Dorham and I used to drink together at a Lower East Side dive called The Port of Call, and Albert Ayler and his brother were guests in my home.

It's appropriate that the central image associated with Rollins is a bridge, because the beboppers, like the hip hoppers—those who are not pushed into a music that degrades by avaricious record producers—have established a bridge that reaches back thousands of years to the sound of the mother drum, the root of all black music.

But sometimes it seems that in a white supremacist society, constantly on guard against minorities gaining the upper hand, even the creators of one of the country's homegrown music are denied credit for their invention. The PBS series *American Experience* is currently running a program about the history of New Orleans. From the visuals one would gain the impression that whites invented jazz. Photos of great black musicians like Jelly Roll Morton, Louis and Lil Armstrong,

King Oliver and others roll by without the musicians being identified. All one has to do is notice the names associated with the production to realize the problem.

Q: *There aren't many survivors from the great bebop revolution. Who is still left?*

A: Well, J.J. Johnson and Max Roach, Milt Jackson, Percy Heath and his little brother Jimmy. There's not that many of us left. Art Farmer, who I guess would be around my age. Johnny Griffin.

Q: *Do you guys have a survivors guild? [Laughter]*

A: No, we don't have one. We should have something like that, 'cause in the old days in Harlem, they used to have all these clubs and everyone would be together, to help guys. There should really be some kind of federation. But people just see each other now and then, you know.

Q: *You've said your mind is like a computer—you have different programs and you snatch from every place. Tin Pan Alley, country and western—very eclectic. Do you consider your music to be at all political or satirical, like poking fun at institutions that take themselves too seriously?*

A: Yeah, oh sure. Of course. I got a lot of criticism for "The Freedom Suite," especially when I went down South on tour and we were playing mainly white colleges. A lot of people had me against the wall, asking, "What did you mean by that?"

Q: *We still get that with gangsta rap, and I remember the horrible things they used to say about bebop. When middle-class black people listened to bebop, they said the music was strange. They didn't like the culture, they didn't like the style; just a lot of hate.*

A: In a way, because of the guys in that day using drugs and stuff, they might have associated the music with that culture. So maybe I can cut them a little bit of slack.

Q: *Let's talk about music here. One critic, Gunther Schuller, said that your method of playing, through melody rather than running harmonic changes, was a radical concept. What did he mean by that?*

A: I guess what he's talking about is thematic improvisation. In other words, if I played "Mary Had a Little Lamb," [*sings the melody*] I might play for two hours from that same song, variations on that theme. What he meant was that I didn't just play the melody of a "Mary Had a Little Lamb" and go into the chord changes. I kept it as a theme. I think that's what he meant. But at the time that he wrote that, I didn't know what he meant. I might have understood it, but it was so strange to have someone tell me what I was doing that it sort of tricked me for a minute.

Q: *Describe your apprenticeship with Coleman Hawkins. I know he influenced you a great deal.*

A: I would say Monk was more like that. Coleman, he was sort of . . . I didn't really work with him. He was just my adult. But I actually used to go to Monk's house after school and rehearse with his band and stuff, so with him I would say it was more like a real apprenticeship. He was like my guru. Monk would say, "Yeah, man, Sonny is bad. Cats have to work out what they play; Sonny just plays that shit out the top of his head."

Q: *In the old days, the players and the gangsters were the real patrons of the art. And if you had talent, they would get you gigs in their clubs. Then a new kind of drug came on the scene. What was the impact of heroin on the jazz scene?*

A: Devastating. Devastating.

Q: *When you got in trouble, was that peer group stuff?*

A: To an extent, but you know . . . Bird was doing it, Billie Holiday was doing it, but especially Bird. That's why Bird was such a distraught figure. Because cats were copying him, and he knew it was wrong but he couldn't stop. So we figured, Yeah, man, Bird is doing it, let's go and get high. And I got strung out. I got fucked up. I mean, that's normal when you don't know better.

Q: *But you overcame it.*

A: That was a rough one. The person that gave me pride to overcome it—besides Bird—was my mother, who stood by me after I had nobody. After I had ripped everybody off. People would see me coming down the street, they'd run. But my mother stayed with me all the way. And Charlie Parker.

Q: *You had a great reputation, but you went to Chicago and worked as a laborer. How did you feel about that?*

A: Well, I had messed myself up so bad and burned all these bridges, so when I went to Chicago, I went there to kick my habit.

Q: *And then you went to the government rehab center in Lexington, Ky. And afterward made your comeback.*

A: I came out and I was thinking about Bird, and what happened when I was in there. I thought, Boy, wait till I come out. I'll show Bird that I'm cool. And then he died while I was still in there. But anyway, I came out and still had to struggle with cats saying, "Hey, man, come on, let's step out," but I won that struggle. I wanted to work, and I had to come all the way back out myself. I knew how far down I'd been, I did janitor work and all of this—well, what else was there to really do?

Q: *What about your relationship with club owners?*

A: I was blackballed by a lot of these people.

Q: *Why?*

A: Because I was what you would call an uppity nigger or whatever, so a lot of these cats were keeping me from playing festivals and shit. This was for acting up and asking for money. Some cats be so glad to play that they don't say nothing.

Q: *People are so happy to play that they lower the standards.*

A: It's not just in the past, either; I'm going through this shit all the time. They just called me to do a commercial for this car, Infiniti. They wanted us to go to Czechoslovakia to shoot it. There's no speaking; it would be this actor and myself sitting down in a jazz club at a table, and there'll be some Czech jazz musicians up there playing and then a voice-over about Infiniti—something like that. So naturally I didn't do it. I mean, for me to just be validating white jazz music. I'm not going to put myself in that position. I'm *glad* they still think I'm viable to do it, but I'm not gonna do that shit, man.

I did one commercial, some time ago, where I was playing on the bridge for Pioneer. They said, "Sonny Rollins really went to practice on the bridge and became excellent, like our product"- something like that is cool, where I'm identified and the people know it's me playing. But to sit down and validate somebody else's shit, it's just not *right.* It would get me a lot of exposure, it would be cash, of course, but I reached the conclusion a long time ago that I'm not rich, I'm not going to get rich, I just want to make enough to make it. Fuck trying to get into that race. I don't want it; I don't even want to speak to those people about it 'cause I don't like them.

Q: *Was that like a revelation—some sort of spiritual thing that led you to do that?*

A: It happened because I was getting a lot of publicity at the time. I had a band with Elvin [Jones] and I was playing these places, and I remember the place I played in Baltimore and people didn't really get it, so I said, "Man, I'm not really doing it. I got to get myself together. First of all, I'ma go back and woodshed." That's why I went on the bridge. Some cat, a writer, was up across the bridge one day and saw me playing, but nobody wouldn't have even known it if it hadn't been for him. That's how it happened. It didn't have anything to do with trying to make it public.

Q: *Why are you so hard on yourself?*

A: I'm hard on myself because maybe I been around a lot of great musicians, and I don't think I'll ever be at the level of some of the people I been around. So I'm trying to reach that level, I'm trying to reach a level of performance, and that's what it's about.

Q: *They used to have something called the pat juba in slavery days: The white slave owners made two black guys beat each other up and one survives, and the masters stand around and watch. I think that still goes on. When it comes to blacks it always seems to be a competition, fighting to see who's going to be the diva, like they're having a diva war to see who's going to be accepted. There can only be one dancer, or one writer, one musician. They tried to do that with you and Coltrane, to play you against each other.*

A: We didn't react to it. Coltrane was beautiful, a very spiritual person. He was like a minister. We were thinking about music. It was the writers who influenced the friends who . . .

Q: *Was it just a few writers who did this?*

A: Probably. Remember when Coltrane and I came out, I was popular before Coltrane. We used to be referred to as the angry young tenors—we were against, like, the Stan Getzes, the *Birth of the Cool*, we were sort of a reaction against that. That was still going on at that time, so we were the angry tenors and nobody was thinking about that shit. But I noticed that without even realizing that's what they were doing in slavery days. I noticed that you could never have more than one person up there at a time.

Q: *Let me ask you about gangsta rap.*

A: I like the content of rap because it's the black experience; what they're saying is the truth. Not everything—I'm talking about the political stuff, of course. We have to accept that 'cause that's what's happening.

Q: *What about the style, all this mixing and sampling and stuff they do?*

A: Well, they sampled some of my stuff. This group Digable Planets did some of my stuff. I heard it in a store; I heard somebody playing some of my stuff.

Q: *How do you feel about that?*

A: It's okay, it's all right, I just don't want to be ripped off. I need my money. So I like the political thing and I like some of the rhythms that them cats are playing. I can use it. I'm not an old fogey.

Q: *What about the controversy at Lincoln Center, where they're accusing Wynton Marsalis of reverse racism? Some of the white musicians say he didn't hire enough of them and that some of the white musicians can play better than black musicians. What do you think about that?*

A: I think jazz has done so much to bring people together, but jazz is only an art form. You can't change a society, unfortunately, so regardless of what Wynton does at Lincoln Center—Coltrane did all these records, Billie Holiday sang regardless, the society is still backward on racial matters. I like to be democratic; I have a white boy playing in my band right at the moment. But it's not a personal thing. I find people personally who are great, but the oppressive society just makes it impossible to be real with people. It always fucks everything up.

February, 2006

After the VIBE interview, I kept in touch with Sonny. We've been corresponding over the years. He sends me these elegantly written letters in longhand on yellow legal paper. In 2000, he was seventy years old, which, given the depressing statistics about black male mortality, is like being Methuselah. In 2000, I interviewed him again for "Modern Maturity," a magazine published by the AARP. The black editor, who requested it, left the magazine so the interview wasn't published. Our most recent interview took place on February 12, 2007, as an update for this book:

More accolades have come Rollins' way since these interviews were conducted. There was a *New Yorker* profile written by Stanley Crouch. Rollins along with composer Steve Reich will receive the 2007 Polar Music Prize, the international award founded in 1989 by ABBA's publisher-lyricist-manager Stig Anderson and currently regulated by the Royal Swedish Academy of Music. Rollins will receive the award from King Carl XVI Gustaf along with one million Swedish crowns (equal to roughly $140,000 US) at a gala ceremony scheduled to take place on May 21st.

His latest album, *Sonny, Please*, was released in 2006 by his own label, Doxy. It was nominated for a Grammy, but wasn't the recipient of one, perhaps because an independent label doesn't have the political clout to determine the outcome of such awards. Just as it was odd that Paul Desmond (of whom I have been a fan since a teenager) received a Downbeat award when Charlie Parker was alive. Biographies of Colin Powell and Ralph Ellison show that no matter what black men might achieve, they will still be subjected to slights and indignities. Unlike white Jazz musicians, black Jazz musicians don't have white cultural nationalists like Francis Davis providing a cheering section for their accomplishments. When *The New York Times* did a gushing puff piece on Ella Fitzgerald wanabee, Diana Krall, they mentioned the great jazz diva Abbey Lincoln only in passing. When I debated Francis Davis on WBAI radio, he challenged many of my comments. He is the kind of white critic who becomes upset when a black intellectual has a better grasp of a subject than he. I mentioned that Rollins told me that he sold more records in Japan than in the United States. Davis heatedly disputed this comment. The day after our debate, CNN announced that jazz sales were higher in Japan than in the United States, probably because jazz shows that blacks are capable of highly sophisticated abstract reasoning. Such admission by millions of Americans would challenge the cherished belief among many that blacks are creatures whose actions are motivated not by reason but by instinct, the kind of racist charge made against the largely black jury that acquitted O.J. Simpson of murder. Not only are hundreds of thousands of whites living in trailer parks hopped up on the idea that blacks are prone to a congenital feeble mindedness, but intellectuals who are on the payroll of think tanks.

Having studied Jazz theory for nearly ten years, I would compare jazz improvisation to high-speed chess. I had a chance to talk to Rollins on February 12, 2007, the day after the Grammy Awards were announced, during which Smokey Robinson was limited to a half a song while inferior performers were given extended time to compete with each other over who could scream the loudest at the audience. Sonny was in Germantown, at the home that he shared with his late wife. (They bought a house one hundred miles away from New York City, because they wanted "to get away from people.") Sonny says that when she was alive and he went out on the back porch at night to practice, she'd come out and turn on the lights for him. He misses her turning on the lights. From his comments in the interview, Lucille Rollins was his right hand. I asked him whether his not receiving the award for the Jazz category for which he had been nominated had anything to do with his forming his own record company.

"It might have," he said. "It's possible. That's a good point, because we did have a nomination. But you know that's okay. I don't expect anything from these people."

Q: *Your first instrument was the piano. One of your compositions, "Nishi"—a blues, on "Sonny, Please"—was written in the key of F on the piano.*

A: That's G for me. Sometimes, I play blues in F. Other times in B flat and E flat.

Q: *Charlie Parker and John Coltrane have their trademark chord changes. For Parker they can be found on "Blues For Alice," and for Coltrane they're in "Giant Steps." Where are the Rollins changes?*

A: I haven't gotten to the Rollins changes. This is something that I have to establish before I get out of here. I would say that the Rollins changes are still evolving.

Q: *You sang a motif that appears in his songs repeatedly.*

A: That's something that I do? [*Laughter*].

Q: *Frequently. You said that on "Sonny, Please," this was the first time that you became involved in post-production, mixing and mastering.*

A: First time in a long time. I used to do it. I hate listening to the stuff after so many years, I got my old lady to the point where she could, and I trusted her, and she liked to do it and so I said okay, you take care of that.

Q: *That's a tedious process.*

A: Very tedious. See when you have to listen to your own work you become critical. You know.

Q: *Did you take some things out?*

A: Yeah. We kept the stuff that was the best we could get or else we'd still be in the studio [*laughter*].

Q: *How much time did you spend recording?*

A: We spent nine hours recording. It took a couple of days to mix it.

Q: *I'll bet Lucille used to insist that everybody show up on time.*

A: Oh yeah, you know Lucille grew up with that American work ethic.

Q: *She handled the caterers and all that stuff?*

A: She made sure that every thing was done on a business level.

Q: *Who does the managing now?*

A: I'm doing most of it and my nephew Clifton Anderson helps. He plays trombone with the group. He's the next generation and so he helps me with the computer stuff.

Q: *His style reminds me very much of J.J. Johnson's.*

A: That's his man.

Q: *Why didn't you use the piano on "Sonny, Please"?*

A: Sometimes I do sometimes I don't. I have been identified with the pianoless trio. That was my claim to fame in Jazz. I switch back and forth piano to guitar. I'm in a guitar mode right now.

Q: *That piano player on* Without A Song: The 9/11 Concert . . .

A: Stephen Scott.

Q: *He's smoking!*

A: Another brother, man, he's not doing anything—he's not out here—there's not enough work out here for people.

Q: *You mean with his talent?!*

A: I know. It's shameful man. It's a shame. You have to be fortunate to have talent and be able to get your life together.

Q: *A new biography of Ralph Ellison shows his contempt for bebop.*

A: He got conservative toward the end of his life.

Q: *He says you can't dance to bebop. I first heard of Bird when he came to Buffalo to play for a dance. He played at a place where people had an inclination to get into fights. Cut each other. Pimps and prostitutes.*

A: He's wrong. Because when we first came out cats used to do a dance called "The Apple Jack."

Q: *I remember "The Apple Jack." Cats used to stand in one place and slide their feet around, sometimes lifting the cuffs of their pants. They did "The Apple Jack" in Buffalo when Jazz At The Philharmonic came to the Kilenhans Music Hall, this seddity white supremacist space. After that bebop was banned from Kleinhans Music Hall [laughter].*

A: So you *can* dance to bebop.

Q: *He also says that bebop leaned toward dissonance. Most of the stuff I've heard doesn't come from the outside; it's played within the key.*

A: That's unfortunate because someone whom he would like, Duke Ellington, was very much into Be-Bop. His main man was Bud Powell.

Q: *The problem with his stance is that with the enormous power Ellison was given, he was able to deny beboppers support that they should have received.*

One of the greatest concerts I ever attended was Sonny Rollins' free concert at Central Park, August 27, 2007. Victor Hernandez Cruz arrived to find Sonny playing before an audience of a couple of thousand people in the rain. He had been on the stage for about forty-five minutes when we arrived. The crowd didn't want to leave and so he did encores, which lasted about as long as the original concert. After the performance, Victor, one of the wisest men I know, said, " Now I'll have a good night's sleep." It might have been the last great concert another man heard: I saw the late Ed Bradley walking out of the park. He was alone.

Q: *You must have been up on the stage for over three hours at that Central Park Concert. You're 76 years old! Where do you get the stamina?*

A: [*Laughter*]. I'm not sure. I'm like Lionel Hampton. They had to get him to the stage in a wheel chair. Once he got up on the stage he was ten years old.

Q: *The encores were as long as the original concert.*

A: [*Laughter*]. That shows that I don't think about anything but the music.

Q: *I wrote you that during the Central Park Concert I thought you were playing the theme from "The Amos and Andy Show," but it turns out to be similar to the actual Noel Coward piece that you played, "Someday I'll Find You." But the melody sounded similar to the theme of that show, "Angel's Serenade." I thought that you were having an inside joke.*

A: [Hums the theme from The Amos and Andy Show, demonstrating his encyclopedic knowledge of music whether popular or underground. He's able to hip-o-cize music that most would consider corny.] We used to listen to Amos and Andy [laughter].

Q: *I loved it. Unlike the material today, which is all gangbanging or presents black men as lethal sexual predators, it presented different classes and types of African-Americans, even though the middle and upper classes were ridiculed by Kingfish. Are you going to travel to Sweden to collect the award from the King of Sweden?*

A: We're accepting that. We're going over there in May.

Q: That's great! That's really great!!

A: I like that because it has nothing to do with politics. It's all about merit. I like that kind of prize. This other stuff is a lot of bullshit politics. Sweden and those European countries appreciate the music and when they give you a prize you know that's what it's about.

Q: You still touring?

A: I'm off right now, but I go back in April. I'm trying to take care of my house up here, take care of my taxes. Things that I have to do by myself.

Q: Jackie McClean died since we last talked. What are your memories of Jackie?

A: [The interview was light-hearted up to this point. In the following section, however, Rollins voice began to crack a bit as his thoughts turned to the musicians of his generation who have died.] We go back so far, we sort of came up together, we enjoyed Miles together, we were all hooked on drugs together, and—I didn't really know he was that sick, I still can't believe that I can't call Jackie up and talk to him, I can't comprehend that, I know his voice and talking to him, it's something that I haven't come to terms with yet, it's like a lot of people that you know well—one good thing he's always there, all I have to do is think about him, you know, it's a big thing in life, that kind of eases the thing about losing people like Miles and 'Trane. I've had dreams about Monk and 'Trane.

The dream I had recently was about Walter Bishop, Jr., the pianist. I saw Walter in the dream, it's like you know it's him, but he looks different, but then I realized that it was him. It was like he was in another sphere. Jackie and these other people—they're still close to me and they're still part of life to me.

Q: Sonny, what do you want you legacy to be?

A: Well my legacy is to be a guy who got himself together after being messed up. Stopped drugs. Someone who did what he wanted to do. I went on the bridge and quit the scene. I used my conscience to do what I needed to do. That's what I'm proud of. That's what I represented. The music part—that's a talent—of course I worked on it. But the other part—trying to get through life, that's where you really have to bust your ass. That's my legacy to me.

Q: *Thanks, Sonny.*

MICHAEL JORDAN

12

By Chris Rock
Moderated By Rob Kenner
February 1997

MIKE CHECKA

*The world's greatest ball player goes one on one with the
world's most fearless comedian. It's not going to be pretty.*

What's left to say about Michael Jordan? Second only to
Jesus Christ in one popularity poll, he's gone from
Tarheel to titan, dominating courts and commercials
and everything in between. He came out of retirement
to spank the entire NBA and even learned to live with Dennis Rodman
(which probably helped him prepare to battle with monsters from outer
space). He also seems to have come to terms with the loss of his pops.

But don't sleep on Chris Rock. He's the man who clowned Suge
Knight on worldwide TV. He's the voice of that obnoxious little puppet
who blows up Penny Hardaway's Nike commercials, plus he's had TV
specials and movie roles and sung a duet with Barry White. Most
recently he rolled out *Bring The Pain*, a hip hop comedy album produced by Prince Paul and his own self-titled talk show on HBO. *What!*

Mike and Chris first met on the set of *Saturday Night Live* in
1991. "Everybody on the show had some stuff for Mike to sign,"
recalls Chris. "I was the only one who didn't fuck with him." Jordan,

who was surprised by the grueling rehearsal schedule, says he won't be making a repeat appearance: "They better replay that one."

We hooked them up again last October in a plush Manhattan hotel suite at an impossibly early hour. Over-caffeinated publicists scurried through the halls making nervous noises into the cell phones pressed to their ears—much to the amusement of Michael's usual entourage. Rock showed up a half hour late, helped himself to some fresh-squeezed juice, and started making fun of the promotional material for Mike's new fragrance (!)

Jordan entered the room tapping his wristwatch and scolding the funnyman. That's where we join them now . . .

JORDAN: Don't you have a watch yet, man?

ROCK: *The limo didn't show up, and a black man still can't get a cab.*

JORDAN: Don't worry about it, bro.

Q: *Okay, what similarities do we have? You're 33, I'm 31. I'm born in Brooklyn, you're born in Brooklyn. Family from the South, family from the South. Lost my father four years ago, you lost your father . . .*
A: Three years ago.

JORDAN'S DRIVER: You jump high?

Q: *I can't play ball for shit. It's sad, my ball playing ability. But I can fake it—play for the exercise. Alright, Michael. Michael, Michael, Michael, Michael. Let me ask you this: Do you think O.J. did it?*
   [Laughter]
   And no matter what your feelings are, would it stop you from playing golf with him? Every time I've seen O.J, he's had golf clothes on.
A: I don't know if I would play golf with him. I don't know him that well . . .

Q: *O.J. is actually like the first Michael Jordan, in a sense. This black athlete, super-popular . . .*

A: I would say either O.J. or Dr. J. They crossed a lot of color barriers. I think he and Dr. J were the first to integrate from a sports stand-point. But did he do it? I'm just like most of the people, I think that . . . a lot of evidence may point in one direction; but the court spoke. If they said he was innocent, then he's innocent. I let it drop there and move forward. Shit, no one will ever truly know, 'cause no one was there. He's innocent as far as I'm concerned; I'll take the word of the judicial system.

Q: *Now if someone accused you of murder, would you call Johnnie Cochran?*

A: Right now I would. In a heartbeat. You kidding me, why not?

Q: *Johnnie Cochran! You got a plug from Michael Jordan! Okay, famous-guy stuff: People always give you suggestions. It's like, you got a skillion dollars, you're the best ballplayer in the world, but still people will walk up to you and say, [Lil' Penny voice] "You know what you need to do?" What suggestion pisses you off the most?*

A: Actually, anybody that tells me how to spend my money, I think that's really insulting. I've earned this money; you didn't help me earn this money. You wanna tell me to put it here, here, or here. I think to some degree that's an insult.

Q: *You left school early to play ball, then you went back and got your degree.*

A: True.

Q: *Tiger Woods just dropped out of school to play golf and no one said shit. Baseball players are encouraged not to go college. Do you think people fuck with the black athlete a little too much in basketball?*

A: Look at what athletes are weighing against college: an opportunity to make a *lot* of money—a lot more money than some of these people with Ph.D.'s and all the masters degrees you can have. Basket-ball is one industry where you can get paid for potential. Not for things that you've done on a professional level, but the *potential* of being a great player—and you can be set for the rest of your life. Some people don't like that. But we didn't determine that. You can't really criticize these kids for making these decisions. If you have an opportunity to go out there and grab for that pot of gold, why not go for it? But you have to have your own objectives. You want to do it? Great. You want to go to college? That's great too.

Q: *But do you think it's unfair the amount of attention paid on basketball players who don't go to school?*

A: I think it is unfair when you focus so much on basketball.

Q: *People drop out of school every day.*

A: Every day.

Q: *Shitty jobs.*

A: That is true.

Q: *My brother dropped out of school to drive a truck—no one batted an eye.*

A: Nobody jumps on the baseball players because they very rarely jump from high school to the majors. They go through the minor leagues, then they come into the ranks of the professional baseball players. But college basketball players come straight into the pros.

Q: *So it's jealousy?*

A: Sure, some of it. I would think so.

Q: *See! Jealousy. Now, baseball is going through a popularity thing right now. Even if they didn't have the strike, baseball is having a hard time reaching the youth. My feeling, baseball has not learned how to embrace the "asshole athlete." If Charles Barkley played baseball, he'd be on nine teams. Matter of fact, they might get him out of the league. Do you think baseball's way too conservative, like they don't know how to make certain personalities work for them?*

A: I think to some degree, yes. I mean, for instance, with Charles you can say what you want to say, but he's probably one of the best players to play basketball.

Q: Ever.

A: I can't think of a baseball player who has that personality . . .

Q: Well, you got Albert Belle, who gets booed in every stadium in baseball. That same personality in basketball, he's the Man.

A: Sure, he's Dennis Rodman. Not to the point where he cross-dresses, but the way he plays. And his teammates love him, but everybody else hates him.

Q: Do Dennis Rodman's teammates love him?

A: Well . . . they respect him. I wouldn't call it love. I mean, where Dennis goes, we know he's probably going to some strip joint or some other weird club. We all understand that. Just so when we come back to practice the next day, he's ready to do his job. We don't question what the hell he's been doing up to that point. We can't baby sit him. Everybody knows that coming into it. He don't throw any curves.

Q: But baseball can't handle that type of personality. They won't accept it from a black athlete. They will embrace an asshole like Lenny Dykstra all day. You know, he can crash cars, drive drunk [dumb-ass voice] "He's a player. He's the kind of guy ya love to have on your team." If Lenny Dykstra was a brother, he'd be a bellhop right now.

A: I don't know Lenny, *[laughter]* but you may be right.

Q: I like Lenny. I like him, but you know. Anyway. When was the last time you were truly uncomfortable? Feet wet something vicious, car broke down, trying to get a boost somewhere?

A: Last time? Baseball was an uncomfortable situation. It becomes uncomfortable when you're in situations that you're not familiar with. But I put myself in that predicament, and I enjoyed it. I got comfortable just by learning more about the game, but initially it was uncomfortable.

Q: It reminded you of before you got paid?

A: Well—not quite. *[Laughter]* I mean, before I got paid I still had the skills *to* get paid. Baseball, it was a whole different thing: I was trying to obtain the skills. The money part wasn't the emphasis. I was getting paid maybe $200 a month, so quite naturally it wasn't the money. It was just the idea of picking up something new. Playing a game you haven't played for 14 years. Everybody's more or less got their own opinions about why I was doing it. And why I shouldn't do it. Instead of just giving a brother an opportunity to go out and do what he can. He's not hurting the game; if anything he's helping the game.

Q: *It was cool you went to the minors. That was the cool part. If you'da gone straight to the majors, it would've been, like, Ahh, come on.*

A: I had a great time. Shit, it was a lot of fun for me. I'd do it again in a heartbeat.

Q: *What makes Michael Jordan laugh, TV, comedians?*

A: I watch you. I watched your HBO special, and I've been mocking every damn thing you did on it. Especially that one, "I looove black people. I *love* black people, but I hate them fuckin' niggas." You gotta give me a copy of that special, man. I'd carry it with me everywhere, 'cause I know a *looot* of niggas who don't know . . . *[Laughter]*

Q: *Okay, this is worth getting up in the morning. He likes me and Cochran. All the sales are going up. Okay, you're 33?*

A: I'll be 34 in February.

Q: *Okay, so when you were in high school, Run-D.M.C. was really big. Run-D.M.C. was the shit.*

A: Oh, sure.

Q: *Any rap you still into?*

A: I don't listen to much rap. I'm more of a mellow man. I listen to Anita Baker. I listen to Toni Braxton. That type of sound.

Q: *In high school, though, were you down with the king?*

A: Little bit. KC and the Sunshine Band was still . . .

Q: *KC—really?! That's right, you're from North Carolina.*

A: C'mon, man. I ain't from the big city. I didn't know nothing about no rap music. *Shee-it.* Lionel Ritchie was still hot back in those days. I had heard of Run-D.M.C. back in high school days but not to the magnitude of a *city* person.

Q: *You said "city person."*

A: Yeah. I was a country brother. I was born in Brooklyn, but I stayed nine months. I don't even remember it. At all.

Q: *Here's a weird question. You lost your father; I lost my father. Do you think somewhere in the back of your mind, like, this is God's punishment for being successful?*

A: No. I think it's God's way of telling me that I've gotta make some mature decisions without the support system of a father. When you have to make decisions, you always talk to your parents, 'cause they've known you ever since you was a snotty-nosed kid. Now I gotta make decisions myself with the lessons and the teachings that my father had given me over the years that I was around him. So it's a test. I think it's a test.

Q: *You and I, we're part of the fortunate crew of black men who actually had fathers.*

A: True.

Q: *So, I mean, to lose a father when most people you know—or a large percentage of the people you grew up with—didn't even know their father. Either their father didn't hang around or just cut the fuck out. What pisses me off is whenever I see a guy as old as my father who ain't shit. I go in the old neighborhood, and I see like a fuckin wino, 60, alive and just chillin'. But my pops is gone. Does that piss you off at all?*

A: Same thing to me is when I see someone who had a child and doesn't take care of that responsibility—who'd rather run away from it—now, that pisses me off. If you were there to lay and make that baby, you've gotta pay the price. You have a responsibility for that child. You shouldn't be running around and being selfish— enjoying the rest of your life while that kid's suffering and the wife or the girl is suffering. That's just sad. And that won't help the black community. Certainly that kid's gonna entertain a lot of different problems as he gets older, 'cause he didn't have two parents there to teach him. That's our problem in our society today. One of 'em.

Q: *Do you feel people put too much pressure on you to be a leader because you're black? Like, no one says, "You know, Italians needs to do more for Italians."*

A: True, especially with athletes. We've been given this position. We didn't campaign to be role models, but we accept it and try to do something with it, even though it's added pressure. We feel an obligation to give some type of guidance to other people. But the true role models are the parents who see these individuals every single day. We only do it from a generalization, from a distance. We gotta speak to so many different people. Kids need individual attention. It's just a bail out when they try to give it to us.

Q: *We are not role models. We are people who are popular to kids at a young age. Nobody likes you when you play like shit. Nobody likes me when I'm not funny. Your parents are the most important people in your life. And whoever you around is who the fuck you're gonna act like.*

A: Exactly.

Q: *Okay, James Jordan Foundation opened in Chicago. What's that all about?*

A: You know, you've been to a Boys and Girls Club. What we try to do is give kids an outlet to get off the streets. You know all the shit we used to do when we was at the Boys and Girls Club? It let us vent our frustration, our anger, instead of turning a gun toward someone else or getting into gangs. That's what it's all about.

Q: *Okay, you're doing cologne here. I don't have anywhere near as much money as you—and I probably wouldn't do cologne. They'd have to give me a looooooooot of money. A looooooooooooooooooooooot of money. A ton. Do you realize no man has ever done cologne, in the history of cologne? Suave guys like Sean Connery don't do cologne. Gay men don't even have cologne. You'd figure some gay* guy would have a fragrance by now. Little Richard would have Tutti-Frutti. "Tutti-Frutti by Little Richard. Smell all fruity." Okay, what am I trying to say? Do you think this is too far—at all? Did your wife talk you into it? 'Cause my woman has talked me into many a thing. Did Juanita talk you into this?

A: Do you wear cologne?

Q: *Yes, I wear cologne.*

A: Right, so you enjoy fragrance.

Q: *Yeah.*

A: Well, I enjoy fragrance. And I think the whole concept was, let's see if you can create a fragrance that everybody can associate you with. For years, athletes were known as sweaty, dumb jocks who wore sweats all the time and tennis shoes.

Q: *Now basketball players get the most girls. And they always wear suits.*

A: So the awareness of fashion is starting to change. It's not just a woman's thing. I know 20 years ago this might be a gay thing, but 20 years later, I mean, look . . .

Q: *We've seen your kids—we trust you. We're not questioning you. [Laughter] Dennis done got in there now.*

A: Oh, *noooo.* That's an exit. Do not enter.

Q: *Oh, man—okaaay. You got enough money of course. So you had to do this 'cause you liked it.*

A: I loved it. It's a creative thing. When we did the Air Jordan shoe, same thing. Hadn't been done. Innovative. Kinda weird at first. Next thing you know, it has a life of its *own.* We're hoping the same process happens here. You got a bottle, didn't you?

Q: *They sent me a whole thing . . .*

A: Pass that out to some of your friends in Brooklyn. Some of 'em could probably use it. *[Laughter]*

Q: *What endorsements would you never do?*

A: I would never do anything like Rogaine. I mean that's just hoping

and wishing that I can get an Afro next week. Or, I wouldn't do cigarettes, cigars. I don't want to project something that's viewed neg-
atively by a lot of people—but I love cigars. *Shee*-it, I'd smoke a
cigar in a heartbeat. I smoke 'em, but I wouldn't endorse 'em. And
condoms. I mean, even though everybody gotta use them. But they
too small! They gotta get some bigger ones. I'd endorse the big
ones. *[Laughter]*

Q: *"Hi. I'm a pro basketball player. As you know, we get lots of pussy."*
A: We use Double X.

Q: *He's a married man, but, you know, pro basketball player. What's the
craziest thing a fan ever did to get your attention?*
A: Lie down in front of my damn car. I had just gotten to Chicago.
Everybody wanted an autograph, but I had to be out. This girl laid
in front of my car and said, "I'm not *leaving.* I'm not getting up
until you give me an autograph."

JORDAN'S DRIVER: She's dead now. *[Laughter]*

Q: *Okay, I guess the owner's the most powerful guy . . .*
A: Oh, [Bulls owner] Jerry [Reinsdorf]?

Q: *Then it's you and [coach] Phil [Jackson).*
A: Phil, then me.

Q: *Phil, then you, okay. Here's a question: B.J. Armstrong's your man.
Did you ever think about trying to pull any strings for him to not get
traded?*
A: B.J. and I were probably the tightest of all of us on the team. I'd
known him since 1983. Pippen and Horace [Grant] were over here.
Bill [Cartwright] and everybody *else* were on their own, but me and
B.J. always hung out. I knew he and Phil didn't get along, so as
long as I was there I was able to soothe the tension between them.
But when I left, that's when things went totally off track. They
were at each other's throats. B.J. wanted to be a scoring point
guard and Phil wanted him to be more of a setup point guard.

When I came back, things were so messed up, nothing I could've done would save B.J. from being traded. [Bulls Director of basketball operations] Jerry Krause told me that they were gonna leave B.J. unprotected [in the expansion draft]. I said, *You gotta be crazy.* Next thing you know, they put him on the wire, and they snapped him up in a heartbeat.

Q: *First guy picked.*

A: First guy. And it pissed me off, too. I told Jerry at that moment, *You knew what was gonna happen. You knew he was gonna be picked. That was just your way of soothing tensions between Phil and B.J.* If I wouldn't have retired those two years, B.J. woulda never gotten traded. He still lives in Highland Park right near me. I think he's happy. He's got his money. He's got three rings. He has an opportunity to play the way he wants. I'm happy for him . . . But I hate it. That was my boy.

Q: *Well, I guess that about covers it—unless you wanna talk about Bugs.*

A: Don't ask stupid questions. Y'all are fine, man. You venture on the stupid questions when you start talkin' about Bugs. You all been different so far, and I like it. Now tell me about these Yankees. Y'all Yankee lovers? That was some game last night against the Rangers.

Q: *Yeah, but you hate to win on an error because you think . . .*

A: *Shee-it.* Are you kidding me? That's like winning on a missed free throw. *[Voice rising]* Are you kidding me? A win is a *win.* Are you a Knick fan?

Q: *I'm the biggest Knick fan.*

A: They gonna be all right this year.

Q: *Aw man, you* know *they gonna be I-ight this year.* [Laughter]

A: Don't go crazy now. It's just the same guys in different uniforms. They ain't have nobody that we haven't bust in the past. So what's hot, man? What you got new coming out?

Q: *Me, I'm doing a TV show. Like an Arsenio-type thing on HBO.*

A: Oh, cool. You got me. I'll watch it in a heartbeat.

Q: *Plus I'm getting my new act together to go on tour. Got some new Lil' Penny commercials coming out.*

A: You know what Barkley says about Lil' Penny?

Q: *What?*

A: He says, "Damn, Penny don't have *no* personality. That's why he gotta have a little doll!"

OPRAH WINFREY 13

By Harry Allen
September 1997

OWNED BY NOBODY

*The most powerful woman in television sits down for a
wide-ranging discussion with the Media Assassin. Mr. Allen
admits that he "fell in love with Oprah from the moment
she herself took my microphone, put it up her blouse, and
pinned it to her collar." Here are two of the world's greatest
interviewers doing what they do best.*

If there's one person in this world who can testify to the power of
Oprah Gail Winfrey, it has to be Jan Karon. She wrote a book, *Out
to Canaan*, that jumped onto the *New York Times* bestseller list
last April. You know the drill: Oprah picks a title for her Book Club;
significant portions of her 15 to 20 million daily viewership rush out to get
it; stunned publishers watch sales go vertical. But here's the really bugged
part: Oprah didn't pick *Out to Canaan*. Her pick was Sheri Reynolds's
The Rapture of Canaan. The Winfrey-led march to the stores was so massive that people picking up the *wrong book* still put it in the Top 15.

As chairman of Harpo Entertainment Group, as well as host, star,
and supervising producer of *The Oprah Winfrey Show*, Winfrey is the

most successful woman ever to enter the field of television. Having won 25 Emmys, her talk show—the highest-rated in history—is seen almost everywhere on Earth with an electrical outlet, from Afghanistan to Zimbabwe. An Academy Award–nominated actress in 1985 for her turn as Sofia in *The Color Purple*, she will soon produce and star in an adaptation of Toni Morrison's *Beloved* under a new five-year motion-picture deal with Disney.

What has brought Winfrey her success, fame, and stupefying wealth—estimated at $415 million—is her gut, her solar-plexus sense of what makes riveting television. That and her willingness to live out her travails—battles with eating and sexual abuse—in front of millions of strangers while making them feel like friends.

At 43, she continues to take whatever risks go with her stated goal: "follow the truth." Fundamentalist Christians criticized her for her role in Ellen DeGeneres's "coming-out" episode. And after last year's "Dangerous Foods" show led to a plunge in cattle futures prices, Texas ranchers hit her with a $6.7 million lawsuit.

I met her in Chicago, near the end of one of her famous 16-hour workdays, as her cocker spaniels, Sophie and Solomon, traipsed about Harpo's comfortable headquarters playing with squeeze toys. Her medium-size office, filled with pillows and done out in soft burgundy and cream, was deeply scented by the Casa Blanca lilies that filled one table. She answered every question—even the tough ones—with candor and grace.

Q: *Few people ever reach the rarefied atmosphere that you're in—and those who do often find there's not too much air up there. How do you psychologically navigate the day-to-day reality?*

A: I'm a very simple person, a simple woman involved in a very complex business. The secret to my success and understanding who I am and how I operate is understanding that I am grounded in a power that is greater than myself. Even as a little girl in Cassius, Mississippi, I already felt that my life was bigger than my surroundings. I remember I used to help churn the butter, and the smell of lye soap on the back porch, and crackling bread and all that. I remember looking through the screen and watching my grandmother boiling clothes in the big, black iron pot, and knowing somewhere inside myself that my life would not be that life.

Growing up between Mississippi and Milwaukee and Nashville, I became an orator, starting early in the Baptist churches and speaking Easter pieces and all of that from the age of three. That is where I developed my sense of value and self-worth, through speaking to audiences. Reciting from the time I could speak, *Invictus* by William Earnest Henley when I was seven, all of the sermons of James Weldon Johnson all the way through high school.

Q: *Did you ever talk your way out of a situation?*

A: Yes. When I was 6 years old, all the kids came to beat me up, and I talked my way out of it by telling Bible stories, talking about Jesus of Nazareth. So then I got labeled preacher. And I remember leaving Nashville to go to Baltimore—22 years old—and speaking at a church. I was going to pack up and leave the next day, and I preached on the sermon of "I don't know what the future holds, but I know who holds the future." Even then, I felt that there was something bigger than myself.

I've never seen myself as a celebrity. Celebrity is something other people see from the outside. Anybody with any sense, who is a celebrity, doesn't see themselves as a celebrity. I am still the same person I was at 22, at 17. I just have more life experiences. I see myself as a person who has accepted the possibilities of my life and tried to work with the possibilities of my life.

Q: *Over the last few years you've talked about the possibility of ending the show, or doing something else—as though you're looking for new challenges. Even Alexander the Great at one point stopped and cried because there was no more world left to conquer.*

A: Oh, I don't feel that at all. I feel that there's so much more. The other day one of my producers was saying to me, "Maybe this is the end. Maybe these were the glory days and this was a great 12 years." And I said, Maybe it's the beginning. If you had asked me 10 years ago to define what this Oprah Winfrey show would become, I could not have told you. I have a certain way of being in this world, an instinct about doing what is right for me at a particular time. And my whole goal in life, even when I couldn't articulate it, was to follow the truth.

Q: Do you still consider yourself a religious person?

A: Raised fundamental Baptist, but over the years I've grown to understand that there's more to God, that God isn't as narrow as I was raised to believe, that the world of God is in everything that is good. I feel a deep sense of connection to the spirit that is greater than myself. I don't do anything without consulting with that spirit, that power, that force.

Q: How do you do this consultation?

A: It varies. Now I'm in the process of doing *Beloved,* and actually say a prayer every morning to the power of God that is everything, and to the ancestors. I collect slave memorabilia—slave documents, slave bills of sale, and lists of ownership from slave masters. And so every morning, as I'm preparing to do this film, I light a candle to the slaves, and say out loud the name of one of them. Because my goal in doing this film is to honor the lives of those whose stories were never told. And to be able to bring that to the screen with great truth, and a sense of honor and integrity that they would appreciate.

Q: How important is it to you that Hollywood accept you or recruit you as an actress?

A: Not at all. I don't think that that will ever be a reality for me. First of all, there's not a lot that Hollywood is doing that I'm interested in doing. And I'm in the most glorious position of being about to create work for myself. I've had this project for ten years, waiting on the right moment.

Q: Why are you powerful?

A: I really don't know the answer to that question. It's a tough question for me because I don't see power the same way other people see power. I understand the perception, if you have money and planes and homes and stuff . . . I think that I am powerful to the degree that I have maintained my truth, and allowed that truth to influence other people for the good.

One of the most incredible stories I ever heard was a black woman who had— You know, when I lost all the weight I sold all my clothes; $400 pairs of shoes I sold for five dollars. And this woman said to me that she could only afford to buy a pair of shoes. All she had was five dollars.

Q: You were selling these at the studio?

A: No, I used a hotel, a grand ballroom thing—*so* many clothes. But later this woman was in the audience, and she told me this after the show. She said, "I came to your charity sale and I couldn't afford anything but a pair of shoes. I'm a size 7½ and you're a size 10. And I've been through some difficult times this year," she says. "My husband left me. I'm trying to raise my kids. And there are lots of times when I think that I can't make it. And when I think *I can't make it . . .*" [*whispering*] "I go in the closet and I stand in your shoes." [*Barely audible*] "And I believe that I can."

That, to me, is what power is. Somebody seeing my life, and seeing that there are obstacles that I have overcome, and believing.

Q: When those words came out of her lips, what was your reaction?

A: I embraced her and I said, "That is the best thing I have heard in my life. I would like that on my tombstone." And she said, "Oh, but it's the truth. I have those shoes." And she says, "I've never told anybody else this story, but sometimes it's late at night—" [*whispering, weeping*] "and I'll just go in the closet and stand in your shoes."

Q: Why do you weep?

A: First of all I think what that must be like, to feel like you can't make it. And then to think that your pair of shoes offers strength

VIBE

preview issue

is **treach** naughty by nature or nurture?

ll cool j bares his soul, not his chest

bobby brown: call it a comeback

white people who think they're black

naomi campbell sings the blues

September 1992: Albert Watson's iconic black and white portrait of Treach,
the front man of the New Jersey rap trio Naughty By Nature, announced to the
world that *VIBE* was about to change the game by presenting hip hop culture

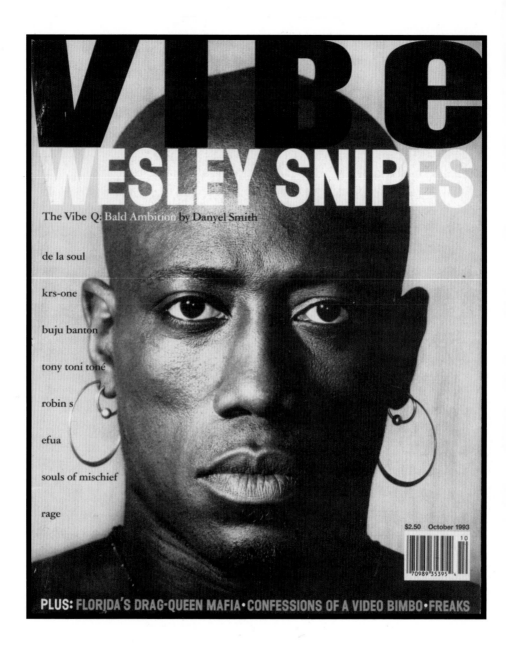

VIBE

WESLEY SNIPES

The Vibe Q: Bald Ambition by Danyel Smith

de la soul

krs-one

buju banton

tony toni toné

robin s

efua

souls of mischief

rage

$2.50   October 1993

PLUS: FLORIDA'S DRAG-QUEEN MAFIA•CONFESSIONS OF A VIDEO BIMBO•FREAKS

October 1993: Wesley Snipes's silvery dome, captured by photographer Christian Witkin, made a bold artistic statement and expanded the magazine's coverage beyond music to actors like Snipes, whose performance as Nino Brown in *New Jack City* made him as much a hip hop icon as Al Pacino's *Scarface*.

VIBe

GEORGE CLINTON

The Vibe Q by Vernon Reid

Chaka Khan:
Every Woman
(and then some)

**THE FUNK HALL OF FAME PLUS: A TRIBE CALLED QUEST • BOYZ II MEN
APACHE INDIAN • JOHN LEGUIZAMO • ZHANÉ • RIDDICK BOWE • HEAVY D'S BEDROOM**

November 1993: When George Clinton appeared on the cover of *VIBE*, the funk was stronger than ever, thanks in part to Dr. Dre's masterpiece, *The Chronic*. Introducing young rap fans to the Funkadelic mothership connection is a perfect example of what *VIBE*'s mission is all about.

VIBe

WHO'S AFRAID OF ICE CUBE

THE VIBE Q BY JOAN MORGAN

BLACK POWER DRESSING:
CYNDA WILLIAMS AS ANGELA DAVIS

ROBIN QUIVERS: KEEPING AMERICA
SAFE FROM HOWARD STERN

ROBBING
BOB MARLEY'S
GRAVE

TEVIN CAMPBELL
BLACK SHEEP
SARITA CHOUDHURY
CUBA GOODING JR.
THE PHARCYDE

SATURDAY NIGHT FEVER:
BRAVE NEW WORLD: THE AGONY OF THE ECSTASY
THE HISTORY OF TECHNO BY MOBY
PLUS: 10 DISCO DIVAS

March 1994: From his groundbreaking work with N.W.A, to his solo masterpiece,
AmeriKKKa's Most Wanted, Ice Cube kept it real—right down to his black power
Afro-pick. Yes, this is the same Cube who's since become a Hollywood player

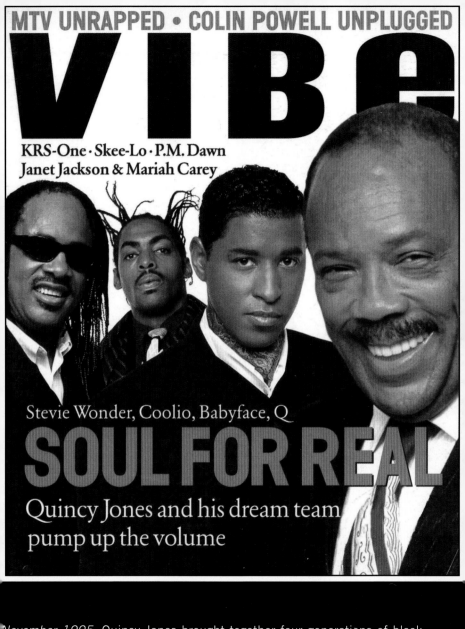

MTV UNRAPPED • COLIN POWELL UNPLUGGED

VIBe

KRS-One · Skee-Lo · P.M. Dawn
Janet Jackson & Mariah Carey

Stevie Wonder, Coolio, Babyface, Q

SOUL FOR REAL

Quincy Jones and his dream team
pump up the volume

November 1995: Quincy Jones brought together four generations of black
music—from himself to Stevie Wonder to Kenneth "Babyface" Edmonds to
Coolio—for his first appearance on the cover of the magazine he founded.

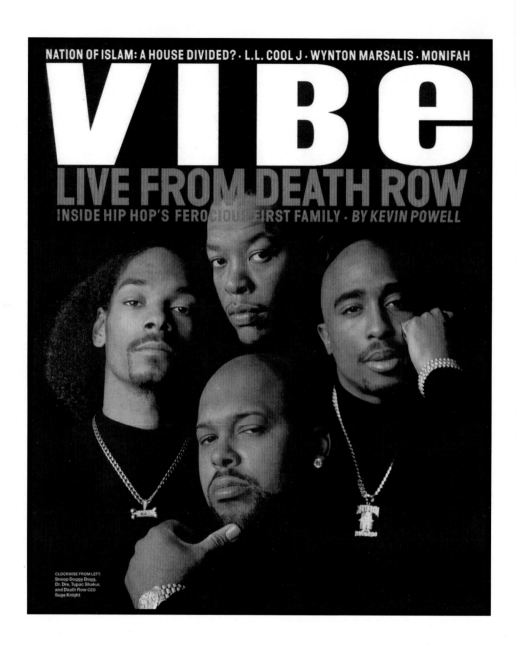

February 1996: One of the most memorable covers in *VIBE* history was this image, reminiscent of the *Casino* movie poster, featuring label boss Suge Knight, production genius Dr. Dre, rap superstar Snoop Dogg, and recent signee Tupac. The cover captured the fleeting moment when Death Row was on top of the rap world.

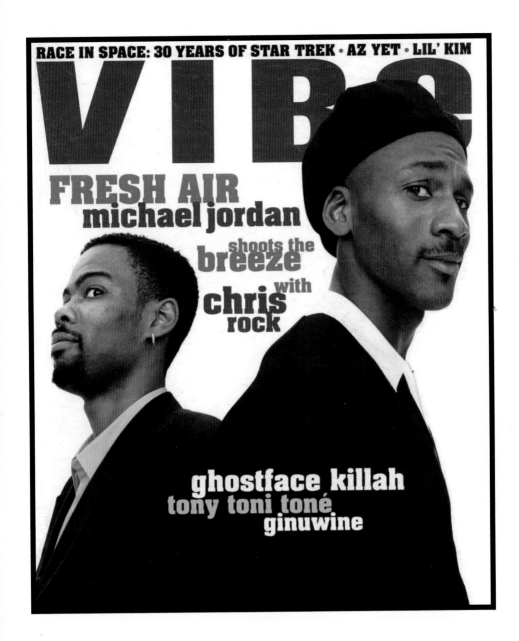

VIBE

FRESH AIR
michael jordan
shoots the
breeze
with
chris
rock

ghostface killah
tony toni toné
ginuwine

February 1997: Although he's a big sports fan, Chris Rock showed up late to his interview with Michael Jordan because, he said, his limo didn't show up and "a black man still can't get a cab." This may be the only existing picture of Air Jordan in a Kangol.

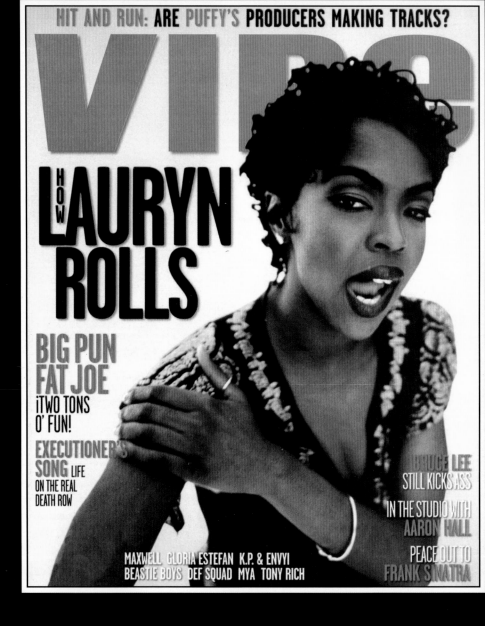

HIT AND RUN: **ARE PUFFY'S PRODUCERS MAKING TRACKS?**

VIBE

HOW LAURYN ROLLS

BIG PUN FAT JOE
¡TWO TONS O' FUN!

EXECUTIONER'S SONG LIFE ON THE REAL DEATH ROW

BRUCE LEE STILL KICKS ASS

IN THE STUDIO WITH **AARON HALL**

PEACE OUT TO FRANK SINATRA

MAXWELL GLORIA ESTEFAN K.P. & ENVYI
BEASTIE BOYS DEF SQUAD MYA TONY RICH

August 1998: On the verge of releasing her sensational solo debut *The Miseducation of Lauryn Hill*, L-Boogie appeared on *VIBE*'s cover and spoke with Karen Good about the breakup of The Fugees and the start of her newest adventure—motherhood.

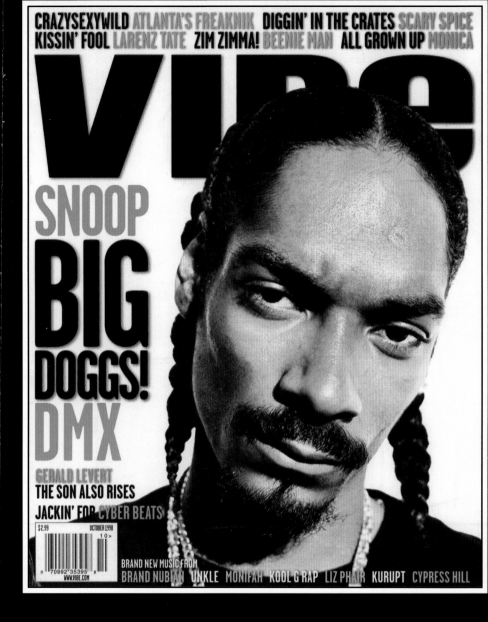

VIBe

SNOOP
BIG
DOGGS!
DMX

GERALD LEVERT
THE SON ALSO RISES

JACKIN' FOR CYBER BEATS

$2.99   OCTOBER 1998   10 >

0 70992 35395 9
www.vibe.com

BRAND NEW MUSIC FROM
BRAND NUBIAN UNKLE MONIFAH KOOL G RAP LIZ PHAIR KURUPT CYPRESS HILL

October 1998: Having recently jumped from Death Row to Master P's No Limit
Army, Snoop Dogg was just turning a new page when he appeared on *VIBE's*
cover for the fourth time.

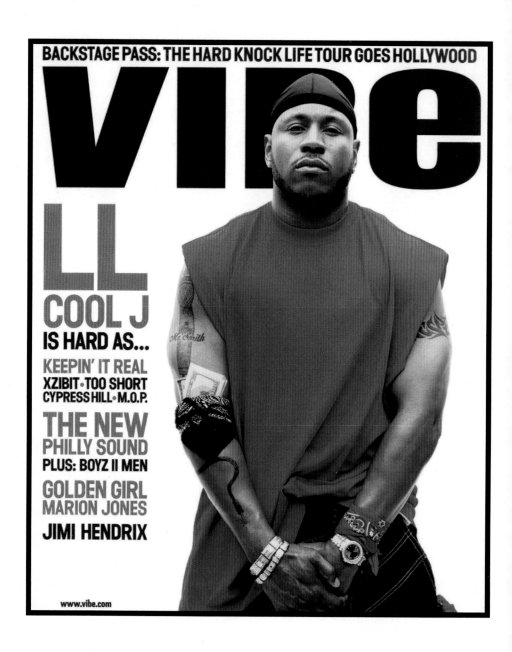

October 2000: Though he was entering his third decade in the rap game, L.L. Cool J never looked stronger than in this Christian Witkin cover shot. His rap skills—and ego—were strong enough to call that year's album *G.O.A.T. (Greatest of All Time).*

March 2002: By the time he made his second appearance on the cover of *VIBE*, The King of Pop was becoming synonymous with scandal, but *VIBE*'s Regina Jones took us back to the music, and reminded readers why Michael Jackson will always be irreplaceable.

VXBE

cover **1** of **10**

> biggie/tupac <
the heroes

September 2003: When *VIBE* celebrated its tenth anniversary, the occasion was marked with ten different commemorative covers. The first one had to go to Biggie and Tupac, two of hip hop's fallen heros. Wish you were here.

VIBE

GGGGG UNIT!

50 CENT Can he survive his own rage?

SHOCKING CONFESSIONS OF PRO ATHLETES
"We treat women like they want to be treated"

ERYKAH BADU'S Common sense

PLUS: Dating Obie Trice, Starstruck celebs

U.S. $3.99/CAN $5.50 FEBRUARY 2004

February 2004: When 50 Cent said he was going to get rich or die trying, he meant it—and he brought his boys Lloyd Banks and Young Buck with him. G-Unit covers always fly off the newsstand, and this one was no exception.

September 2006: Janet Jackson's fourth *VIBE* cover made more news than all her others. That's what happens when you go topless at age 40.

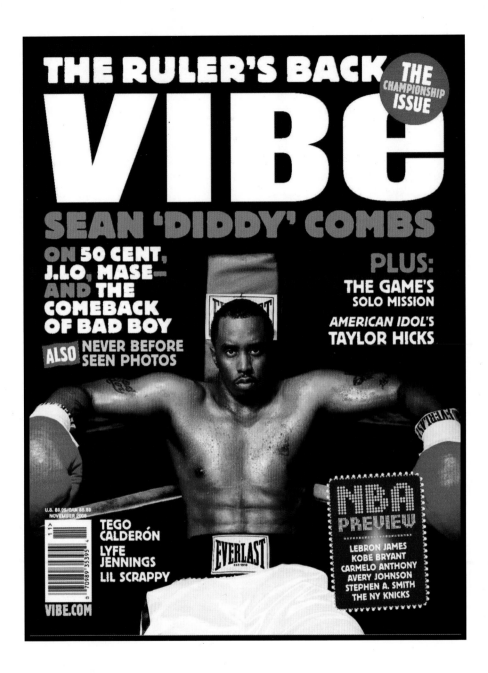

December 2006: These days folks call him Diddy but we've known him so long we still call him Puffy. Whatever you call him, Sean Combs calls himself the last man standing.

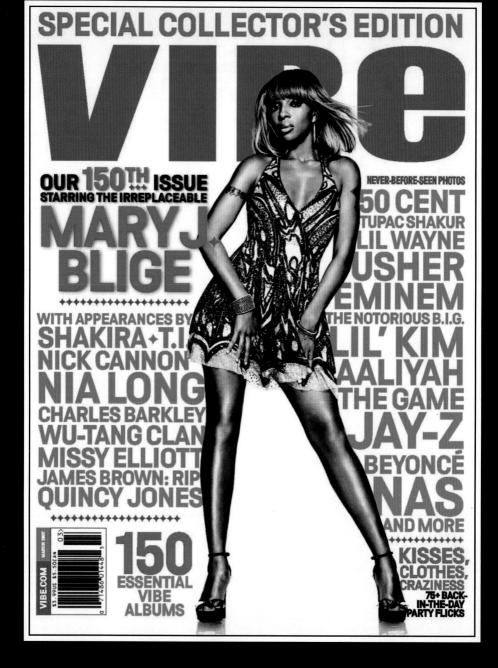

March 2007: Mary J. Blige graced the cover of *VIBE*'s 150th issue with this stunning photograph by Matthew Rolston and an interview that proved once and for all that it is possible to come back triumphantly from the brink of despair.

to somebody. And so I weep for her and I also weep for myself, because that is exactly the way I wanted to lead my life. Exactly! All the Emmys and all the shoes in my closet and everything that I might acquire doesn't mean as much to me as the woman who says, "I stand in your shoes and I believe I can make it."

Q: *How materialistic are you?*

A: That's not an easy question now, because I have so many material things. I remember in Baltimore when I used to walk around with a fake Rolex watch and a fake Louis Vuitton bag and I was 22 years old and I thought that material things somehow created value for you as a person. But I never wanted to live beyond my means, so when I was making $50,000, I drove a Chevette because I could pay cash for it. And I remember speaking at schools to children, and kids would say, "How come you don't have no Benz?" And I would say, "Well, for a Benz, I'd have to have a car note. But this I can afford to pay for." So I remember a couple of times, like, not wanting to disappoint the kids and I'd park a block away so the kids wouldn't have to see the Chevette.

I don't at all feel defined by material things. If I never bought another pair of shoes in my life I'd be okay. I really am at the point where I hate excessiveness. I hate toasting 4 pieces of bread if you really only needed 3! I'm sitting at a hotel in New York, and I love the Four Seasons, but the guy brought me a cup of cappuccino and raisin toast, and the bill was $25.62! And I said to him, "Yes I can afford it—I mean, *please*, I'm sittin' at the Four Seasons in the largest suite—but you yourself know that this bill is too high!"

Q: *You don't feel $25.62. It's not even an atom to you.*

A: No. I don't feel $25.62, but I understand that it's too much to pay for a cup of coffee and a piece of toast. And that doesn't mean I wouldn't spend a million dollars on a painting that I really loved.

Q: *And not feel that either.*

A: And I wouldn't feel that either. But if I felt the painting was worth it, it would be all right with me. I buy no art because Monet did it or because Van Gogh did it—I only buy what I love. The painting that means the most to me is a painting I have in my home done by Harry Roselin in 1904 called *To the Highest Bidder*, and it's a black woman on the auction block with her child. That painting is in my living room to remind me of who I am, where I've come from, and how far I had to go. I saw that painting and I thought, "I must have this."

Q: *Do you buy a lot of art?*

A: I do. I was introduced to art by Bill Cosby, because Bill Cosby told me [*imitating his voice*] "One day, sis, you gon' get sick a shoes!" Bill has been a great mentor for me, Sidney Poitier has been a great mentor for me, when I was going through difficult times, when black people were telling me my show wasn't black enough . . .

Q: *Has that stopped?*

A: Yeah. For the most part. Bill told me this, and Sidney told me this too, that you will outlive it. Sidney Poitier sat me down, I was at Quincy's house as a matter of fact, and I used to be really distraught about it, because no matter what you do, you can never do enough. And Sidney said to me, "It's because you're carrying people's dreams. And the expectation is so high." [*Whispers*] "You're carrying people's dreams."

Q: *Did you not understand that?*

A: I think I didn't, because I came from a world of needing to please. You know, I'm a Southern black girl. You try to do whatever you can to make everybody happy. Especially when you're black, because the expectation is extremely high. I was in my late thirties, almost forty, before I realized I can't please everybody.

And I broke all the rules. I wasn't thin. I wasn't light-skinned. I didn't have a thin nose or thin lips. Nobody could explain how I got to where I was. They knew damn well I didn't sleep my way there! And all I did was talk! I didn't sing, I didn't play basketball, I didn't fit anybody's stereotype. And so of course I was going to cause people to look at themselves.

If you look like Jane Kennedy, and you become host of *AM Chicago*, people say, "Oh she got it 'cause she pretty," which is unfair to Jane Kennedy's talent. But if you look like me, coming into Chicago in 1984, overweight with a Jheri curl, nobody could explain it. I was as shocked as everybody else that I'd gotten the job. And so it caused people to look inside themselves and say, "If she did that, what does that say about me?" All resentment, all jealousy, is based upon "What does this mean for me?" So I understood that, but it was very hard in the beginning. And I used to apologize for it in many ways. I think I held onto the weight as an apology to people. But then I realized that I'm owned by nobody. That I'm only God's child.

Q: *You've acquired a reputation as being a lavish gift-giver.*

A: I have a very generous spirit—always have. When I was a kid, if I had a candy bar, I couldn't enjoy mine unless you had one too. If I was going someplace, it wasn't as much fun unless you could share it with somebody else. I love the fact that I was born when I was born, and how I was born. Black, female, 1954, Mississippi . . .

Q: *Poor.*

A: All of it, because had I not had that, I don't think I would have this grand appreciation for what I've been able to acquire. I have kept a journal since I was 15, and in recent years have decided not to focus on the things that bothered me, but to focus on what I have. And I've encouraged the entire country to do the same: look at what you have, not what you don't have. That has brought such bounty to me I want to share that with other people, to say: "This is how you get it! All the time you think you're thinking about making more money, what you're really thinking about is money you don't have. Start appreciating what you have, and you will begin to see that you have more." [*receives a call from her best friend, Gayle King*]

Q: *What's the Gayle connection?*

A: She's worked in television for as long as I have. I was 22, she was 22. She was a production assistant, I was an anchorwoman. There was a snowstorm one night, and she couldn't get home. I said, "You can stay at my house," and she said, "I don't have any underwear," and I said, "Mine are clean. You can wear a pair of mine." And that was it. Stayed up all night talking, went to Casual Corner the next day, bought two sweaters, $19.99. She was like, "Awesome! You can buy two and not think about it?" Oh yeah baby, cause— [*snaps fingers*] I'm making twenty-eight thousand! [*Laughs*]. It was fabulous. We've been best friends ever since.

One of my favorite Gayle stories is last year we were in Florida, and we were going to the mall for my birthday, and we passed a car store. I said to the driver, "Stop this car now." We both got out, and we looked at this car, which was a convertible black Bentley. Cream interior.

Q: *They're about $180,000.*

A: This one was more. It was called a Bentley Azure, a sports thing. So we walked into the place and bought the Bentley. This was a Casual Corner moment, only transferred to a Bentley. We're sitting there trying to figure out, "Gee, this color, that color . . ." and I go, Gayle, this is the car we saw. This is the car that caused us to stop and say, My God, what is that car? And I bought the car.

Q: *Do you like driving the car?*

A: I never go anywhere. Go to the store, get some peaches. I've had the car now a year and a half and I don't have a thousand miles on it yet. But it was fun. It was a Casual Corner moment. The car cost $329,000, and Gayle's saying, "We gotta get it for three!" [*Laughs*] And I go, Gayle, really, is it gonna make any difference?

Q: *Does it feel different to drive a Bentley? I mean, is it nicer than your Chevette?*

A: I'll tell you what really is fun. When me and Stedman and the dogs are in it and the top's down—that is a cool thing. And I'm wearing my Tina Turner wig, trying to hold onto it to make sure it doesn't come off! *That* is a cool thing. Just the whole idea of it.

Q: *You mean, "This is outrageous, I can't believe we're doing this?"*

A: Well, what's outrageous—sometimes when I'm flying in my G4 . . .

Q: *That's your Gulfstream jet, right? How many seats is that?*

A: It seats 14.

Q: *How much does that plane cost?*

A: I'm not gonna discuss *that!* Jet etiquette means you never discuss how much the plane costs.

Q: **[Laughing]** *Okay, now I know.*

A: Jet etiquette! Jet etiquette says you *don't* do that! But some-times—and I get a kick out of this—there's all black people on the plane. Just the other day, the flight attendant was passing out some lobster and I said, "We still black! It's not like we turned white! We still black, y'all! Oprah's still black!" It's like, who knew?"

Q: *Do you understand the effect of stories like these? You're the richest black person in the universe.*

A: Am I? Let me think . . .

Q: *Yeah! I mean, except for Mobutu, but he got all his money from the CIA!*

A: I always think of other people as being rich. It's not a concept that I'm attuned to.

Q: *How much are you worth? $415 million is a figure I've heard—*

A: That's pretty accurate.

Q: *A lot of black people wonder why black people as wealthy as yourself don't centralize wealth. Why don't Bill Cosby and Oprah and Prince and Eddie Murphy and all those other people get together?*

A: Because we are individuals. And I think the expectation shouldn't be any greater for what I do with my money than you ask Donald Trump to do with his.

Q: *But inevitably the follow-up statement is that's what the white boys do.*

A: And what does that have to do with me?

Q: *You don't see pooling our resources as a racial or even a humanistic imperative?*

A: No, I do not. I don't think that what black people need necessarily—certainly economics is a major part of what everyone needs to survive. But what we need is to change the way we think about ourselves. That is true for both the African-American culture specifically, and for humankind generally. Human beings don't understand that we are just spirit in the body—I see that as the number one problem facing the world. Everything else grows out of that.

Q: *There are people who would read this and say, "She's talking around the very real fact of what money does and what it can do."*

A: For some people, merging might be the answer for them. My goal is to do what I can to change the way people think about their lives so that they can hold the highest, grandest vision for themselves. I believe the way to do that is through education. And educating in a way that you don't just teach memorization skills, but you teach people how to *think*. That's why a lot of my money, and interest, is in education. I'm just getting ready to combine my forces, so to speak, with the organization Better Chance. They find black children in the 6th grade and place them in college prep schools around the country. They find the kids who *want to make it*.

Q: *Is this a black-run organization?*

A: Mm-hmm, sure is. A Better Chance.

Q: *Is that fact important to you?*

A: Yes. It is important because that's who I am. Not to say I would exclude them if they included other children—they're predominantly African-American but they certainly include children of other cultures.

Q: *One of the professors who knew I was going to speak to you said: he had a chance to speak to Oprah Winfrey, he would ask, "Why don't black entertainers and athletes endow historically black colleges and universities?"*

A: A hundred men at Morehouse. I'm putting a hundred men through school at Morehouse.

Q: *On an ongoing basis?*

A: On an ongoing basis. Set up an endowment so I could do that. My alma mater, Tennessee State University, set up a scholarship fund in my father's name. But I think many times college is too late. That's why I try to figure out a way to work with kids who are younger.

Q: *Do you feel any pressure to "give back"?*

A: If you look back through any journal that I've written for the past fifteen years, my constant prayer is for the power that I call God, all that is God, to use me. Use me. That is always my prayer. Always has been. That I be used as an instrument for that which is the will of God. I don't think you can do any better than that— whether that is through economics, or scholarship funds, or combining with whoever. I feel no guilt. I feel no pressure.

Over the years, long before I made a stand three years ago about taking the high road, I have consistently been concerned about the images that were portrayed and presented through the media. That's why it was so hard for me to be a news reporter. If I'd go to cover a black person's home that had been burned down and a woman would be standing outside, rollers in her hair . . .

Q: *And crying.*

A: I'd ask her to please go and change her hair. Would you please take the rollers out of your hair? Would you please speak up? You go to a man on the street and you need to get opinions from different people—I would always make sure that the person who was black was the most articulate person in the group.

Q: *Some people would say that's a petty concern in the light of dire circumstances. I mean, if your house has burned down . . .*

A: No. No, it's not a petty concern. Because the reason racism is so prevalent in this country is because of the images that are presented on a daily basis over the airwaves, throughout the media.

They think we can't talk, we can't speak, a lot of people think we're not feeling, thinking, emotional, caring human beings.

So to the criticism that I used to receive about you're not doing enough for black folks, I'd say, "You don't understand how it works." If I do a show talking about parents concerned about their kids going off to college, and on that panel we have a black father protesting the way his daughter was being treated, we don't say "Here is a black man who cares about his child." But you put him in the same arena with other people who are also being portrayed as loving, caring, nurturing parents . . .

Q: *You humanize and normalise them.*

A: And that is why racism exists—because the slave master was allowed to dehumanize us. To make us less human, less feeling, less caring, less than they were. It is the humanization that breaks down barriers.

Q: *Is it so white people now feel these people are human? Or black people feel that they're human?*

A: Everybody does. It's no different than when I first went on the air and people used to call me up on the air and say [*Southern voice*] "My God, gal! Ah neva knew a colored gal could talk like that."

Q: *Do you remember an interview you had with Frank Perdue?*

A: That is not true, that Frank Perdue called me a baboon or something. That's one of those urban myths.

Q: *What actually happened?*

A: What actually happened was he came on, he talked about chicken, and he left. And I said to him, "You know, you kinda look like your chickens." And then the urban myth became that Frank Perdue told me, "Well, you look like a gorilla." That is not true. And it is also not true that Liz Claiborne came on the show and said anything about black women's behinds, nor is it true that Tommy Hilfiger came on the show and said if he'd known that black people were going to be buying his clothes he wouldn't've made them—all just urban myths.

Q: *Why did you pull out of Families for a Better Life?*

A: That's a great question, and I really appreciate your asking. I didn't pull out. I still have my foundation. It's the For Better Life foundation. But I was not prepared for the enormous responsibility of running an organization that needed to completely revamp thinking. To help people change the way they thought about themselves, about working, about family life, about home ownership. I wasn't prepared for what that took.

Q: *What were the objectives of the organization?*

A: I wanted to take 100 families out of the projects on my own. Get them into homes and have them become self-sufficient. I thought I could do that in three years. After a year, I'd spent so much money, and I wasn't seeing any movement with the families, and I thought, "I've just become the government." I'm feeding money into a program and I don't know what's happening, and I'm seeing a lot of paperwork but I don't see anything happening with the families! That's why I said I have to stop and re-look at it.

The best example of the failure of the program: I had taken a family, put the kid in school, and he was having problems in school. And I went to the house and I said, "You're not going to school. So tell me, what is it?"

Q: *The alarm clock.*

A: Yeah, they didn't have an alarm clock. And to me that was symbolic that I am in *way* over my head. Somebody wanted me to write a book called *First You Get An Alarm Clock* after seeing that story. I went out and got some alarm clocks, but the alarm clock is symbolic of an even greater issue. You're working with somebody who doesn't have a concept of time, like "We just try to wake up! We just tryin', every day!"

Q: *What would you say to someone who says the only way you could've really come to that conclusion is because the successes you see on your shows seem to happen so quickly.*

A: The successes that I see on my show do not happen quickly. Anybody who's saying that is blowing smoke. A woman said to me one day, "You've changed my life." I go, "Okay, I hear that a lot. What does that mean?" She said, "I used to beat my child. And I beat my child 'cause I was beaten. And I heard you a lot of times say that that's not what you should do. Beating your child is not the answer." She says, "It wasn't the one time I heard it. It was the consistency. Year after year, every time I heard it, every way you said it, the message was: this isn't helping my child."

Q: _Your children are not your children._

A: They're little people. I don't understand why black people can't let that go since that's absolute learned behavior from the slave master. We were beaten until we think that's the answer! But we didn't like it from the slave master, and our children don't like it any more from us.

Q: _A lot of black people thank their grandmothers for putting the lash to their behinds._

A: That's 'cause they don't know any better. I'm not talking about tapping somebody on the butt to get their attention. My girlfriend Gayle was never hit in her whole life. Black as she wanna be. Her whole family, never hit—most shocking thing I ever heard!

Q: _Yeah, me too._

A: And I'm like, "How did you turn out to be a decent person if nobody beat you?" You really should be asking the opposite question: How did you manage to maintain any sense of self-esteem and manage to be such a good person when you were treated so violently as a child? Discipline doesn't mean violence. You could have talked to me.

And I would not have spent years of self-hatred, lack of self-esteem, feeling unworthy, allowing myself to be sexually abused, abused by men, mistreated, and so on and so on, had I developed, as a child, a greater sense of self-worth. That would have come had I not been beaten every day. You cannot tell me that being beaten every day is going to help you. It does not! Cannot!

Q: *Oprah, even the look in your eyes has changed when you're talking about this.*

A: Well, it's just the truth! And it's upsetting to me that people can't see that nothing good comes from violence. Just because we've had millions of wars doesn't mean it was right!

Q: *Do you include violence against animals here?*

A: I don't believe in any form of violence.

Q: *But you wear fur.*

A: I don't wear fur anymore.

Q: *Do you eat meat?*

A: No, I really don't eat meat. But I think eating meat is not the same thing as wearing fur. I have given my furs to other people. I think I may still have one that I wear about the farm when it's brutally cold or something, but I no longer believe in the exploitation of animals for your own sense of "luxury." I don't feel guilty about the days when I did, because when I knew better I did better! But I think the idea of eating meat—eat meat if you want to eat meat.

Q: *You're in a lawsuit right now over this very issue. The issue of even discussing this.*

A: Right, so I probably shouldn't discuss it.

Q: *Can you stand by what you said on that show, the dangerous foods show?*

A: I can say that I was asking questions, as I always do, as a surrogate viewer, concerned about what I was being told about cows being fed to cows. Yeah. I stand by that.

Q: *Do you think these laws against talking about food make sense?*

A: I can't comment on that. I really can't.

Q: *Your eyes say everything, Oprah.*

A: Well, that's good. Because Lord knows—lawsuits? Fighting the cattleman in Amarillo, Texas? Dear God almighty! God be with you, Oprah Winfrey!

Q: *How proud were you when you heard that the beef market had bottomed out after you spoke about this on your show?*

A: Neither proud nor not. I was only asking questions. I was neither proud nor not.

Q: *Did you kind of go like, "Wow!" at your effect? It's kind of like watching a mushroom cloud recede from you at its epicenter.*

A: I'm always surprised at stories of our influence. I don't do anything for effect. The book club was the purest example of just doing something that I felt was truthful. I said, "I'm gonna do it because it's my show, and I think it would be a good thing for some people, because I know what books have done for me." I've never felt that there was anything I could not do because of the color of my skin or because I was a woman. Because I read about women, black women, strong people like Sojourner Truth, who had done it.

The book club has been one of my greatest lessons this year. Because it means one thing to the outside world, and it means something completely different to me. To the outside world it's, Oh, you're selling books and the books you mention make number one. To me it says you can take a little idea that means something to you and it can become something great. That's how you always need to operate—not trying to profit by it, or influence anybody, or bring greater acclaim to yourself. Just, what is the purest idea?

Q: *Henry Brooks Adams once said, "A friend in power is a friend lost." What's tricky about having power and having friends?*

A: Oh, I don't know! You know, this is getting harder for me, because I don't see power the same way you do. I know that the title that is given me is celebrity, but I feel that I am the same person that I was when I came to this job. With me it's about holding a vision for myself. I can drive a Bentley if I want to, or I can fly any place in the world, and I guess that is some people's perception of power, but for me it is how you use your influence for the good.

Just like I said years ago, I don't know what the future holds, but I know who holds the future. When we did *The Color Purple,*

Steven Spielberg said, "Baby, your future's so bright it burns my eyes." So I kinda took that on as a part of my own belief, that the future's so bright it burns my eyes.

Q: *Has success changed you?*

A: Anybody who says, "Oh, this person was changed by money," that is a lie. Money only magnifies who you already are. When you see all these people going crazy over money, those are people who had the potential to go crazy. The money puts a magnifying glass on who you are.

I wonder what happens with these rap stars, for instance. You're living in the projects, and then all of a sudden you get millions of dollars the next day. I had a strong sense of values, a strong work ethic, and success came in increments. I made $100 a week, then I went to $15,000 a year, and then twenty-two. I remember at 22 when I got my first $10,000 in the bank I thought I was home free because my daddy was in his forties when he first got $10,000 in the bank. When Gayle and I were in Baltimore we used to talk about making our age. "By the time you're forty, if you could be making 40,000, you'd be doing pretty good."

Q: *And you did, only you're counting in tens of millions.*

A: Yeah, tens of millions. So I still know what that feels like and understand the meaning of the *dollar*. It's harder to understand the meaning of the *million* dollars if you want to know the truth— you're the first person I've told this to, and I hope it doesn't get misinterpreted. But it's harder to understand what you can do with millions of dollars, and still understand that $25.62 is too much to be paying for a cup of coffee and a piece of toast.

Q: *But even ten years ago, you said "I can allow myself to spend a million dollars this year."*

A: Right—you've done your research. And I remember when one of the Winans called me up and said "Well ain't you just miss somebody?" At the time that's how I was budgeting myself. When you're a kid you say, "God, if I could only have a million dollars." But I understood what a million dollars was. I didn't understand what multi, multi, multi millions can do. What does that mean? I still ask myself that.

Q: *On a recent show you were speaking with Rob Reiner and a psychiatrist about playing music for your child and how it stimulates the growth of neurons in the brain. And you said, "I think rap music might cause brain damage."*

A: Mm-hmm.

Q: *Now when I heard about this comment, and then read it, I thought there were at least two very powerful implications here: one, that children and young people who listen to hip hop music are brain damaged, and two, that indigenous black musical culture is somehow corrupt and degraded.*

A: Mmmmm . . .

Q: *When you said that, Dr. Bruce Perry said "I'm not going there." He didn't touch this subject. Why did you make that statement?*

A: I probably should have thought more about it because it really was personal. I don't listen to a lot of rap music, because it really does not cause me to feel a sense of calmness or to feel particularly inspired. I love all different kinds of music, but I'm not particularly stimulated by rap. I should have thought more about its implications before saying that . . . Now, don't have all the rappers mad at me. I like L.L. Cool J. But he's not considered rap anymore, is he?

Q: *Sure he is—L.L.? He's just not* center *anymore. There's a lot more newer, angrier voices and approaches.*

A: No, no. I'm not that angry. But I accept the fact . . .

Q: *I mean, you've got the Fugees for example. You probably haven't heard Wyclef's new album. I think you'd like it.*

A: I've got the Fugees' album. I like the Fugees. Lauryn Hill was almost my daughter in *Beloved*. She was gonna be the daughter, then she called and she was pregnant.

Q: *And she looks like you!*

A: Yeah, she looks so much like me. And we did our reading together, she was the girl who read the audition. But she got pregnant.

Q: *That's incredible!*

A: She was gonna be the daughter, then she called and she was pregnant. And that's what happened. So I like them, I like The Fugees.

Q: *Let me ask you this. Many times brothers and sisters talk about having to repress a certain part of themselves, a part of their blackness, in order to work with white people. What do you feel you've had to trade off or repress in order to do that?*

A: Not very much, because I truly am a self-made woman who has made myself by being myself. I remember in the very beginning, being hired as a black woman in Baltimore, and them deciding that somehow my blackness was perhaps offensive, because they kept trying to change me. "Your nose is too wide. Your hair is too this . . ." I remember saying, *But this is what you hired.* This is what my nose is like. This is what my lips are like. This is what they look like on camera.

I remember going to try and fix myself, the French perm and all that, and I became bald. But other than that, I would say I haven't had to sell my soul to be myself. I learned early on when I was pretending to be Barbara Walters—thank God I stopped pretending to be Barbara, and understood that the best thing I could do was to let whoever that self was come through.

Q: *But you said "The drums of Africa still beat in my heart."*

A: Mm-hmm.

Q: *Somehow I don't get the sense that all those Midwestern white women in the audience are feeling those drums of Africa. Is there a discontinuity there?*

A: What do you want me to do, go on the air every day and speak to what I feel about all my issues? What I feel about how children are treated in this country? What I feel about the way women allow themselves to be treated in this country? I feel a lot of things—very deeply—that I don't express every day on the air. And because I work in my own way to help change them, doesn't mean there's any discontinuity if I'm doing a show about fashion. What you see on the air is just one dimension of my life. That isn't the full expression of who I am.

Q: *Could there be a race equivalent to the book club? The success that you had with the book club, could there be a way of handling race?*

A: I've tried everything and will keep trying. Last year Diane Sawyer and I talked about doing a big series on race and never could just come together—what is the best way to do it? How to try to bring together the racial divide?

Q: *I still think the image of you, standing next to a half-filled aquarium with marbles, and pulling out one black marble and saying "This is how much genetic material is responsible for race, or skin color." I think that should be in the Smithsonian.*

A: The marble was good. In the early days, we did the brown-eyed / blue-eyed experiments, those were good. But recently, during the Mark Fuhrman show, I said on the air that Mark Fuhrman was not an aberration to black people, and got the worst hate mail of my career.

Q: *While discussing this with a member of your audience, you said, "If I go any further I'm gonna get in trouble."*

A: What I meant by that is people are *so* uneducated, that it is so *easy* to have *anything* you say be misinterpreted and not understood. Because the racial divide is *so* great. You should see the mail I got after that show. *Vile* things. Like "That's the reason God hasn't given you children, so you can't spread your racist hatred." I mean just vile things.

Q: *What do you do with all that mail? Do you keep it? Shred it? Donate it to the Schomburg Center?*

A: Someone has it here. I can tell you the people with the greatest job security here are the people who handle the mail.

Q: *You're at a restaurant and you overhear someone order the Oprah Winfrey. What does the waiter bring out?*

A: Mm-mm-mm. It's um . . . Some mashed potatahs [*her voice changes*] and it's some smothered chicken. Maya Angelou made it. Cause she dun't just smother the chicken, she suffocates the bird. It's some okra on the plate. It's some turnip greens with spicy cha-cha pickles. It's corn bread, very thin crus'. It's uh, sweet potatahs with marshmallows in it. It's some ice tea [*laughs*] not like a whole lot of sugar, but it's like half lemon, half ice tea. And that's what the Oprah Winfrey is.

Q: *And you eat it with your fingers?*

A: Nope, you don't eat it with your fingers.

Q: *What do you consider holy?*

A: Oh . . . *great* question. I'm gonna write that down. That's a good question to remember to ask somebody—What do you consider holy? *Mmm. Great* question. [*She begins writing*] I got many pens. These are my Bulgari pens that I love. What do you consider holy?

All that is good. [*She clicks the pen cap, puts it down, rips off a page of paper*]

All that is good I consider holy. I keep a journal every day to honor that which I consider holy. To honor the holy moments. To honor the *things* that bring holiness to me. And so on any given day, that can be, you know, the perfectly smothered chicken and the feeling that that brings and the memories that that conjures. Or it can be sitting in complete silence in the grass with my dogs. Or walking through the woods with Stedman, or really *seeing* the moon. Or having somebody hold the door for me, and me saying Thank you, and having that moment of human-to-human connect. Or sitting with Toni Morrison in a room, talking about slavery and what it meant—*really* what it meant. And understanding where I've come from, and that I have been carried. *Been carried.* By the spirits of those who've come before. And that my life is a continuance of theirs. And understanding that connection. That my life is bigger than my own, that it doesn't just belong to me. I consider that very holy.

And one of the reasons I feel moved to question what comes next for me is because our history has shown that we owned nothing. We had nothing. We were able to maintain nothing. And so when you reach a point in your life—black woman born *colored* in Mississippi who has acquired all of this—I ask, Was it just to have *shoes*? Certainly not. I don't believe He brought me this far to leave me.

Q: *What is proof to you of God's love?*

A: *Oh!* My God. Don't even go there with me. Don't—I mean, please. What is *proof?* Our existence. [*long pause*] Our very existence. [*whispering*] Our very existence—that's it.

Q: *What is proof to you of God's wrath?*

A: Oh, there *is* no God's wrath. I don't know God's wrath. I know *man's* wrath. [*Pounds table*] I know man's inability to connect to God's love, to understand God's love, but I don't know God's wrath. The God I know has no wrath. The God I know has no wrath.

LOUIS FARRAKHAN 14

By Farai Chideya
September 1997

THE CHARMER

The controversial leader of the Nation of Islam goes head to head with VIBE's National Affairs Editor for a point-blank discussion of race, religion, power, and hip hop.

He's been called a savior, an anti-Semite, a radical, a healer—and by some critics, just plain evil. Born in 1933 in the Bronx, New York, as Louis Eugene Walcott, he became a Calypso singer called "The Charmer" before devoting his life to the Nation of Islam and moving to the top of its ranks. Minister Louis Farrakhan is arguably the most powerful and charismatic leader within America's Black community. His 1996 Million Man March drew black men from around the country and from all walks of life—ex-cons, teachers, students, businessmen. He preaches black economic self-sufficiency—and has helped lead the Nation of Islam into scores of successful business ventures. But he most often makes the headlines for his comments on race and religion, as when he called Judaism a "dirty religion." He's been described by conservatives as the best hope for leading blacks into the Republican party, and by at least one Black civil rights leader as the equivalent of David

Duke. It is hard to find a more complex, more loved, and more hated figure in contemporary American society.

The leader of the Nation of Islam makes his home in the ornately decorated, Islamic-themed Chicago mansion formerly occupied by the Honorable Elijah Muhammad. On the day we meet, he is attired stylishly but casually in an African shirt and slacks; he looks far younger than his six decades on the planet should allow. We sit at one end of an immense marble dining room table, while associates and his son Mustafa, who wears hip hop gear emblazoned with the Shabazz Brothers label (one of the Nation's business ventures), sit nearby. Despite a hectic schedule that can leave him exhausted (he uses acupuncture to boost his energy) Minister Farrakhan ends up allotting three and a half hours for the interview . . .

Q: *Tell me one thing you have done in your life that makes you the most proud.*

A: The proudest moment of my life is when I decided by the grace of God to submit my will to do God's will, and to give the total weight of my time, talent and energy to the cause of the rise of black people into moral, spiritual, intellectual, economic and political excellence.

Q: *Describe the vision which sealed your decision to end your life as a professional calypso singer and devote yourself to the Nation of Islam.*

A: When persons are faced with great decisions, they sometimes will have a dream or an experience that will point them in the right direction. When I was asked, through Malcolm X, by the Honorable Elijah Muhammad, to choose between my music career and my love for Islam, it only took a matter of five minutes—or less—to decide to give up my music. But I had thirty days to make the decision. So this particular night I decided that I would give the full range of my gifts and get it out of my system. And so I played the classical violin, jazz violin; sang ballads, calypso, blues; danced, told jokes. And at the end of the night, the manager of Pearl Bailey and Billy Daniels was in the audience, and he came and offered me five hundred dollars a week, which was a lot of money at that time. That night I had this dream or experience where I saw two doors. Over one door, which I could see clearly into, was a mound of gold, and over the door was written SUCCESS. The other door was titled ISLAM, and it had a Black veil over it where I couldn't see what that door held. And in this dream, or experience, I chose to follow the door of Islam, though I knew not where that door would ultimately take me. Forty-two years later, here I am, by the grace of God, where I never thought I would ever be. And the lesson I learned is whatever you give up for God, you never lose.

Q: *What would life be like if you'd chosen the other door?*

A: Making music, and making people happy with my entertainment skills, because that is what I thought I was born into the world to do. But I am so grateful that I have found the door of truth so that I could make my people happy with a knowledge of self, and a knowledge of God and a knowledge of the time and what must be done, to make a meaningful difference in the lives of countless tens of hundreds of thousands of persons in America and throughout the world. I probably could have done this musically, but never could I have raised the level of consciousness of the nation as God has blessed me to do with the word of truth. And now, that I am playing my violin again, through words and music I hope and pray that god will bless me, in the final years of my life to make an even greater contribution to the freeing of the human spirit here in America and throughout the world.

Q: *Recently you've been involved with a different kind of music, hip hop. You hosted a summit to try to heal the east coast/west coast rivalry which Ice Cube and Chuck D, among others, attended. Some politicians and critics see rap as the most evil form of music in America. Do you?*

A: It is the mode of expression of the most marvelous generation that we have ever produced. This young generation is the generation of fulfillment of the hopes and dreams and aspirations of a suffering people. If there were no slavery and no suffering there might never have been the spirituals. If there were not this suffering and this longing for relief and closeness to God, there might never have been gospel. If we had not lived this experience there might never have been jazz and be-bop and blues. So hip hop is another of the expressions coming out of our experience. Our youth have become an organized force, at this present moment, in many cases, that force is destructive. Rage is a weakness but properly directed it is a force that can propel a nation upward. And this is why America has always made greater advancement whenever she could provide the American people with an object of rage: Hitler, Mussolini, Hirohito, the Kaiser in World War I, the Cold War with Russia. And now there's an attempt to make Iran, Libya, Iraq, China, Cuba the world's bogeymen. And so, when you channel anger into a force to bring about change, that can take a negative thing and turn it into something positive.

The Honorable Elijah Muhammad was a master at this technique. He made us angry at White people for the evils that their fathers had heaped upon us, but he never allowed that anger to manifest itself in anti-social behavior. He turned that anger into a force for self-correction and self-development. He turned that rage on alcohol, on drugs, on illicit sex, on the buffoonery and clowning that we had become accustomed to seeing, and he forced us, through this anger to become impassioned over learning. And I close this point with the example of Malcolm X. Malcolm, as you know, had a vile historical beginning until he met with guidance and turned his life around. And the same Malcolm who was great in the low life, became even greater in the high life. And now history records Malcolm X, not as the gang banger, not as the pimp, not as the armed robber, the hustler, but history records the marvelous transformation in his life that helped to transform the lives, and is *still* transforming the lives of tens of hundreds of thousands of human beings.

Q: *What are your future plans with the hip hop community?*

A: We wanted to put together a tour of East-West artists, traveling on both coasts and in the center of the country. This can bode well not only for the youth of the black community but the youth of the Hispanic, the Asian, and the white community as well, because the characteristics of young people today are universally the same, in terms of their anger, their frustration, their rage and their disappointment with the leadership, spiritually, politically, economically. So, again, we hope to get the youth together to put out an album which speaks to the peace that they have embraced. We hope that some of the proceeds from this album will go to the mothers of Tupac Shakur and Biggie Smalls, and to build some meaningful institution in the name of those who have died but have not died in vain, because if we pull the youth together, whose blood was shed to bring them together? You know, as a Christian, we talk about the precious blood of Jesus Christ, which was shed for our redemption. What about the blood of Tupac and Biggie? That is sacred blood.

Q: *Do you have either a projected date for starting work on this album or a projected lineup of people who you think will be participating?*

A: Many have started working on the album, on their participation in the album, already, we hope to have another meeting to pull our brothers and sisters together.

Q: *You said that the hip-hop tour would reach out to not only black youth but even white youth. What can white Americans do to foster racial equality? At one point, a young white girl asked Malcolm X "What can I do?" He said, "Nothing"—and later regretted it. If you were asked by a white teen, "What can I do?"—maybe somebody who comes to the tour—what would you say?*

A: I would say that every human being should get involved in the process of atonement. Black youth are in a depressed, oppressed, suppressed condition. White youth, who did not bring our fathers into slavery, or put us into this condition, are in a somewhat privileged position because of the evil, really, of their fathers. No, they are not responsible for this condition, yet in the atonement process, they have to take responsibility to right the wrongs. The native Americans suffering on the reservation, how can white youth help in righting the wrong? The blacks that suffer in the ghetto, how can white youth help to right the wrong? One of my sons is a recovering addict. And I was blessed to go to a particular institution where he was graduating, after having finished the course that they had given him. And I was asked to address the group. There were blacks, whites, Hispanics, Christians, Muslims and Jews. Here they were in a condition that caused them not to think of their color, their background, their ethnicity, their education or the lack of it, their sex or sexual preference: they were dying from crack addiction. And crack cocaine produced what the revealed religions could not produce. Now if the drug can make them one in struggle against it, then what needs to be introduced is the spiritual, universal component that on the highest level can do what crack has done at the base level. And that will involve the youth of the entire world. And that is why this October 16th the world's day of atonement will have its focus on youth. The young, gifted, and atoned.

Q: *Tell me about how the Nation of Islam's theology perceives whites, which as I understand it, correct me if I'm wrong, were created by a scientist named Yakub, and are evil. If they are evil, how can they even be approached as members of the struggle?*

A: First, I think there's great and grave misunderstanding of this aspect of the teachings of the Honorable Elijah Muhammad. White people exist on this earth, they are a physical, economic, social, political, military reality. The question is asked, "whence came the white race?" They are not considered natives anywhere on the earth. They are not native Africans, they are not native Australians, native New Zealanders, native to the islands of the Pacific, they're not native Americans, they're not native South Americans. So if they are not native, or natural to, that part of the earth, then we give them Europe as a place to their birth or rise into their greatness. They had an origin in the world. And scholars and scientists agree that they have as a parent, the black man and the black woman. That's not racist, that's an absolute, mathematical, biological, genetic, historical, anthropological truth. Now the process by which they came into existence is the science that we have to talk about and the purpose for their entrance onto the world scene.

Now if you look, the whole world of man and mankind has been affected by the presence of whites. Freedom is good, justice is good, equity is good, righteousness is good. Now, the question we have to ask is, "Have whites in general been good to the principle of freedom where the darker people are concerned?" Answer: No. "Have whites as a body been good to the principle of justice where the darker people are concerned?" No . . . If you look at the moral laws laid down by the prophets of God, have, as a body, they lived up to that? The answer, of course, is no. "Well, Farrakhan, what about you black people?" Well, in reality, neither have we, okay? But, they being the leaders, and the power that builds the institutions that shapes the direction, they have to bear the heaviest responsibility because they are the people in power. Now, can that condition of evil and rebellion to divine will and law be changed? The answer is yes.

Q: *Even for whites?*

A: For anybody who will come under the transforming power of the Messiah. And that's why the scriptures and the writings of Paul says "any man who comes to Christ becomes a new creature." Well, how in Christ do people become new, and why must we be made new? So that to be a real good Christian you must be born again, right? Well, to be born again, what does that mean? Can I enter back into my mother's womb for the second time? Of course not, but it is here. The re-birth starts with the presence of a knowledge and a wisdom that can kill the mind that produced you as an evil person. And that is why Jesus, from the Christian vantage point, is the most important human being that ever lived because in him and through him all human beings have a chance to become new. Whites, blacks, the whole human family can become new. Malcolm did not offer that young lady the chance because at that time in our spiritual development we were so angry with whites we wouldn't offer them a door out if we saw it. But here, you know, if I am a man of God, I cannot speak in a way that deprives any human being of access to that which will bring that human being into the favor of God, regardless to their color or their past.

Q: *Do you believe that your thoughts have changed or evolved over time? When Malcolm X returned to America after having experienced Islam in the Middle East, he said that the destructive "white" attitude could be purged through belief in Islam. You were among those who criticized him.*

A: I never criticized that, because we knew that. We always knew that there were White Muslims all over the earth. And the Honorable Elijah Muhammad, in many of his writings, said they are our brothers in faith.

Q: *What are the differences between the NOI's orthodoxy and Sunni Islam in relation to race?*

A: We believe in the Koran, which is the basis of belief of all the Muslims, but what we cannot divorce ourselves from is the social, political, and economic context in which Islam was introduced to us in America.

Q: *Could you ever foresee a day in which the NOI has white members?*
A: It has white members now.

Q: *Really?*
A: Not the NOI, I can't even say that, but under the leadership of the Honorable Elijah Muhammad many whites accepted his teaching and today there are many whites who accept what I teach. They don't join the mosque, but there will come a time when every human being who is a Muslim will be considered a member of the NOI. The NOI is every believer in Islam anywhere to be found on the earth. They are black, brown, red, yellow and white. We are the lost members of that nation.

Q: *How are women treated within the Nation of Islam? Are they expected to be submissive to men, who hold most of the leadership positions?*

A: The word submissive has become an ugly word, when in reality it is what Islam is, submission, but it is submission to the will of God. Black women have been independent of black men, and in submission to whites . . . Look at the men, look at the girls. Who's in the colleges? Who's filling the schools? It's the girls. Who's downtown working in the businesses? It's the girls. Who's getting the book learning? It's the girls. Who gets the jobs? It's the girls . . . They're docile, see? Now, you're in submission alright and you don't even realize that you're in submission . . .

I'm in submission to the will of God. My wife is in submission, in submission to the will of God, she submits to her husband if she thinks I'm right and I submit to her when I know she's right. And it ain't about submission to my maleness, it's about submission to what is truth and what is right and what is in the best interest of us as a people . . . My mother? Baddest black woman in the world. She made me. In the family, the male figure is the authority figure: in African society, in Asian society, in European society, wherever. God gives the male a degree of authority over the female.

Q: *Let's talk about anti-Semitism. To my mind, one of the best books on the Nation is* In the Name of Elijah Muhammad. *It was written by a Swedish professor Mattias Gardell, who defends you against some of the attacks by the Jewish watchdog group the Anti-Defamation League [ADL] but points out other instances of anti-Semitism by you and your followers. Can you ever dialogue with the ADL? Or is it a situation where neither side is willing to lose face by talking to the other?*

A: It is not with Farrakhan a question of losing face. We've already lost our face if our face is buried in falsehood. If pride and arrogance stop us in the perennial and infinite search for truth and more truth, we've already lost our face because our face is false. Humility makes us to know that we are not absolute in anything that we claim to know, there is always room for growth: among the Jews, among the blacks, among scholars and scientists. Okay? I say that to say this. I have said to the Jewish people, I am willing to sit down with you. Don't give me preconditions, because I know you are used to crushing people. This one, you can't crush. Don't give me preconditions, let's sit down and talk, you are a scholarly people, you couldn't be where you are if you didn't have great knowledge.

Q: *But weren't those pre-conditions—as expressed by the ADL's director in the days before the Million Man March—simply a disavowal of racism and anti-Semitism?*

A: If you can show me where I am in error, it is nothing for me to stand before the world and apologize. For having misstated, been erroneous, in my preachments. That is the right thing to do. But if you will not dialogue with me you cannot show me the error of my ways. And if you are as wise and intelligent as I know you to be, surely you can show me the error of my ways if I am willing to be shown.

Now, my argument with the Jewish community is not out of hatred. I have the deepest respect of this people who are at the head of just about every field of human endeavor. [But] I do not like, nor will I ever accept, the inordinate degree of control, that members of the Jewish community have over black intellectual, black political, black art and culture and its expression, that control, they would never relinquish as Jews to an Irishman, an Italian, or somebody else, over their life, over their intelligence. Black intellectuals are not really free to speak. I can get a better interview from a white person who doesn't have to kowtow to somebody who may or may not be Jewish. When the owners of your publication happen to be Jewish, then maybe these words won't find their way into publication because it seems to be a necessity to paint me as anti-Semitic. Which I detest. Not only the term being applied to me, but I detest the very act of hating someone because of their faith, tradition or the color of their skin, or their ethnicity. I detest that and if I were that I would detest myself. But what I detest is inordinate control.

Let me give you an example of what I mean. Michael Jackson, a very beloved and wonderful human being, is hurting. So, in his lyric, I think it was his last album, it's called *HIStory* and he talked about "do me, Jew me, Sue me, Kick me, Kike me, don't you Black and White me." An expression, just a line. *but*, the wisdom, or, I would call it the paranoia of those in the record industry and others, said "no, you cannot put that out." Think about that, just those lines. And they made him go back in the studio and change that. That's power! But at the same time, my little hip-hop brothers can call my sisters bitches and whores and talk about their genitals and sex and degrade themselves and that is promoted worldwide. But my little brother can't say "Jew me do me, kick me Kike me." See? Somebody is concerned about themselves and they are in control. I don't like that. I don't like that kind of control over black political thought. Black art expression. I don't *like* it.

I intend to fight it until it exists no more because until that control is broken you will never be free. If you can't write what you think, say what you believe, preach what you believe without fear of censure from the censurer than you are not free, you are not really intellectually free. Look at the control of Black college campuses and black college presidents. I don't like that control. I'm a free black man. You may not like what I say, but you will never stop me from saying it. See? I'm free. I hope you are as free to write as I am to speak and I hope that those who will read what I have said will not so edit this piece that it won't be worth a damn after it is printed.

Q: *You don't have to worry about that.*

A: I gave this man from Harvard, Henry Louis Gates, a six hour or more interview, and what I read in the *New Yorker* magazine was trash. Well, what is he trying to protect? Why would he sit here and call me brother and all that kind of stuff and then write that garbage? No balance. We all have to please a boss, I have to please one too, but I thank God for my boss because my boss wants me to tell the truth in season or out of season, and I like that, because I probably would fight my boss if he didn't want me to preach the truth.

When the sister from Washington D.C. went to Time Warner, C. Delores Tucker, to fight them in a dignified way over promoting this insanity, they told her something about cultural freedom and, you know, what may be offensive to one is not offensive to another and blah, blah, blah, and so the beat goes on. Now I want to see, will they be as interested in promoting the good that the hip-hop generation will produce now, will that get the amount of play that the gun has gotten? That the bitch and the whore and the funky this and that has gotten? The vile language? Will something better get the promotion? Now, there have been positive rappers and they have sold millions and millions of records, Public Enemy, Big Daddy Kane has done some good work and conscious rap, a lot of them, you know, Eric B, and . . . who? Rakim, and others, have done very positive things. You know, we're not expecting them to become gospel hip-hoppers, you know, all we're saying is let's promote that which inspires a people to higher consciousness and actions, that ennoble a people, not degrade a people.

You know, I was in show business, it's different today than it was when I was in it. As a calypso artist I used to wear the kind of costumes that opened and showed the chest and when you danced you moved your hips and your waist, and I was on television they would keep the camera from here up, you're not supposed to show any sensuous kind of movement to the public, well, television has gone along way since then. My point is, it is not necessary to sell sex in order to show your gifts and talents and skill. Once you put peoples minds in the gutter, and you feed and you feed and you feed them filth, they begin to eat at the slop trough of human degeneracy. And so they may think that that's the only food that there is. Ask any pig. Is there any other food than slop? His nature makes him just wallow in the slop. Well that's the way we have become, it's not our nature. Give them something better and they will grab a hold to it.

The same way these three year olds . . . I have grandchildren, great-grandchildren, that can recite the raps. I can't even decipher the words the brothers are talking so fast, but the children, they got it, three and four years old. What are they saying? Suppose you put something positive, something that inspires them to see themselves in a better light? If they can talk about funk and shake your booty, and want that thang and all this, at three and four? Of course you can't make them say something better. There is an old saying, "man is what he eats." Jesus said, "as a man thinketh, so is he." If you feed people food which is filthy, how can their bodies, which is a temple, be clean? If you feed the human mind filth and garbage what do you expect as the expression from filth and garbage if that's what I'm hearing 24 hours a day? Then my actions will flow from what I'm being fed. And what I hope to see is that all of us who are record producers, who are managers, who are agents of talent, recognize that we are feeding a public and what comes from that feeding—in terms of the actions of the people—we have some responsibility in that. So if man is what he eats and I'm the one that's cooking and I'm the one that's choosing the food that the man eats, well if I choose the food and cook it and put it before the man and the man is hungry and eats the filth that I cook and choose and provide. And when that man is sick and dying as a result of that food I have some responsibility in his death. And I want us all to see that in the atonement process we have to accept responsibility for our words and deeds.

Oh, I am considered the bigot, the hater, the anti-Semite, the unrepentant one who is the embodiment of evil from their vantage point, some of the Jewish leaders, look at the religion of Islam. You cannot find one member of the Nation of Islam that has been involved in any hate crime, anywhere in the country. Here in Chicago, a young man, two young men, were beaten, one, just a few weeks ago came out of a coma, the people that beat him were Catholics, came out of the Catholic church. I was in Philadelphia in Gray's Ferry where one of our sisters and her son and her nephew were beaten by a gang of young whites who came out of the basement of a social hall of a Catholic church. I challenge them, find me one Muslim under my leadership, that has been involved in a hate crime anywhere in the fifty states of America, and we're in every one of them, and I know you can't find me one. So who is the real hater, the real bigot? If we are so hateful of the Jewish people, why can't you bring me one Jew that a follower of Louis Farrakhan has beaten, or robbed, or broken into their homes, or sold their child drugs, or picketed their stores? You can't find it.

Q: *Why have you been so successful in reaching out to inner-city black youth and to prisoners?*

A: Revolutionary change rarely starts at the top. New ideas always find root first in the poorest members of that society. It is no different today than it was during the time of Moses, Jesus, Mohammed and the prophets. The prisoners—of which there are 1.6 million in America, the largest prison population of any civilized society—most of them are black or brown and men. The Nation of Islam offers them a doorway out of hell.

Q: *What about politics? After interviewing you on his show, CNN's Bob Novak, a conservative, said of you, "He struck me as somebody who would like to find some reason to lead his followers into the Republican Party." True?*

A: I guess when you look at a mountain, depending what side you look at you describe it as you perceive it. That is Mr. Novak's perception. I'm not trying to lead black people into the Republican party, but I do want to lead them out of the plantation of the Democratic party, you, know? I don't think that black people should be in the hip pocket of any party, but should spread themselves in all the parties and then if that doesn't get them where they need to go, lets unite all the dissatisfied elements within the country and produce a party that will speak to our own needs. But, no, that is his perception and the poor man [Novak] has suffered just from saying a kind word. Anybody who says a kind word about Farrakhan, beat him down. That's terrible.

Q: *The media has definitely been critical of you. But do you consider the criticism an asset with blacks who already distrust the media?*

A: Yes. The bible says "no weapon formed against the righteous will prosper." There is nothing that the media has done that they perceive as negative against me that hasn't turned out to ultimately been good for me.

Q: *Tell me about your "World Friendship Tour." You visited scores of countries including Libya, the Sudan and Iraq. Members of Congress called for legal action. Why?*

A: Fear. Those in power fear any connection of black people in America with the broad international community. They do not want any links of us with the struggle of our people worldwide. And if you look at the history of every black leader who became international, they were deported, imprisoned or killed. Paul Robeson. W.E.B. DuBois. Marcus Garvey. Malcolm leaves the nation, although while he was yet a member of the Nation of Elijah Mohammed, he visited Africa, he visited the Middle East, we were going to link the struggle of the blacks in America. If you look at the old *Mohammed Speaks* newspapers it always had on the masthead two black men linking hands around the globe. That is something they never wanted to see. Malcolm, vilified and assassinated. Look at Martin. Martin Luther King was fine as long as he was integrating lunch counters but when he internationalized the struggle by tying the poor people in the rice fields in South East Asia to the poor peoples' march in America for more justice, he was assassinated. With 40 million or more descendants of Africa, if we became politically and economically mature, America would never have the policies towards Africa she now has. And that is why the linking of us with Africa is dangerous to those who suck the blood of Africa and keep our people in a weakened state in America.

I started in Ghana, I went to Nigeria, I went to Libya, I went to Senegal, I went to Gambia, I went to Zaire, I went to South Africa, I went to Mozambique . . . I went to the Sudan, I went to Saudi Arabia, I went to the Emirates, I went to Iran, I went to Syria, I went to Iraq, I went to Turkey, I went to Malaysia, and I came back to the United States. But my tour was labeled a "thug fest." I visited Jamaica, Trinidad, Barbados, Guyana, Surinam, Cuba, Canada. I visited these countries but the only ones they could pick out was Iraq, Iran, Libya, Sudan, Cuba. He visited the rogues, therefore he's a rogue.

When any of the religious leaders in America visited North Vietnam, visited Moscow, visited North Korea, even visited Cuba, they were on their humanitarian work of spreading the gospel of Jesus Christ, as though Farrakhan has no gospel to spread. Huh? Now the pope has opened up relations with Libya. One little blurb in the paper. Now is the pope involved in a thug fest? He's on his way to Cuba. Is the pope now hanging out with thugs? See. Look at this double standard. Because I am black I can't have a motivation that is of God and spiritually motivated. I must be lining up with the enemies of America to do harm to my country.

The last thing I want to say, is my trip to the Sudan, in an article that appeared in VIBE trying to link Farrakhan with slavery in the Sudan. It was very malicious. I've been to the Sudan on at least what, four occasions? The most I've ever stayed was seven days. Nobody mentioned slavery to me as an issue.

Q: *But does slavery exist in the Sudan? A black reporter from the* **Baltimore Sun** *documented buying child slaves in the country.*

A: I don't know. If slavery exists I want to know. So we're taking a team there, very soon. Because if slavery exists I want to condemn it, I want to add my voice to those who condemn slavery. But now let me ask a question: Does slavery exist in the United States? If so, where? What about slaves in Louisiana today? Or Texas today? Or in parts of Mississippi and Georgia and Alabama today? Are there still blacks in virtual slavery on plantations in America right now as we speak? What form does this slavery take? We got to look at all of it. Slavery must be condemned but let's condemn it all. Is working a person for hardly any wages, wages that disallows them to live, is that a form of slavery? Is cocaine and the sentencing, check it out, where for a rock you get 5 years and you can have, how many grams of powdered cocaine and you get probation or whatnot? Is this a new form of slavery? Let's condemn it all!

JANET JACKSON 15

By Danyel Smith
November 1997

JANET'S BACK

*Miss Jackson talks with VIBE's Editor in Chief about the
pleasure in pain—and vice versa.*

The whole thing is, she's not fat.

Right up until the moment I see Janet Jackson—in a penthouse suite at New York City's Four Seasons Hotel—people are telling me that they've heard "Janet is fat now." They heard on the radio, or some other reliable source, that Janet had been seen leaving KFC with buckets of Honey Roast. That her butt was wide, her tummy plump and mushy. "She's changed" is what they whispered gleefully. "Janet said, 'I'm eating what I want.' She said, 'Fuck a Versaclimber.'"

They wish.

When she walks into the sitting area of her suite—waist wee, eyes lined, lips laced bricky brown—she looks like she has since she Lost The Weight. She's a 31-year-old woman who got her nose done when she was a girl of 16; she eats fatless soul food prepared by the chef she's employed for ten years now; who walks the treadmill, counting the calories burned, tallying the surreal miles towards Global Stardom.

She lives in Malibu with René Elizondo Jr., her lover of eleven years. Talks about her antiques. About her dissatisfaction with the way she's dealt with mental trauma. Talks about hitting a boy when she was thirteen because he took her food.

Whatever she talks about, it's slowly. She pauses before she responds. Enunciates. When you do that, you might sound too slow to yourself, like you're talking through molasses, but to the listener(s) you sound serene and confident. Thoughtful. Prepared. Too prepared, maybe.

And because these are cynical times, because "celebrity news" is ubiquitous, and it all looks like it was shot in the same studio, with the same clip-on mikes and harsh lighting and camera shot that makes celebrities and those that comment on them look like they're all chest and head. And because every "big" album is called "classic" before it's even in the stores, and because every "major" label's publicity/marketing/video/radio plan meticulously is orchestrated to force folks into purchasing a song collection like Janet Jackson's new *Velvet Rope*, (and because this magazine is component of that system) it's easy to start believing that we are all being manipulated into thinking Jackson's new album is art—pure emotion manifest—when the songs are really just an indestructible, strategically designed platform from which to maintain world pop domination.

Q: *So, what's up with this album?*

A: A lot of it is about pain. I don't know if it's something that we developed as a family but I developed this way: if I was ever in any kind of pain, I'd find a way to brush it aside. Eventually it caught up to me. Actually I should say the album took 26 and a half years, because there's one incident that I won't go into that happened to me as a kid. It took me 31 years to do this album—my entire life. I had to run grab a tape recorder because I couldn't write as fast as it was coming to me.

Q: *When you were four and a half! You're not trying to go into it at all?*

A: No.

Q: *Have you been talking to yourself mostly? Getting help from your boyfriend? Have you reached out to a professional?*

A: René helped me a lot. Then I was in the desert one day [on a trip, with René], and I met this guy. He's in his 50s, and he's a cowboy, and he's full of wisdom. The way that I see him is as my Obi-Wan Kenobi.

Q: *We should all have one. Just from one conversation?*

A: Yes. The day our paths crossed, he looked at me and told me about me.

Q: *Did he know who you were?*

A: Yes. He's not *psychic*. He *saw* me. I felt like I was ass-out, butt naked. I was sitting in front of this man who I had just met like a half hour ago, crying my eyes out. There are times when you don't feel deserving of what you have. Feel fraudulent. For me, it has to do with my past and my childhood. I didn't feel good enough.

Q: *Even when you were selling like 10 or 12 million records—*

A: Even then. People thought I was pretty, I would say, Yeah, right. There's a song that's not on the album called "God's Stepchild" . . .

Q: *So you feel like a stepchild?*

A: *No.* But those are questions I asked myself. I know I'm not God's stepchild. God, he wouldn't play favorites.

Q: *Was your childhood too difficult? Should another girl have the life that Janet had?*

A: I wouldn't want them to.

Q: *Was it the stage and the cameras? Was it your family?*

A: It was everything. I started working when I was seven. When I was ten, I had a serious full-time job. I had a contract with a studio, and I had to be there on time every single day until the show ended.

Q: *This is when you were "Penny" on* Dif'frent Strokes?

A: Yes. I enjoyed it, but were there days I was lonely? Hell yeah! I missed my family. I missed Michael. He was doing *The Wiz.* We had a hiatus coming up, and I remember asking mother if I could go to New York and visit him because I missed him so much, and we did. I went to Studio 54 for the first time, with Michael.

Q: *You went to Studio 54 when you were ten?*

A: Ten years old. The only kid sitting up in the place, seeing people pretty much butt naked. I was loving it.

Q: *You had a* life, Janet.

A: I was having a great time. But I could have swung in another direction. I could have gone to drugs, or drinking. There was cocaine everywhere back then. Someone could have said, Hey try this.

Q: *You don't regret your life though?*

A: I don't regret it at all

> *Check in the mirror my friend*
> *No lies will be told then*
> *Pointin' the finger again*
> *You can't blame nobody but you.*
>
> *—"You"*

Janet is not just a voice. She sings (her voice is pretty and small), and she writes. She comes up with melodies. She makes music. Janet says she's always resisted taking credit for her writing. She says, like she's admitting to a misdemeanor, that this album is the most personal, wrenching work she's ever done. And you know with that "Man In the Mirror" reference on "You," she ain't talking to nobody but big brother Michael, and she even sounds bratty and semi-mad—just the way Michael did circa 1987 in "Leave Me Alone." The song is spat out over a snatch from War's 1973 "Cisco Kid." That "*was* a friend of mine" vibe.

Q: *Are you feeling competitive with your brother Michael?*

A: Yes.

Q: *Is it hard for you?*

A: Because we're brother and sister?

Q: *Yes.*

A: No. Because it's business. I love him. He knows that.

Q: *Right . . .*

A: I know that he loves me.

Q: *Was that hard for you to come to?*

A: That was very hard for me to come to, and I didn't realize how—how do I say this correctly—how much business it was with he and I until a few years ago.

Q: *It's hard for me to say this because it's your brother.*

A: Go ahead, say it.

Q: *Michael is a legend in his own time. There will never be another Michael Jackson.*

A: Right.

Q: *I just don't know if there is a Michael Jackson right now.*

A: Right.

Q: *The Jackson right now is Janet. I'm wondering how you deal with that.*

A: It's hard for me. That voice inside my head starts talking. I ask, What did I do to deserve this?

Q: *To deserve all this adulation?*

A: Yes. I've called my mother and asked her. She said be thankful. So I try not to question it. I used to do that all the time because I felt guilty.

Q: *For being a winner?*

A: I felt very guilty for being a winner, when maybe someone else in my family wasn't doing as well as I was.

Q: That must be hard.

A: There are lots of times where I would ask, God why can't you just make us all be on the same level? All of us—win just a little bit, but all be on the same level. Why is one of us excelling more than the other?

Q: Did you feel this way before Control? You know, when Michael was Mr. MTV and Mr. Thriller—did you wish even at that time that everybody could be even?

A: No!

Q: You wanted to be a star?

A: Yes! I wanted to be a star! But I was so happy for Michael. I remember when he did *Thriller*—he had a serious sound system in his car. He played the album for me there. I'd never heard anything like it.

Q: How old were you?

A: A teenager. I was so stoked for him.

Q: Does he get excited about your work?

A: From what I hear, yes he does.

Q: From what you hear? Have you guys had good talks recently?

A: [No response.]

Q: I guess I'm asking are you guys friends right now?

A: Are we friends? Yes. Are we enemies? No. Have I spoken to him recently? No, I haven't. It's kind of embarrassing. I hate to say how long it's been since I've even seen my brother—two years. But he's on tour. I haven't even seen my new nephew.

Q: Janet!

A: I know. It's horrible. I know.

Q: Are you guys going to be all right? As far as brother and sister.

A: Yes. It's nothing like that, it's just that when everyone was invited to the ranch to meet [Michael's son] Prince, I was doing the album, and I was at the end of it, and there was no way I could even come home for the day.

Q: That's kind of deep.

A: It is. I mean the last time I saw my brother and spoke to him was when he was in the hospital.

Q: When he was on tour and collapsed?

A: No, no, no. We did "Scream" since then. I'm talking about when he was in the hospital when he was supposed to do the show for Pay-Per-View or HBO or something—it was the night of the 1995 *Billboard* Awards, and I was supposed to receive an award that night. I didn't even go accept my award. I went straight to the hospital.

Q: You haven't seen him since then?

A: I haven't seen him since then. I haven't spoken to him since then.

Q: Did it have to do with that "Scream" single? I thought your voice was mixed down kinda low. I wondered why I couldn't hear you.

A: I wondered why you couldn't hear me either. We went back [after the session] and put my vocal up more, and it sounds better. That's pretty much all that I can say because I don't know what really happened. I wasn't there.

Q: Because you were singing when you were in the booth, right?

A: Oh, yes. I recorded my part in New York, and I didn't like it. So I sang it again, in Minneapolis at Jimmy and Terry's studio where I felt comfortable; [Michael] was there too because he wanted to re-sing his as well. He re-sang his, but his first pass at it in New York was the shit. I don't know what happened, but I felt I was mixed down, too. It sometimes happens, you know. Then they pushed it up. I wish they would have pushed it up a little bit more. As far as the video goes, I think it was the best video out. But it didn't have anything to do with me being in it or anything like that.

What about the times
You lied to me
What about the times
You said no one would want me
What about all the shit you've done to me
What about that?
"What About"

So what is the *Velvet Rope*? Art? Hype? Maybe, as with Janet's breakthrough album, 1986's *Control*, it's both. The 21-year-old's new-found command of self, combined with Jimmy Jam and Terry Lewis' superpop music—combined with the power of a huge entertainment conglomerate—connected with over five million fans. *Rhythm Nation* had less of a clear mission statement (maybe it was about looking fly in '80s black), but the music was fierce, the big-budget videos were mesmerizing for the time, and she sold another umpteen million units *and* played to sold-out arenas around the world.

Four years later, *janet.* was "about" Janet's blossoming sexual-ity—but was it really? Or was it just calculatedly "hot," and "sexy"—a big vibrator for our rhythm nation's collective clit. (Batteries not included.) It's hard to think *janet.*—with beautiful songs like "Always" and "That's the Way Love Goes" was all spin.

And now, with *Velvet Rope*, it's all about Janet Jackson getting into her "self." She writes songs that allude to some unnamed child-hood trauma, talks about what hurt she's "locked away in her mind" all these years. She sings of hiding all this pain—and that segues really nicely into the idea that she herself is semi-getting-into "pain" as arousal. She, and her long-time love, have written a bunch of songs about that. Is this some stuff invented or exaggerated or strategically timed so that we have a reason to care? Not to accuse her of making up trauma for the sake of drama, or fetishes just to flourish—but you can't help thinking that real life needs a remix in order to go platinum.

❖

Q: *What about your self-esteem? Most people assume that you feel perfect.*

A: That's furthest from the truth. I have never felt attractive.

Q: *What about after you lost the weight back in 1990?*

A: Did I feel better about myself after losing the weight? Yes I did. Did I still feel ugly? Yes I did.

Q: *People didn't tell you were ugly when you were little, did they?*

A: No. That's just the way I felt when I looked in the mirror. I was shocked when René and I got together.

Q: *What brings you joy, then?*

A: René brings me joy; work brings me joy.

Q: *You've been with René for a long time.*

A: Since 1986. We were friends for like four or five years before that, like best friends.

Q: *You guys have a good relationship?*

A: We have a very good relationship, and it's due to us being good friends in the beginning. Then I started looking at him differently. It's weird to kiss your good friend for the first time. It's also hard work—

Q: *To keep a relationship going.*

A: We work at it.

Q: *Did I see you at the Essence Awards with a diamond?*

A: Everyone thought it was an engagement ring. It was a birthday present.

Q: *Do you like not being married?*

A: I'm not afraid of marriage. I just like where we are right now.

Q: *[Phone line beeps] Janet, hold on for one second.*

A: Sure. It's okay.

Q: *I just told my cousin Khalief that I have Janet Jackson on hold. I've got a lot to deal with—a few family issues tonight.*

A: Don't worry. I can understand family issues.

> *Everywhere I go*
> *Every smile I see*
> *I know you are there*
> *Smilin' back at me*
> *Dancin' in moonlight*
> *I know you are free*
> *'Cause I can see your star*
> *Shinin' down on me.*
>
> —*"Together Again"*

"Together Again" is a big, perfect, Donna Summer ode, all "MacArthur Park" and "Last Dance," and you just know the spirit of Ray Vitte (who played the DJ in *Thank God It's Friday*, and who died of some kind of overdose) is dancing on his celestial ceiling.

Janet Jackson gives it all the way up in this, her tribute to friends who have died of AIDS-related illnesses. I mean, not to compare it to other extremely beautiful songs that play with our general despair, but that song her brother did, 1991's "Gone Too Soon," about the little blonde boy with AIDS? "Together Again" tops that. Puffy's chart-destroying "I'll Be Missing You"? "Together Again" kills that. This four-minute song is true disco dying for a 21-minute extended mix. The joint is hot to death. Literally.

The joy "Together Again" inspires, the way it makes you want to swing and dip and bounce and skip—you can't believe it's about seeing people in heaven who have died so horribly. And then you cry while you dance because you know you have little faith in "heaven," and death is everywhere and that's why you play your music so loud. Because otherwise, why go on?

"I was very cynical in the beginning," says Janet, in an industry trade sheet, of Puffy. "I was sittin' back thinking, 'How much pain is he really in?' It's seems like he's taken his and ran with it. Part of me wondered if it was really real. But only he knows that—and God."

Q: What was it like working with Q-Tip? Do you like his voice?
A: I love his voice. I know René is probably sick of me saying, "God, I love Tip so much." He was real quick in the studio.

Q: So you, Tip, and Joni Mitchell—
A: I spoke to Joni over the phone and told her we used her sample. Everyone kept saying don't even bother. I called her up myself, told her how much of a fan I was and how my brother Randy introduced me to her work. When we were kids, Randy was a really big Joni Mitchell fan.

Q: What's your favorite Joni Mitchell song?
A: "Be the Black Wings." I absolutely love it. As a matter of fact, Joni called and asked me to be on her tribute album. She said, "I read in an interview that you were a fan. So I want to know if you want to do this song."

Q: So you did that one? The "Wings" song? How was it?
A: I like it a lot. I just hope she does. That's one of the hardest things to do because to me you just don't touch greatness. It's like, leave it there because you can't go any place with it. For her to ask me was such an honor.

Q: Speaking of how you feel about not touching greatness, I'm wondering how come you're not working with Puffy? How come you're not working with Babyface?
A: It's a loyalty thing, for one. Not just that, though—Jimmy and Terry and I work well together. I feel as a team there is still more within

us to give. Though that's not to say that if I were to do something with Babyface that I would be unhappy with Jimmy and Terry. But if it's not broken, why fix it?

Q: *Like Joni says, I guess sometimes you don't know what you've got 'til it's gone.*

> Follow the passion
> That's within you
> Living the truth
> Will set you free
> —"Velvet Rope"

Maybe you have hidden this pain. Maybe you're reading *The Story of O* or maybe your man whispering lines from *Beauty's Punishment* by Anne Rice while he's dripping wax on your décolletage. Maybe your left nipple and your tongue are both pierced. Maybe right now it is all about spankings and nipple clips and surrender. Maybe you're wondering why you like to abandon the you you've made up. Why it's fun all of sudden to relinquish your feigned tranquility, and beg for the pain you trust your lover not to give you too much of.

Then you redo Rod Stewart's 1976 "Tonight's the Night" because that song was massive when you were like 11, and you sing it with all the "girl" references intact so it seems to your public you're into girls. And, if some factions of your public are girls into girls or boys into girls who are into girls—they know you support that. Maybe this sticky marketing convolution is from whence your new art came. Maybe, in this day, it's from where all art comes. Or maybe you just want to outdo Madonna.

Or maybe Janet Jackson really feels lonely. Because she sounds more convincing, more alive, more supa dupa, on "I Get Lonely" then on *Velvet Rope*'s bland-ass title song, better than when she's singing about any of that push me pull me fuck me from behind "Rope Burn"/

"My lips hurt . . ." stuff. I mean, it's fun and all, but Janet's "velvet room" is the ho-hum part of *The Velvet Rope*. She says herself, she wants to feel a "soft" rope burn. Because truly, when it's gotten down to ropes—feel the heat or get out the kitchen.

Q: *When was the last time you had a big laugh out loud?*

A: When I get tired, I get so giddy I start crying. I laugh so hard, I can't breathe; and then *that* becomes funny to me. The last good time that I can think of, was just last month. Renee was pretending to be an actor in a film, he had a cigar in his mouth. It was so funny, I couldn't stop. On top of it, we had wine. Wine makes me giddy, too. Just a couple of sips and . . .

Q: *You're gone?*

A: I'm a lightweight, is what they tell me. When I take a couple of sips, you know how it normally goes to someone's head? With me, It goes in the opposite direction.

Q: *[Laughing] So it's on after that?*

A: I'm telling you. Literally, it will take two sips and, Oh my God!

Q: *You're looking for René.*

A: *Somebody!* I'm just joking.

Q: *I'm curious where sex fits into your life now.*

A: Are you kidding?

Q: *Do tell.*

A: [*Laughing*] Please could I not?

Q: *So is sex about bondage and domination for you now? Are you and your lover playing with power?*

A: [*Laughs*] You mean, like, pain? Are we into pain?

Q: *Yes, are you into pain, Miss Jackson?*

A: No, no . . . I have a high tolerance for pain.

Q: *You think so?*

A: That's what I'm told . . . how would I possibly know that, right? I guess from the things I've gotten pierced, I suppose.

Q: *In some of your photos you look strong and in control, and in some of them you look like you're giving up your power. Do you know what I mean?*

A: I believe I know what you mean.

Q: *There's one picture of you where your wrists are up and tied, I'm wondering how you got to that place.*

A: It's a part of me. On this album, you hear that. For instance, about [the song] "Rope Burn," someone said, "You know, that's a painful thing." But it says "soft rope burn"—nothing to really harm a person. I'm getting deeper into my fantasies, into what I like and don't like, that's the other side of this album.

Q: *So, the album is somewhat about you looking at the past pain in your life and coming to terms with that, and some of it is about Janet's own personal fantasies.*

A: It all goes back to feeling special. There's a song on the album called "Anything," it's about pleasing a man. There are people who are into pleasing others, and people who are into being pleased. Some nights you feel one way, some nights, you feel another. Pleasing someone else and seeing them enjoy—you become aroused.

Q: *What's your idea of ecstasy? Is it the old candles and flowers?*

A: It's all that. There's a point where you could go too far—I'm not into that *real* painful stuff.

Q: *The idea of a velvet rope to me is like, you're constrained, but nicely.*

A: Exactly. It's soft. Instead of it being crass, there's still something classy about it. The candles, the flowers, the wax, the ice . . .

Q: *The whole nine.*

A: Yeah. Trying new things.

Q: How did you come to name the album, The Velvet Rope?

A: That's what I've been exposed to all my life. That's what I still see every single day in my life.

Q: Which is what? Pain blanketed with a nice little covering?

A: That need to feel special. There are two sides to the velvet rope: those who want to be on the other side and those who *are* on the other side.

Q: It depends where you're standing.

A: Take a nightclub: those outside of the club, waiting to be chosen—they wish they were inside. Once inside, they thinking they're the shit. But there's another velvet rope—the V.I.P section. They wanna be in that section, but they can't.

Q: Does anyone ever get to that point where they're finally on the side of the velvet rope that they want to be on?

A: Where the grass is greener?

Q: I guess you never get to it.

A: I don't know. We're all born special, and somewhere along the way, we lose knowing that. We want that specialness. When you feel special, you don't need a rope to validate you. You know who you are.

Q: You're always on the right side, if you have your own rope.

A: That's where I'd like to be.

> Sittin' here her with my tears
> All alone with my fears
>
> —"I Get Lonely"

"I Get Lonely" is a gigantic voice-y song that takes you right up into the spirit of Dru Hill's recent Jermaine Dupri–remixed "Sleeping in My Bed." The song starts with the beautifully overblown chorus—"I get so lonely / Can't let / Just anybody hold me," and after that, it's official, you're singing it until next year, until the next *real* R&B pop jam. There're like 40 Janets singing the chorus and she harmonizes with herself like she's The Pips. Honey butter. This is where she wins. Makes pop. Art. Hits you where? In the head the heart the booty.

So why do people dis Janet? Is it that when a person gets so large—at a certain point, they can no longer be trusted? That the art gets trite automatically?

There are no questions about who Janet is when she's making music like this (or 1989's "Escapade" or "Miss U Much" or a long list of others). Janet Jackson is not just Michael's sister—because so is LaToya. And Reebie. Janet is Janet is Janet. And maybe when you get that huge—so big that you've got to look for you in your own life— nothing is regular anymore.

Q: *Can you imagine a day when you put out a record and people aren't interested?*

A: It can very well happen with this record. The applause *will* die, it happens to every single person in this business. It's like in my song, "You." *Does what they think determine your worth? By getting this applause, are you worthy? Without the applause, are you worthless?* And that's what a lot of artists have trouble with. Maybe their music is not what it used to be. Maybe people aren't paying as much attention to them as they did in the past, but those happen and you have to understand that you're special, and it's okay. I'd rather for people not know what I am, what I have, or who I am, and to accept me for me.

Q: *Do you ever have that option?*

A: Sometimes I do, sometimes I don't.

Q: *Have you gone through things with friends, where you realized they were just being your friend because you were Janet Jackson?*

A: Hell, yeah. Or just being my friend because of I lived right down the hall from my brother Michael when I was younger.

Q: How do you know when somebody's your friend?

A: I think the truth comes out. You can't fake it forever.

Q: Is there any place you can go where you're not recognized?

A: [*Pause.*] I don't know.

Q: Any place where you can walk the streets and no one points at you?

A: [*Pause.*] So far it hasn't happened. So I don't know if there is.

Q: I'm just curious because—

A: Would I like it?

Q: Would you?

A: I can't have my cake and eat it too.

TONI MORRISON 16

By Robert Morales
May 1998

IT WAS WRITTEN

The Nobel Prize–winning novelist talks about Oprah,
Tawana, rage, rap, rebuilding, and how to live in the world.

Y‍ou know her books. So imagine going to her luxuriously spartan Manhattan crash pad, where Toni Morrison sits you down at her kitchen table, makes you a cup of imported herbal tea, and chain-smokes fiendishly while she tells you stories:

A black seminarian she knew had been tutoring some urban New Jersey black kids. As he was telling them some basic facts about slavery, he noticed that they kept giving him a strange look. Finally, one of them said, "Man, are you kidding? You mean black people were brought here as slaves?" *And they laughed.*

"These kids were twelve and fourteen," Morrison points out. "They knew about racism and being black, but they did not know . . ." She cocks her head from across the table and gives *you* a look: "I want to know who skipped that part."

Then she's switched gears, and you're both laughing at the general outcry over O.J. Simpson's recent interview appearances. "I think Geraldo ought to give O.J. ten percent of his salary," she cracks. Then she'll swear you to secrecy and share some truly hilarious (non-O.J.–related) insight, and while you're laughing at *that*, Morrison warns: "If you print that, I will sue you and I will kill you." *And she laughs.* [Some time after this interview appeared, she published her assertion that Bill Clinton was the first black president in *The New Yorker*—but it wasn't as funny.]

"No person is only *blank*," Morrison explains later, when answering if she feels pigeonholed by the definitions (first Nobel Prize–winning black feminist author) of literary critics. "When I was a little girl, I was walking down the street in Ohio. A man came up to me and said, 'Are you a Willis?'—referring to my mother's maiden name—'I thought so, by the way you walk.' And I knew he knew my family. It was a comfort to be identified as a Willis. I moved to New York and people said, 'What do you *do*?' So you say 'I'm a writer, teacher, editor, whatever'—but you know that's only a *part* of who you are."

Perhaps it's the way she so keenly divines "who you are" that makes Toni Morrison such a force with which to reckon. From her first novel, 1970's heartbreaking, pigment-envy classic, *The Bluest Eye*, to her most recent, the gender tragedy *Paradise*, the 67-year-old writer has fearlessly explored the pitfalls of self-limitation, as well as the horror that is not being seen for who you are. Morrison isn't an easy writer, and she is often the bearer of unwelcome truths. It's the weight of her talent that makes Oprah Winfrey curl up with these obsessive, violent parables—then gets the TV personality to recommend them to middle-American homemakers. (Winfrey has produced and stars in Jonathan Demme's feature film version of Morrison's 1987 post–slave era ghost story *Beloved*, due out this fall). And her genius is surely what makes it such a trippy privilege to sit with her for hours and shoot the shit.

Q: *So.* Paradise *is the story about this women's commune in the '70s, and all these completely screwed-up guys who—*

A: Got it wrong.

Q: *—who got it wrong and feel they have to butcher these women. The thing that struck me was, What if this book had been written by a man?*

A: That's interesting because I think some people have noted a strong feminist theme in it.

Q: *What if it was the same text, and if Toni Morrison was a guy? Would it be attacked by NOW?*

A: But I think that I do write with a very good male sensitivity, because I don't have axes to grind. I'm not that judgmental.

Those men who mounted that assault were in error, and they came from a whole history of black men and women who were better than that. Much better than that! It's a parable of the so-called '60s, really, when the threat of women—free with certain kind of license—was real. And, in a closed, protected, religious society of any kind, that was a major threat. So that patriarchal values, whether they're white or black, would have been hostile to any collection of women who seemed not to need male control.

But there are all sorts of dialogues that have not yet taken place within the group. There're generation conflicts; there are class conflicts.

There's a budding conversation about young black girls in the entertainment world, the rap singers, the dancers, and their contribution to the culture versus their not-contribution, you know, counter-contribution, and another group of women, who consider themselves quite liberation. That discussion hasn't taken place yet. Those differences.

Q: *I wanted to ask you about the violence that women seem to vent today. You know, I just heard that my cousin's 15-year-old daughter got arrested for killing a cabbie in Florida.*

A: Oh, my!

Q: *You know? And this is right after these other teen girls up in the Bronx killed a cabbie and then were caught bragging about it.*

A: I think women have been in a *rage* for a long time. And they just didn't have any guns. But now we have the guns! [*Laughs.*] The rage of women is still staggering to me. It's different from I guess earlier days. But, you know, in the African-American culture, women were much more walk-on-water aggressive types than white women ever were, anyway. They really took things into their hands, and they were not about to go slowly into that abused life. You know, if you listen to [blues] lyrics, it's always, "If you start it, you have to finish it, because I'm not going to take it lying down." So that feeling of confrontation with whatever was out there, or whatever men or it proposed, has been a very strong survivalist strategy among us.

However, some of it's a little wanton now, it's a little narcissistic, a little prideful—there's the "He Done Me Wrong" or "She Done Me Wrong, Therefore Kill." Or, there is the "He Done Me Wrong, Let Me Get Out of Here and Make My Life Over." The latter is the one that I grew up with. The other one seems sort of narrow, and self-absorbed. The slaughter of somebody who was mean to you, or didn't like you, or hurt you in some way. The slaughter. I mean, it's the uselessness of another person's life. That to me seems very recent. The rage has always been there, but the management of it is different. Now, you know, it's quite easy to not manage it, to terminate the argument.

Somebody has to talk to those girls. You know what they need? They need to go out to Bedford Hills [Correctional Facility] and have some conversations with some of the women, young women who are there. That is the most helpful conversation they could possibly have. They don't need me or some authority saying, "Don't do bad things." What they need are some of the people who have *done* the bad things.

I have been to Bedford. What struck me was, when you see women in prison, whatever their dealings are among themselves—just the notion that men in prison have on their walls pictures of women. Women in prison have on their walls pictures of children.

Anybody's child. All kinds of children. And they adopt one another. It would be interesting to see some dialogues between the young gang members, women, girls, and some older black women who have been there.

Q: *What about the huge rise in what they call neo-natocide?*
A: Is that babies or fetuses?

Q: *Babies.*
A: Babies. Well, you know, we have told those young girls in very clear terms that what you are doing is immoral and expensive and a burden to society and a blight. We have told them that there are ways in which you can avoid doing this. So what these girls are producing, in their minds' eye—*they* thought it was a baby. But in fact in turns out to be a disease. A horror. An embarrassment. Something that no one wants.

When I was a young girl, black girls had children—it was a scandal, but they took care of the children. Somebody took care of those children. They didn't put them in the orphanage. Somebody took those children and raised them. And people could appear, even in my own family, ten and twelve years later, claiming to be the daughters of various people, and my mother said, "Come on in." Now that's not true. So that they're bearing something that, when they deliver, is already something that society has contempt for, because no one wants to pay for it. So their connection to that child is sometimes immediately distorted because it's not a person, it's not a human being—it's a terrible, terrible illness. And you have this violent reaction; the body even sometimes has a violent reaction to the carrying of it. And we are not putting our arms around those girls.

Listen: I heard, and have heard for years, that a female who is pregnant by the time she is sixteen has no chance of getting any cancer of any of her reproductive organs. Now, I asked an oncologist about this, and he said it seems to be so. Now, I thought now suppose it is so. I don't know if the baby has to come to term, but any female who is pregnant by the time she's sixteen, has no chance of her getting these major cancers. Now that's interesting information, isn't it?

Q: *That's amazing.*

A: What would happen to social policy? What would you do with your daughter? All I'm saying is that we're not looking at this right. We're looking at it from a Republican-who-doesn't-want-to-pay-taxes point of view. They don't care about those girls, they care whether they pay for them. That's all.

We fought a long time to have "women taking care of children" understood to be work. Now it's understood to be something else. Do you remember this British nanny case, and there was a lot of complaint about the mother not being home with the child, and she should have, this professional woman. She should have been home with her children, said some people.

On the other hand, if she was a poor black woman, she should *not* be home with her children. She should work. Even if that work is taking care of somebody *else's* children. So that the contradictions and the deceit in that discourse, you know, boggled the mind. No wonder nobody can say anything, because the signals that one is getting from public discourse, government discourse, cultural discourse is meaningless because each sentence contradicts the other one.

Now, Breast Cancer Month just passed, you know, all sorts of shows about who has it, and what to do about it. That what I said was never brought up. I mean . . . it's very interesting. I haven't found physicians yet who said, "Oh, no, no, no." [*She pauses for a moment then laughs at herself.*] "Toni Morrison is a kook who sits around . . ."

Q: *No, we haven't got to the "Toni Morrison is a kook" phase yet. You still have a ways to go. But, you know, it's one of those things where if a white man were saying that, he'd be stoned.*

A: I can away with it.

Q: *Tawana Brawley made an appearance recently and New York newspapers seemed aghast that so many black people believe her story.*

A: Something happened to Tawana Brawley. And she was *fifteen*. I have never forgiven the people who betrayed her.

Q: *Well, who do you feel betrayed her?*

A: When have you ever seen an *alleged* rape victim's picture in the paper? Never. That child was fifteen. I don't care what she was doing . . . something terrible happened to her. And everybody is busy saying something *didn't* happen—she invented it. I mean, it's just unbelievable! At the time that happened to her, I had a lot of white women friends call me up to get me to sign on to Hedda Nussbaum as a victim of her abusive, manipulative husband. And I would ask them, "What are you doing about Tawana Brawley?" And there was always this incredible silence. No one even . . . *This is a little girl.*

But what is interesting to me, at the moment—and has always been—is this overwhelming urgency to sweep that under the rug. I mean, just *urgency* to make sure it never happened. That's very alarming to me. Why is the media all in it? Why is everybody in there determined that it was hoax? From the beginning, you know?

Q: *Well, why is it acceptable to believe Oliver North if you're white, but not to believe Tawana Brawley if you're black?*

A: Exactly. [*Laughter.*]

Q: *The media freaks out because so many black people believe that there're all these conspiracies against them.*

A: I wonder why? [*Laughs.*] Oh, no kidding. No, something terrible happened to her, and I've always wanted to tell her that it hurts me to think that there was no respite for her. No haven. Nobody she could talk to. Her going to join the Muslims was inevitable, it seems to me, under those circumstances. The truth was co-opted by several diverse groups. *A* truth—that suited their agenda. And Tawana got so lost in it.

Q: *What was your reaction when Oprah's Book Club picked your 1977 novel,* Song of Solomon, *and it sold zillions of copies?*

A: I was astonished by that choice. But somebody last year asked me, didn't I feel *awkward* being in the company of some of the titles that she had chosen. I said, "Hey, listen, the remarkable thing about Oprah's Book Club is not just what you think. But it returns the novel to what it *was*." Remember when they told women "don't read it, it might give you ideas"? It was a thing that men said was dangerous for women. Also, novels are always associated with sleep and death. You know, people say I dipped into it before I went to sleep, or it's on my bedside table.

But listen—Oprah Winfrey said to her 20 million audience, "Turn off the television, it's *okay* to do this in the central part of your day." No more, "Oh, you know, I *used* to read, but now I don't have time." And it means they can talk about it, and they can be confused about it, or they don't have to understand it, they can fuss about it. Now that's returning novels to narrative, or public discourse.

But the consequences of it are twofold. One, it makes the active reading for all those people that we think we have disdain for—the publishers certainly do, they never talk to them. The publishers talk to the man who run Barnes & Noble, they don't talk to those people out there, that she talks to. *Those* people, many of them, have never been in a bookstore, and are intimidated by going in a bookstore. And book shops all over the country are saying, "You know, we're getting people that we have never seen come in bookstores before."

This is something coming from someplace else, saying, "You don't know what you're doing if you can't sell to these people." That's the implication: You publishers do not know what you're doing if you can't sell *800,000 copies* of a book to these people.

Oh, all right, she's done it for twelve months or whatever. But there is no book that she has mentioned that hasn't been purchased at that level.

Now, I have thought about this a lot because I wondered who is going to buy my book because Oprah says so. Then I realized that most book shows on television miss the point because they're teacherly, I-know-it-you-don't, elitist. It's not open, friendly, we're both in this together. And it's off-putting for the non-reader, non-browser, non-academic person.

The bestseller sells to people who *don't* buy books. That's why it's called "best." You know it's out there when people who buy two books a year, buy it. Not just buy it, but actually read it and talk about it. I was in a chat room—it's amazing what's going on out there: quarrels and interrogations, a marvelous series of conversations from hundreds of people about *my* book. It's a dream.

It's sort of like when I was an undergraduate, when you used to fight about books—that kind of fervor, that kind of passion is out there. I don't need this sort of cool New York critical eye. It's something else.

Now whatever that is she's tapped into, has always been there, and nobody knew how to get to it, or work it. But Oprah just reads books, and she reads them all the time. And, she just likes them, for all sorts of reasons, some good, some perhaps not. But it almost doesn't matter, because the phenomenon is the thing and I am not going to do what authors triply do to themselves, which is to identify so quickly with an elite, so that they're pleased because only ten people read them.

I was wondering if there's another talk show host who could establish a book club?

Q: *Jerry Springer.*

A: [*She feigns innocence.*] You think?

Q: *Has her purchase of the movie rights to* Beloved *and* Paradise *changed you in any way?*

A: Not really. I had reservations about selling *Beloved*, because it wasn't an option, it was an outright sale. But I thought it was interesting that there was a black woman in the world who could buy the property and just write the check. Every other option was sort of "Can we go beg a white guy?" and this was something so different that it was just seductive. She wanted *Beloved*, and she got it. She went in her pocketbook . . . [*Laughs.*] I am very wary—not just of people, but of people in media. And she is forthright. It's like being in the company of the genuine article, as opposed to the *developed* one. Oprah is evolved.

Q: *What are the reasonable expectations that minority readers should have toward minority writers?*

A: They should not be easily seduced by calls to simplistic arguments, and, you know, I guess you call it black exploitation—where you sort of use your essentialism in order to get attention that way. They should pattern it after the demands of the music, complicated, simple, but easily demanding. Early black music was not tampered with by other forces. The best floated to the top. And the critical audiences, the demanding audiences, were black. You couldn't get away with junk when you were delivering to a black audience. That's the way I feel when I write. I can't get away with silly stuff, patronizing stuff, misleading stuff.

As a writer, I don't play that game. Of course, a lot of people don't read me because I don't play the game, but it has to be the highest possible standards, like the precedent that we have, which is obviously in music. My feeling is that wherever minorities enter into a previously all non-minority field, they *always* raise the standards. You can never play basketball like that again, ever. You can never play *this* after Coltrane. We always make it harder and better. And I think that's true—if we let it be—in literature. The promise has been filtered through other gazes and other eyes, but once it gets unpoliced and not so much about celebrity, when the work itself is unpoliced—and it has to be in your feedback, the tough black readers; even if there are only four, that's what you go for.

I know how to write difficult esoteric books, and I probably *do* write them. But I'm always, *always* focused on the story, the plot, and I think those books that are well done can be enjoyed by non-discriminating readers. And there also is a lot in there for very fastidious readers.

Q: *As a writer, who do you think of as your peers?*

A: Oh, there's a woman I used to edit that I always thought of as my peer, she died recently—Toni Cade Bambara. I just miss her in every single way. She was for me, artistically, the closest. And I still sort of identify myself with that whole generation of emerging black women writers. Whether Book A or Book B I liked, it was that whole movement. I was not early. I mean, Alice Walker published before I did. Maya Angelou published before I did. June Jordan had published. Lucille Clifton was publishing. But I feel a part of that community. Sonia Sanchez.

And I'm just delighted because there's so many other women who are a third of my age who are doing it. And seeing that happen after 20, 25 years is the best news there is in the world.

Q: *Who do you like now?*

A: Well, I like this girl A.J. Verdelle. There's a girl who wrote this interesting thing called *Push*.

Q: *Oh, Sapphire?*

A: Yeah, interesting stuff. I like the later books of Jamaica Kincaid. June has a new thing out. Lucille, I did her book, *Generations*. And now I saw a book, somebody handed me a galley by Gayl Jones. I haven't heard from her in years and years. It's called *The Healing*. I mean, this is fantastic stuff these people are still doing, because a lot of people aren't. You must know that most of the young people now, when you ask them what art thing they want to do, if they don't do music, they want to make movies.

Q: *They want to go where the money is.*

A: That's right. They don't want to sit around and do this long and boring, isolated, no-money job.

Q: *Do you have an opinion of rap as an art form?*

A: I find it totally compelling. I don't know why. It's a stopper, as they say. But I don't have a lot to say about what is probably the most interesting part of it, which is the language. My sons listen to it all the time, and I keep saying to them, [*Laughs.*] What was *that* again? It's like when they used to hit—you know, do graffiti. And I'd say, "What does that mean?" They'd say, "Mom, the point is that it not be overtly clear." It's like an underground railroad of communication. And that's when I found it fascinating—not only in the sounds, but what was going on.

Recently, it seems to be so over-merchandised that it's being driven by something else other than maybe the performer's interests. There's something about it that seems a little slick right now. I'm not sure that I'm right, but it doesn't have that *unpoliced* quality. Now it looks like the police are there telling them *how* to misbehave. It feels so marketed. I like to see everybody get rich, but I hate to see the whole field manipulated.

But I have to tell you, I have heard rap in practically in every language in the world, there's *nothing* like the rap that comes out of this country; I've heard it in Russian, German, French—it's really everywhere. It's just amazing how they can come up with playing the music against the music. [*Laughs.*] The *innovation*, it does my heart good to see that happen.

Q: *What do you think of someone attacking the form, like C. Delores Tucker?*

A: All young people's music is hated. I mean, even Mozart. Jazz. Their music was despised—because they were young. Rock. Blues. Like reggae was when it first came over here. So I always have a healthy respect for young people's music because I know the part of it that makes other people shudder is the part that means it's new.

I like those arguments a lot. When there's a big canvas and a map and something happens, and everybody is in it, because that's the only way something new and something resolved, or unresolved—it doesn't all have to be resolved—happens. It's the *not* talking that's a problem for me.

Somebody told me at the Million Women March, there was an interesting attack by Sister Souljah on some of the young rap girls, and their response, *and* some Christian-singer-type woman—all quarreling with each other. I like that kind of interrogation among these various streams. I mean, I know it's sort of antagonistic, but nothing has only two sides. Think of a young girl, like Lil' Kim, versus an older Sister Souljah-warrior-type versus, you know, someone who wants to sing Bessie Smith . . .those conversations can be quite valid. We have to talk about this stuff. And besides, people change, you know? One day Lil' Kim will be 50.

Q: *That'll be an interesting day.*

A: And she'll sit around and say, "You young people today [*laughs*] are *outrageous*."

Q: *Are you religious?*

A: I have a problem with institutions. I don't have a problem with faith of certain kinds. Magic. Meanings behind the meanings of things. Incoherence. Power—you know, all these aspects of religion. But I have a problem when it gets institutionalized and frozen, and becomes formidable. So I say that I'm religious because I can't deny my perceptions. I'm a Catholic, and I have been very much involved in my mother's church, which is AME. And so I have always gone back and forth between Catholicism and Protestantism. And, I guess. ended up *nowhere*—except I feel nevertheless as though I am a deeply religious person.

Q: *Do you get the sort of thing that I remember García-Márquez talking about—how people would ask him what the angels in his stories symbolized? And he answers, "Well, they're angels." [Laughter.]*

A: Well, they think I'm sort of mystical, and . . .

Q: *But they don't get that you're not kidding.*

A: No, they don't. I'm not kidding, you know. I've had visions. I think many of us have. And some people may not recognize them as such, but those of us who are interested in an enchanted world . . . Even physicists talk that way. When they get to "The End," their language becomes wholly theological: A "hand" being back there where they can't get it. So the language runs in that area when you're very, very deep into practically any discipline, scientific or not. But the other thing, of being deliberately *alert to* or just *available to* sights, and inner voices. If you're really clear and focused, it *seems* as though the universe cooperates and reveals to you the ways of which to go. [*She shrugs, and smiles ruefully.*] Now, what it means is that the mind is fantastic and fabulous. Each brain reads the world a certain way. I can, I suppose, become a total rationalist and eliminate a large part of life's experiences, or my own imagination. I choose not to do that.

I think I'd like to exhibit the best qualities of my grandparents and my parents, which was a very shrewd, practical, down-to-earth approach to life, *coupled* with a religion that placed them on the moral high ground—and *added* to that a dash of the magic, of reading the world, and understanding its science as some kind of conversation that they were having with the universe. That's the way to live with the world.

Q: *What about when spirituality gets confused with a kind of X-Files reality where people need to believe just about anything?*

A: Well, spirituality is like anything else. It's hard work. You can't just become a great net and just *attract* everything. You have to work at it as if you were going to law school, medical school, or whatever else—if you want to be a brain surgeon. You have to think about *those* things very carefully. And some of it is innovative, and some of its laws already passed down and information you have before you. But spirituality requires the same amount of intense intellectual brainpower to think about it. It doesn't mean you just sort of drift off into Tarot cards, and you want something other than your own mind to tell you what do to. It's an active-aggressive relationship. It's *all* you, you know?

Q: *You're rebuilding the house you lost on the Hudson River a few years back. Having your home burn down—it must be like a death.*

A: It's very sad, and the sadness goes on a long time. Somebody was asking me the other day for pictures of me and my sons. I had to go through it again and say I don't have any. Or, if I do . . . it's somebody *else's* stuff.

Q: *So you don't con yourself into thinking of it as a liberating experience.*

A: Well, we've made a better house, but we lost a lot of things. Not in value, but the irreplaceable things. And my memory's failing, so I *need* all those little documents.

Q: *Did you feel like you had to start all over?*

A: I was rocked. And I thought about Native Americans, some of whom say, "When a house burns down, *leave.*" So I thought, Okay, I'll sell it. But it has such a lovely aspect, on the river . . . I put it on the market, but then I thought: *I've written all these books to the sound of that water, and the water is in my dreams. The weather was never bad on that river—I'm not leaving it!* So then I changed my mind.

That helped a lot, to rebuild that house. For a while I couldn't talk about the fire to anybody—except people whose house had burned down. [*She starts to laugh a little hysterically.*] It's surprising how many people's houses have burned down!

Q: *I hear it's the latest thing.*

A: My mother's house was burned. I was living in New York then. Her house was set on fire, I guess, and burned, and she was out of it . . . And *she* rebuilt. And I remember her during those months, she was living with my sister—and it was obsessive and debilitating and horrifying.

Q: *Jesus! Who burned down your mom's house? Did they ever find out?*

A: That's an *entirely* different story . . . an interesting one, but I'll tell it later. [*Laughs.*]

Q: *Another thing I wanted to know: You seem so utterly fearless on the page—*

A: Oh, I am fearless on the page. Oh, yes! You mean in real life?

Q: *Yeah. I mean, what scares you? Is that what you write about?*

A: I'm sometimes frightened of that, what I write, but I can't look away. Not there. I will not look away; that's the one place where I'm going to, you know, make eye contact. Just feel it, and do it— it's a free place for me. It's not always safe, but that's the one place where all my little vulnerabilities, and cowardices, cannot come to the surface. Not with the work.

Q: *What about the sense of that place for your characters—where the place is violated? So much of what you write is about people not respecting boundaries. Especially in Paradise, where the place is violated? People move in on it. Are you like other writers in that, you know, you have this conceit that if you put it on paper, you're marking your spot: "This is the line. I dare you to cross the line, and come in."*

A: Part of the history of the race is dealing with personal transgression. You have to remember we were an *owned* people, in the most finite sense of that word. That is unique, and interesting, and the exodus from that is a very complicated journey. Where is the territory where you're free? Where is the territory where you're safe? Where is it that it's *okay* to love somebody else, and know that they're not going to be taken from you, for no reason or nothing rational? The idea of Home, or Paradise, or *mine*, or *this* domain, or language that's ours, *mine*, you know—struggling to hang onto it, struggling to know what *it* is—is an important aspect, I think, of the life that African-Americans have led. And also the fear that somebody can just walk in your house in the middle of the night, and say, "Give me your nephew." And your house is [*she laughs bitterly*]—open. So, there is that constant sense of tension and how to defend it, how to protect it, how to transcend it, or travel away from it. That seems to me to be *particularly* acute among African-Americans, but I think it has resonance for everybody. Resonance in terms of territory.

The biggest thing going on in the world now is the movement of peoples. Not necessarily war refugees, but just *people are moving*. And all of the legislation is to keep them *from* moving or to deal with them once they have moved, or to educate them, or to *not* educate them, or to throw them out or burn them or—you know—whatever. That's what global policy is now about: What are we going to do with the people outside who are now *in*side? Do we keep them? Do we starve them to death and send them back as we have decided to do in the United States, you know, vis-à-vis immigration.

Now you have public spaces being treated as though they're private. Not homelessness but *streetlessness* is what I call it. Privatizing all of public space: parks in which people are not welcome, streets that belong to the buildings, getting people off the street. This man was killed yesterday, right? Picked up in the garbage. A family living out in a lot, I read in the paper yesterday—a forklift ran over them. So the city has to go through the garbage to find the people because Mayor Giuliani said they cannot be in the public view? "We have to get rid of these people." So we have put the human garbage in there with the garbage. It's an intolerable situation. And to have your *garbage home* invaded? I mean, those are real conversation stoppers for me. It's just too terrible.

It's like writing while there's a war on—how can you not mention the war, and what's really at stake? You can't sugarcoat this stuff. And you cannot look away.

LAURYN HILL

By Karen Renee Good
August 1998

BLACK MAGIC WOMAN

Seeking refuge from the demands of superstardom, the Refugee Camp's own Lauryn Hill has gone home. She tells Karen Good all about her new album, her new baby, and what it feels like to experience true deliverance.

There are children here in South Orange, New Jersey. Everywhere. Moist, green grass underfoot and a strong sun. A red brick house, humble, where many burdens have been laid down. It's hard to peer into the black Range Rover pulling up in the driveway, but you figure it's Valerie Hill behind the wheel. Her daughter, Lauryn, is in the backseat, watching over Valerie's grandson, one-year-old Zion David, called "Zi." He's a happy baby who glances long, like he knows something you don't. "Been doing that since he was born," Lauryn will later explain. Zion's eyes, dewy and trenchant, belong to his mother and his Uncle Malaney—soft, yet not quite vulnerable. But the truth that is life has narrowed his mother's glances— she is whole, and centered, and far from an inaccessible shooting rap star.

"Some wan' play young Lauryn like she dumb," she says on her first single, "Lost One" off her solo debut *The Miseducation of Lauryn Hill* (Ruffhouse / Columbia). Lauryn *is* young, but soon she will be a sage.

It was Lauryn's wraith-wrought chat and song that spirited her into our consciousness via the multiplatinum, richly talented Fugees. A day away from putting the final touches to *Miseducation* (named after Carter G. Woodson's *The Miseducation of the Negro* and the 1974 film *The Education of Sonny Carson*), the artist also known as L-Boogie chooses to outstretch her arms in the skies of normalcy, doing the things young mothers and geniuses do. Here comes something magic.

Lauryn teeters gracefully in *baad* five-inch stilettos. ("Oh, I have a shoe fetish," she'll admit later in the kitchen, coyly tilting a heel.) Locks gathered on top of her head, baby positioned on her hip, she greets with a quick "Hey," and walks into this brick house where she was raised and still lives (though now there's also the roomier house five minutes away that she bought her parents). The place where birthday parties played out and family reunions went on. "Give me a second to get it together," she says, which means catch her breath, pee maybe, and pass Zion to her mama, who'll feed him sweet potatoes.

The front steps will do nicely, for we plan to speak easy, even if we have to sometimes shade our eyes from the shining. I pull out my Bible and Lauryn turns to Psalm 73, the one of Asaph-a Levite, musical composer, and leader of David's choir. "Read this," Lauryn says, "and I'll be right back." She disappears inside only to check on Zion.

The Word follows: "But as for me, my feet were almost gone; my steps had well nigh slipped. For I was envious at the foolish, when I saw the prosperity of the wicked . . . When I was thought to know this, it was too painful for me . . . But God is the strength of my heart, and my portion forever."

The last time I saw Lauryn Hill was in Ocho Rios, Jamaica, this past February. Mother Booker's boy—Robert Nesta Marley—would have turned 53 that day. The Marley family crossed over to the venue in wooden riverboats painted red, green, and gold. The I-Threes looked like brides in tiaras, scarves, and flecks of gold. "Buffalo Soldier!" they sang. "Dreadlock Rasta!" and saluted. Bob's sons are beautiful and virile. Rohan Marley, Zion's father and Lauryn's love, is no exception. He watched her backstage as Lauryn joined the Melody Makers, marching and chatting in the language of emancipation. "Happy Birthday, Bob Marley!" Lauryn offered, then remembered "*mi newborn son*" and rewound: "Happy birthday, *Grandpa*! Respect!"

Lauryn Hill comes back; settles on the steps. As conversation unfolds, freckled and Afroed childhood friends will stop by with jokes and stories—as will uncles, a little girl who has a gold nameplate necklace that spells Denesha; and another girlchild, corn-rowed, with a note that says she just finished baby-sitting class. "Come on in!" Lauryn will yell from the steps to waving neighbors in passing cars. "You gotta meet the baby!" To these folks, Lauryn has always been a star. To can go home again. It's okay, even, to want to. Maybe even necessary.

LAURYN HILL: I take my music seriously. There's nothing fictional about what I'm doing. Everything I write, everything I say, is a profession. You're not going to hear me talk about what I have—and what you don't have. My role is to communicate what I experience to the greater world. To me, *Miseducation* is about me becoming aware of the things I was really naive to. I really wasn't thinking about doing a solo album. A lot of people told me to do it.

Q: *People were trying to make you do R&B? Or stick with hip hop?*
A: Some were like, "Girl, just sing." And then you had the people who always thought I was in the wrong crew. There was always a lot of energy for me to do something solo, but to me it was a little bit negative. It was flattering, but it was like, "Cross them cats; get rid of them." But that's not me. I'm not a jump-ship type of person.

Q: *That must have made you feel uncomfortable.*

A: Very. But I was young and naive. And it caused some stress in the group. I felt because I paid no attention to it, that meant other people didn't pay attention to it. Who knows what insecurities are in the minds of people because of what someone says? In my mind, I was happy because those were my boys; we grew up together, I loved them very much. But the hill looks different depending on where you're standing—if you're at the bottom or at the top, or in the middle—you know.

Everybody knew those comments wounded, that they were painful. I chose to ignore them. But it did cause some strain. I think it made [Wyclef and Pras] feel like they had to champion other agendas. Like, just in case I did jump ship, everybody else was going to be all right. The world was a little bit late in discovering the talents of Wyclef. I think they get it now.

Q: *People thought they were just throwaways?*

A: Love and competition really can't coexist in a relationship. So we had to work at that. 'Cause it's either I love you, respect you, and I want you to be happy and win—or it's, Yo, you're my competitor.

Q: *And you being the only woman . . .*

A: Because I was one female and I was surrounded by guys, I got so much attention. We all existed in denial for a while. But when you're in denial, you're sort of stagnant. We stayed on tour for a long time. Tour is interesting because it ain't home, which means it's not reality. It's the road. Every night you play for an audience that's clapping for what you do, so you have this warped sense of self. And when I came home—not because I really wanted to but because I was forced to [by the pregnancy]—I was able to watch Wyclef and everything that went on from the outside in, and now I thank God.

Q: *What did you see?*

A: I saw how they welcome you into Jerusalem only to crucify you. I remember seeing the publicity and the energy go from like, "You thought the girl was all that? Here's the guy who *really* sings." I was just like, *Whaaaat*? I said okay, have I been stagnant for the sake of promoting this "group collective effort"? I was so busy trying to convince the world of how strong we were as a unit.

Q: *How tough of a realization was it?*

A: It was hard. It's kinda like realizing the Easter Bunny is fictional. You go from this naïveté to like, Wow, okay. This is how it works. My energy has always been very idealistic. I've always been in this record business loving what I do, but it wasn't the world. If it didn't work for me, there were other options.

Q: *I wonder how you managed to stay grounded. You're not on no superstar thing.*

A: I actually resent superstardom, because with that comes a lot of shit. Not because I don't want my music to travel across the world— but I'm not a superstar, I don't fit the profile. I can't come into a photo shoot and rip through clothes and holler at people. I think there are people who play that role because they think that's the prerequisite. And that if you're actually cordial and nice and polite, that people'll walk over you. But there's a lot of truth to that. People do take kindness for weakness. Especially when you're female. So a lot of women feel like they have to overcompensate.

Even after selling 17 million records, I still have to convince people that I'm a self-contained unit. I think part of it had to do with the fact that I was with a group of guys who, for some reason, were perceived as being the breath and the life and the reason I do what I do. Granted, we worked very hard together, but I was also an individual, as much as I was part of a group. I think everybody looked at me and thought that because I was such a cheerleader, and because I championed the group so strongly, they thought I had no legs to stand on.

Q: *In your new song, "Ex-Factor," you said "How you gonna win when you ain't right within?"*

A: That's going back to the road, and you can stay there for a long time. But when you come home, you gotta come home. And that's only a metaphor for karma. And that's why the 73rd Psalm is so significant.

Q: *"I was envious of the foolish when I saw the prosperity of the wicked."*

A: You have a lot of people who chase this thing with no end and no morals. As if people with money are better than people without. It's a dangerous way to live your life.

Q: *I remember when you were on the radio and it was that whole [radio gossip] Wendy Williams thing. She was asking and asking are you pregnant. You said to her, "'I know this is your job, but this is my life.'"*

A: I was in the woman's face, and there was no compassion whatsoever. But people who show no compassion will be shown no compassion. I was twenty-one years old. I was happy and confused at the same time. I was trying to figure out what to do with my life. But for some reason, because I was young and successful, that made my personal life something for everybody to know.

Q: *How much do you think you're responsible for giving to the world?*

A: I'm very clear, especially now, that I live my life for God. I love humanity, and every day that's a struggle because the devil—I mean those negative forces—they're always out there trying to give you reasons not to love humanity. It makes you say, Let me go up in my house, close my door, turn my TV on, hug my boyfriend, and hold my child.

Q: *Let's talk about the album. That guitar on the song "To Zion" is amazing.*

A: I've always adored Carlos Santana and considered him a true master. It actually started out for me when I was little. I had his *Abraxas* album. This is how I'm as weird as I am. I was fooling around in the basement one day, I think I was six or seven years old, and I found a Santana 45. I didn't have any records at the time, and I thought it was the most beautiful thing I ever heard. It was so old, it had my mother's name on it from high school. There was always music in my house. My mother played the piano.

Q: *Did you have your own little group?*

A: Please. *Did* I?! We had so many names I don't remember them all. I was always very dramatic. I was very ridiculous. You know when you're just happy to sing? Everything I do I try to do from the heart. What gets me upset in music right now is that we're so hidden behind this whole "I'm trying to be cool and I have to look flawless." But humanity, just by definition, we're not flawless.

Q: *Folks are trying awfully hard to be polished.*

A: When I worked on "The Sweetest Thing," I remember people were like, "What you talking bout? That song is crazy." I was like, Why? You never fell in love? But for some reason there's a level of embarrassment. I appreciate the fact that Mary [J. Blige] has been honest about her relationships on record. She's like, [*sings*] "Every day it rains." And I feel that, because it's not always perfect.

Q: *"A Rose Is Still a Rose" (Arista, 1998) is the first time I heard Aretha use her range in a long time.*

A: Aretha's so *baaad*. When I wrote the song—the rhythm, the syncopation is definitely hip hop—I expected to have to really go through it with her. But she took the demo version, came in the studio, and it was done.

There is usually very little to do within a loop. You can't really go anyplace because you'll be out of tune. I wanna bring the musicianship, the songwriting, back to hip hop. Drums gotta be hard. They gotta be banging. But I want changes. When I went to the bridge in "Sweetest Thing," people thought I was crazy. "What the hell is that?" I said, It's a change. Remember? They used to have those in songs back in the day. There's no reason why Carlos Santana can't pick to the hip hop drums—because he's a musician.

Q: *What is genius to you? Because I read about you being labeled a "diva."*

A: Underneath it is "Bitch!" Understand, it's not you're dope. It's, "Girl, you can sing—Bitch!" Aretha Franklin asked me, "What made you decide to sing?" I said, Well, I knew what I wanted to hear, so why not? She said "Basically, that's what I used to do with Jerry Wexler, but he always got the credit." I started bugging out. I said, So you mean people didn't think for you? She worked intensely at everything she did, and that's when I realized. Record companies are always talking about how they make women. She'll be the next . . . whatever. Brothers are allowed to be kooky and zany and quirky. Diva is just so unspecific. It's like. "What does she do?" She divas.

Q: *Do you feel sexy?*

A: Yes—especially after having a child. There'll be little changes, but I actually feel more attractive now than I did before. I probably weigh the same, but something happens; you just start growing in other places.

I never wanted to be perceived as not being sexy or as being matronly. Please perceive me as a mother. I've always tried to be perceived as a mother of someone, a mother of a nation, a mother of people, a mother of love.

Q: *That's another thing you said to Wendy Williams: "I'm always with child."*

A: Always. But don't make me matronly. I'm twenty-three years old, and I'm blessed to have a child so young because I have a mother in my life and I have the energy. Even though I'm twenty-three, I'm sort of a traveled twenty-three. When I was nineteen I was like, Wow, what else can I do besides have a family? I mean, after you do so much at a young age, you start to realize it's not about doing so much. I have so many friends and associates who say I wanna be a singer, I wanna do this and that. And I say, Please don't let that be your final goal in life, 'cause you'll be so disappointed. There's very little security in the hip hop game.

Q: The average life span is, like, three albums.

A: *Mmmm*—that's horrible. I hope not. We have a lot of plaques, but you'll never see me hang them up, because I don't want to be complacent. I wanna always feel like I can sing this better. And my record company, they're supportive, but I think there's a little "Come on, Lauryn, let's do another 'Killing Me Softly.'" And I'm saying, Let me be young.

Right now I have time to build, and I'm not afraid. My family foundation is very strong, and if for a minute I'm not popular—which is very likely—it's not the world to me. I don't feel like my life has to be over.

Q: Onstage with the Fugees you always seemed like you were holding something back.

A: Remember there was a lot of shared energy there. It was very important for my brothers to shine. And I think for a period of time, I was almost afraid to shine.

Q: Were you afraid of your own power?

A: I think I was. I think people were afraid of my power.

Q: Will there be another Fugees album?

A: I definitely think there will be. We just gotta get into a room to do it.

Q: Do you see each other a lot?

A: Right now we don't. Clef is doing *The Carnival* (Ruffhouse/Columbia, 1997); Pras is doing his thing. And, you know, I assumed the domestic role for a minute, and then I went headfirst into the studio. It had to do a lot with my personal development. I learned some really incredible things about myself.

Q: Like what?

A: My capacity, my threshold for pain, and my threshold for creativity. I was very blessed to have to have done this album by myself. I wasn't going to say, you know, Clef come off the road and let's do this.

Q: *They're not on the album at all?*

A: No, they're not. Only because it's kinda out of context. Because the album is so narrative. I think every woman goes through a relationship which is a great lesson in love. I had gone through one earlier, and it was kinda like my therapy to write about it. I made peace when I created these songs. I've revealed myself because I'm an honest musician.

Q: *There was the rumor that Wyclef and you were going out.*

A: All of us in the group were very close. I don't have a response to that one. We were a dynamic group in the sense that we grew up together. So there will be a lot of love there.

Q: *There was almost a manhunt: Who is Lauryn's baby's daddy?.*

A: I thought that was nuts, by the way. I guess people'd never seen me with a brother in public—other than the guys.

Q: *Do you think it was hard for the public to see you as a woman?*

A: As a real woman? Yeah. [*She laughs.*] I'm allowed a personal life. [*Long pause*] If you're a man in the music business, there's girls throwing their panties at you. And you can either accept it or reject it, and most of the time they accept it because they've never had that much overwhelming attention in their lives. For women in the music business, it's very different. Men are often intimidated by you, or they're crazy. So it's not easy to make connections with real people.

I value the relationships that exist outside this industry. Those people, they just want my attention and my love. So when I try to save my relationships from the media attention, what I'm doing is saving that dynamic.

You know, my boyfriend [Rohan] is like that. I enjoy us going places and not being chased. Or us goin' places and girls not hawking him because he's my man. We're very happy, but we're still very private. I still don't like to talk about it. Not because I don't love him extremely and he doesn't love me, but because I want to love him away from the lights, camera, action. And I want him to love me away from all that. And that's hard when you're all up in it. Mary J. Blige and I were talking about competitive relationships, and they just don't work. It's like, If I can give, please give back. Please.

Q: *How was it working with her? She's on the album, right?*

A: Oh yeah. Mary, she's my sister. I *love* Mary. I feel like I grew up with her, like I *know* her. She's so familiar to me, and that's what people love about her: that she's so familiar. When she sings, she feels it. It's not about perfection. That's the difference between the method and the heart. She strikes that chord.

Q: *Speaking of songs from the heart, I wanted to talk to you about "To Zion."*

A: The lyrics came from when I was sick with the flu and I was terrified because I thought I was gonna give it to him. My mother was like, "Relax." And those lyrics just came to me. "Unsure of what the balance held / I touched my belly overwhelmed / By what I had been chosen to perform." Um, I gotta sing it. [*She sings*] "But then an angel came one day"—sure did. "Told me to kneel down and pray / For unto me a manchild would be born / Woe this crazy circumstance / I knew his life deserved a chance / But everybody told me to be smart / Look at your career, they said / Lauryn, baby, use your head / But instead I chose to use my heart / Now the joy of my world is in Zion."

Q: *Zion, the deliverer.*

A: Names wouldn't come when I was getting ready to have him. The only name that came to me was Zion. I was like, Is Zion too much of a weight to carry? But this little boy, man. I would say he personally delivered me from emotional and spiritual drought. He just replenished my newness again. When he was born, I almost felt like I was born again.

Q: *Was he in the studio when you sang that song?*

A: Oh, all the time. It's extraordinary. How these babies are created, and they come to us and through us. It's hard to put into words. Trust me when I say this, it is the highest form of unconditional love that you can ever feel. When you have a child, it makes you see the flaws in some of your other relationships. There is nothing he could do that would stop me from loving him.

Q: *I wanted you to respond to a quote by M.O.P. "Is this hip hop? / Hell no, this is war / I been trying to tell you that since 'How About Some Hardcore.'"*

A: Yeah, I remember that line. Mmm-hmm. I think people tend to underutilize hip hop. I think hip hop can bring our agenda to the front, but we talk about a bunch of nothing rather than talk about real issues. Hip hop has the potential to be a great forum. We have our own form of communication. But it's a lot easier to ride the middle. Once you stand for something, that means you have opposition. That's not easy. You have to be well prepared. A lot of rappers are very young. And what we exist on is our energy and our fire. It may be naive, but sometimes when we're in the public, we just start speaking about what we feel is right.

Q: *Do you have an agenda with your music?*

A: I want to empower; I want to inform; I want to inspire.

Q: *Inspiration is so important.*

A: It is because there were so many things in my life that inspired me to be who I am today. That's the motivation that inspires us to create. Zion is my inspiration.

I was not raised to be beautiful and not say it. I was not raised to have grievance and not cry out. Some people would prefer to say, "Be pretty and don't talk too much." But you gotta keep talking, or people forget about you, and your agenda. My agenda is to make sure that we're taken care of, and educated, and healthy, and happy.

Q: *And you're happy?*

A: I'm very happy. With a foundation, with a good man and a child, and a family—and I don't have the fear of losing my job. You know how in the office space people are sometimes hesitant to be vocal 'cause they could be fired for what they say? The only person who can fire me is God.

SNOOP DOGG 18

By Chairman Mao
October 1998

LAID BACK

In Snoop's world, hairdressers sculpt 'dos, cold beverages rest on coasters, and jukeboxes jam classic tunes from easier times, proving that, yes, the beat, and the show, must go on. Chairman Mao drives by Tha Dogg's pound.

Enter the domain of the artist formerly known as Snoop Doggy Dogg and one detail immediately penetrates your consciousness. Beyond the black dog insignias that festoon the gates of his isolated Claremont, California ranch house; beyond the tropical fish pond that greets you before you reach the front door; beyond the melancholy image of an upright cardboard cutout of Tupac Shakur defiantly raising his middle finger as you enter, or the Tasmanian Devil doormat that says GO AWAY; beyond the ebullient photos of Snoop's wife, Chanté, and two young sons, Corday and Cordell (aka Spanky and Lil' Snoop), that lovingly decorate the spacious living room (or the platinum certifications, music awards, and Death Row Records paraphernalia that complement them); beyond the game room (known as the Dogghouse); beyond the swimming pool, pit bull yard, and regulation-size basketball court planted to the rear . . .

Beyond the raw awe that Snoopy's dog house offers the eyes, one cannot help noticing the writing on the wall: His habitat is really clean. Impeccably clean. So clean that the notion of not using a coaster for your drinking glass doesn't touch the left side of your brain. So well kept that, if you're lucky, you might even catch the Thin Black Dogg methodically wiping down the kitchen counter or vacuuming. Apparently, a feline Felix Unger finickiness exists within hip hop's most notorious canine. When Snoop notifies you to "wipe your feet when you enter in," as he does on "Snoop World"—the infectious lead track from his latest album, *Da Game Is To Be Sold, Not to Be Told*—he really ain't playin'.

"I respect everything I ever got 'cause I started from nothin'," a bandanna-ed Snoop explains later between puffs of his beloved bomb hemp, his indigenous West Coast twang as distinctive as ever. "And when you start from none, you appreciate everything you get."

And now, Snoop's long and winding road-from reputed Long Beach, Cali Crip to Dr. Dre protégé to rap superstar to acquitted murder suspect to *Doggfather* disappointment to Death Row funk refu-G—has landed him the unprecedented role of underdog and at the doorstep of Master P's No Limit Records empire. Though seemingly inactive over the past year while awaiting his official contractual separation from former boss Suge Knight and friends, Snoop's already acclimated himself to Colonel P's relentless boot-camp production regimen. In addition to *Da Game*, an entertaining and frenetic 21-song anthology of hustler-related narratives, classics revisited, and rejuvenated moments—he's already begun recording his second No Limit long player, *Top Dogg*. Following P's thespian excursions, Snoop is also preparing for his feature film lead debut in the P-produced *Da Game of Life*, in which he plays the first black, mob-affiliated casino owner.

Yet even in the middle of a greater Los Angeles heat wave that's seen temperatures exceed the 100-degree mark, Snoop Dogg remains cooler than cucumber ice cream. Casually attired in a gray sweatshirt and jeans, he takes a seat within his rec room/home studio and shuts his eyes while his hairdresser of six years, Tasha, attends to his braids. A Wurlizter CD jukebox spins a continuous, mellow program of R&B classics. And as '70s soul man William DeVaughn's glossy tenor invites his audience to "just be thankful for what you've got," a Snoop characteristic beyond his fastidiousness crystallizes before me: the unmistakable strains of contentment.

Though he's already enjoyed more than he might have ever hoped for, this Dogg will have his day . . . again.

Q: *People are very curious as to how Master P helped you sort out your deal with Death Row.*

A: Master P and God, the Man Upstairs, made it happen. It's like a marriage. When you ready to get a divorce, [you've got] a lot of good memories, but you ready to move forward. Basically, back then I was lost—searching for friends, searching for wisdom and everything—and now I'm found. Once I found God and found peace of mind, He led me to the direction of Master P and No Limit Records. They did what they had to do to get me out of that situation. And it's business—it's Death Row doin' business with Master P and Snoop Dogg.

[My time at Death Row] was fun while it lasted. I didn't say nothin' bad while I was there, so I don't have nothin' bad to say when I'm leaving. It was all gravy. We did a lot for each other. They made me who I am; I made them who they are. So let's take that for what it's worth and continue to do what we do.

Q: *Did Master P have to buy out your contract?*

A: I don't know the specifics behind it. All I know is that we came to a mutual agreement to where everyone's happy. We had a quarrel; we squashed it. It shouldn't be draggin' on . . . and lives is taken, and there's negativity. I mean, we gotta be examples in this rap game. And I know Suge Knight feels the same way I feel.

Q: *Have you gotten your No Limit tattoo yet?*

A: Nah, I ain't got no tattoos. I ain't even got no tattoos with my 'hood or my set on it. I'm straight. I don't like needles, you know what I'm sayin'? I got my No Limit tank. [*Snoop holds up his chain*] I'm a true tank dog. Fa-sheezay!

Q: *Yet at the end of one of your new songs, "Still a G Thang" you shout-out Dre.*

A: Oh yeah, fo' sho. Get at me on that tip. 'Cause me and Dre, we definitely need to get together, and we gonna get together to make something happen.

Q: *You obviously stay in touch with your people from the Death Row days—like Kurupt and Daz—because you've collaborated with them on their new records. But what's it been like for them to see you move on to your new family?*

A: It gotta be with respect. It's like if we were in the NFL and I wanted to play with another team after winning all these championships with their team. They still would have respect for me. But when the season start, they know I plan to win a championship with No Limit Records. That's my main goal—to make sure No Limit stay on top and Snoop Dogg stays on top. My homeboys is businessmen and individuals enough to stand on their own two feet.

Q: *Would you call yourself a competitive person?*

A: Very. Shit, when [I was a kid] and played Pop Warner football, we went to the championship twice. We lost once, and we won once. We played for the West side, and the year we lost, we lost against our homies from the East side. We was playin' our hearts out tryin' to beat them niggas. And when they beat us, we cried like babies. It was just that serious. But, as men, it's something we can look back on and laugh at.

Q: *I see you've got the basketball court out back with the Lakers' emblem on it.*

A: [*In a disappointed tone*] The Lakers'll be all right next year or two. I still love my niggas. They was doin' too much partyin'. They be in the clubs too motherfuckin' much—rappin' and shit, instead of winning championships. They gonna get it right. They're young. That's what it's about when you young: you gotta have fun. You splurgin', and you havin' your money. Like me, I'm in it to win. Every team I done been on I been winning. I'm trying to be the Jordan of my run—you heard me?

Q: *What do you think is gonna happen this year?*
A: With Michael Jordan or with me? *[laughs]*

Q: *If you wanna address Michael and the Bulls first, go ahead.*
A: Chicago gonna split up, man. Mike gonna leave and go ahead and quit and let the youngsters fight over it. He did what he supposed to. The team's in the death. Everybody gone. So go let the youngsters fight over it, and if he feels that urge to go and challenge the youngsters, challenge 'em without the team. Bring a *new* team to the title—and Michael, show 'em what you really got.

Q: *Sorta like—*
A: What I'm doin'? Exactly.

Q: *So answer the other part. What's gonna happen with you?*
A: I'm gonna show you *[laughs]*.

Q: *P's opened a sports agency. Have you considered trying to bridge all of your different interests as well?*
A: Yeah, definitely, but I think what I'm gonna end up doin' is get with a whole lot of movie stars and get on a whole 'nother level with them—chillin' with big movie stars and flyin' overseas and gettin' on that level. Because my game is real big, and it's elevating. I'm too big to be doin' this small shit. I need to be doin' movies with the top actors, and lead actresses need to be having me in movies with 'em. And doin' big records with No Limit and continuin' to do my thang-thang. Me and P doin' big thangs time after time.

Q: *Which actors provide you with your inspiration?*
A: Fuckin' Al Pacino, Robert De Niro, Wesley Snipes, Samuel L.

Jackson, Denzel Washington. They're some real motherfuckers. Fishburne too. And Christopher Walken. I like him; he's hard. That real shit is what I appreciate and respect, and I wanna be a part of it. I think I can bring something to the table. I love movies. I love gangsta movies. I love good movies. I love classic movies. I love movies from the heart that say something.

Q: *Did you see* Titanic*?*
A: Nah, I didn't see that. Ain't that something? Not even on bootleg. Is it tight?

Q: *It wasn't.*
A: I didn't think it was.

Q: *How about science fiction?*
A: I like that kind of shit too. I liked *Alien*. That shit was hard.

Q: *Tell me something: Do you believe in extraterrestrials or life on other planets?*
A: I think the shit do exist. That's why motherfuckers make movies about it. Every time I see a movie, the shit is *too* real. That's why I'm like, Okay, if I had the chance to make a movie, I would make it real and about what I *know*. So motherfuckers that's makin' extraterrestrial movies must know about that and must *see* that. It is believable. It's the truth. It's here.

Q: *Earlier today, you were watching* Casino. *One part of that film that stayed with me is the beginning, when De Niro has his little monologue about handling the casino. He says, "It was the last time street guys got to run anything. And we fucked it all up." I'm wondering about your reflections on that line.*
A: I've been given a whole lot, and I'm thankful for it. And if I fuck it up, I'm gone. And only *I* can fuck it up. Can't nobody fuck it up for me. So I can get along with that dialogue to the fullest.

Q: *I remember* first *seeing the "Nuthin' But a 'G' Thang" [Death Row, 1993] video back in the day, and I was always thinking how camera-shy you were. Performing for the big screen doesn't intimidate you?*

A: It's what I been waiting for. When we're rapping and doin' videos and makin' records, we're acting like a motherfucker! You gotta look at it like this: It's a mind thing. When we create the music and videos, we're actually creating the kind of movies other people write and do. So instead of cutting that bullshit, we gonna cut some real shit and go straight to the movie game. Snoop Dogg uncut.

The pressure of starring [in a film] is [like starring on an album. There's more motherfuckers that are gonna be watching that album to see how I'ma do on that. That's the major performance right there. I gotta give an Oscar-winning performance on that album, and I think I did good on [my album]. I think I represented to the fullest, and it's unexpected. There's no high expectations on this album. The way it was put together was so fast, it's not like it was set up twelve months ago and you knew about it and you thought it was gonna be the biggest album in the world. It's gonna just come out and do the fuck what it's gonna do. But it's gonna break a lot of shit in half 'cause it's that real shit.

Q: *I noticed in the ad copy that you're now going as "Snoop Dogg."*
A: That's my new persona. Snoop Dogg.

Q: *Is that a part of your agreement with Death Row?*
A: Nah, that's just me. Master P just said, "Nigga, you Snoop Dogg! You ain't Snoop Doggy Dogg! You Snoop Dogg, nigga!" And I'm with that shit.

Q: *Tell me how Snoop Dogg is different from Snoop Doggy Dogg.*
A: Snoop Dogg is more educated, wiser, and more of a thinker—he's more for life. Snoop Doggy Dogg was more for death—and down for whatever.

Q: *Family man is another shift in focus for your public image. What do you tell your kids when they might hear something sideways about you or your past? Has that moment come?*
A: It ain't came yet, and when it does, it's just gonna be as real as life. Me and my sons have beautiful relationships. It's love. That's

all it is. It's nothin' but love. And that's all you gotta know about a kid. A kid just understands either hate or love. If you showin' 'im love, he'll appreciate it and show it back to you. They'll do what they gotta do as kids and get into thangs that they not supposed to. But if you straight with them, they'll be straight with you.

Q: *You mentioned the Man Upstairs earlier. What kind of role has faith played in your life?*

A: Shit, it brought me through every obstacle I ever been against-before I became a rapper and I went to jail the first time, when I was faced with the adversities of the record business and the shit that come along with it. God put me through that. He put me here to do what I do, and I'm thankful for that. I know what I'm here for. And I'ma continue to shine and do for the kids and do my positive dues and make my music for the motherfuckers that wanna hear it.

JAY-Z

By Harry Allen
April 1999

YOU MUST LOVE HIM

One of Brooklyn's finest MCs, Jay-Z still has the whole rap game on lock. Five years before Shawn Carter became president of Def Jam records, just as he made the jump to multiplatinum with his ghetto anthem "Hard Knock Life," Harry Allen found out why the streets are still watching.

Shawn Carter touches it, Shawn Carter flips it. Once he focused mainly on 2.2-pound packages of coke, legend has it, then later, tracks like "Hawaiian Sophie" and "The Originators" with friend/mentor "The Jaz." But these days, the Bedford-Stuyvesant-born Jay-Z flips the sensibilities of both his native Marcy Projects' hard rocks *and* cornfed Iowa farmboys. I mean, think about it: Which was Jigga's greater feat: To laconically pulverize Annie's kettle-drums on "Hard Knock Life," 3-year-old white stage brats in tow, or to make everybody forget that "Tomorrow" was the play's showstopper? To achieve triple-platinum status? Or to make platinum jewelry the new status symbol, and gold seem woefully played out? The twenty-something stylist is possibly the East Coast's most notorious MC since his friend, the former bearer of that name, went to a freakishly early grave, dominating the No. 1 position on the *Billboard* pop charts for more than a month.

In the process, Jay-Z has totally refurbished the meanings of "pop," "underground," and whatever other labels were still left clinging to this potent black culture. Consider: The Lincoln Continental Grandmaster Caz boasted ownership of in his lyrics for "Rapper's Delight" 20 years ago is . . . well, basically, car service today. Realize that the vulgar excess and the tart poignancy of having a $300,000-plus convertible in the middle of the ghetto, while real-life Marcy moppets warble wearily about their lives, can perhaps be reconciled. Perhaps. In short measure, this rapper has delivered the frothy ecstasy of "Brooklyn's Finest," his catalog's sole collaboration with the B.I.G.; the futuristic oscillations of "Can I Get A . . . ," laced with the exotic, alien tones of the scirocco-voiced Amil; the twin sex pieces of "Ain't No Nigga" and "(Always Be My) Sunshine" with partner-in-larceny Foxy Brown. There's "You Must Love Me"'s operatic fatalism, and one minute and fifty seconds of "Friend or Foe," the track over which, in his *Streets Is Watching* home video, Jay-Z single-handedly revives the movie musical from *West Side Story, Oklahoma!, Singin' in the Rain*, and a bunch of musty Elvis movies. He does all this on top of flows as curvaceous as Lisa Nicole Carson, lyrics as hard as the J and Z subway tracks that wend through his old 'hood, and with an eye for detail that makes *The Starr Report* read like a vague summary.

Memorable as those moments are, the most memorable to this writer is one you never saw: co-Roc-A-Fella label heads Damon Dash and Kareem "Biggs" Burke at New York's LaGuardia Airport, baggin' on a male ticket agent wearing a pile of hair that could only be deemed fascist retro-pimp—or just a breathtaking fright wig. With his best friends' snaps and laughter loudly punctuating the large space, Jay-Z used the time before jetting off to the Super Bowl festivities to school the scribe on fame's wearying costs. As in previous conversations, he was warm, genial, and generous with his time, which tends to be the prerogative of real-life tough guys—gentlemen, that is.

Q: *Your album's at 3 million. Will Smith's is at 4 million. What does that tell you about the state of hip hop?*

A: Will did a great thing for hip hop—he brought light onto it, exposed people to it who normally wouldn't be listenin'. Some people are gonna love and stick with Will. Some people are gonna say, "I wanna little more edge to my music." The more educated people are, the more they're gonna look for the cream of the crop.

Q: *Do you mean your own work?*

A: Yeah.

Q: *You wouldn't say Will is the cream of the crop?*

A: Me and Will make different music. He's a very creative person. I think mine has more edge and is more reality-based than his.

Q: *What would you say to those who say your latest album is, in many ways, a Puffy album with incredible lyrics?*

A: People could say that about "Hard Knock." Puffy could probably use that, hut I can't see Puffy rappin' over "If I Should Die," or "Can I Get A . . ." Nah. No beats that I've ever heard him rap to was similar to "Can I Get A . . ." or the Too Short record or the Bleek record or "Paper Chase." I can't see him rappin' to none of those tracks.

Q: *In what ways would you say your life is the same as the average brother working hard at UPS?*

A: There's more similarities than not. it's a demanding job. People imagine every day is shrimp, lobster, and champagne—but I'm in marketing meetings, we're arguin' constantly, I'm fightin' to get records played, videos played, get vinyl in. It's not easy. Not to knock anyone who works at UPS.

Q: *Could you ever go back to the life you lived before?*

A: I don't think any rapper can go back. You can be a car salesman, a bank teller—I mean, really good jobs, and people are still gonna look at you and be like, "You used to rap; what happened?"

Q: *Would you ever go back to selling drugs? How much are you trying to downplay the fact that you used to sell drugs—especially now with your increased visibility?*

A: It's a part of me. It happened. I don't regret it. It shaped me as a person. It's a thing that, whether I rap about it or not, exists. So I'd rather shed light on the situation—in an indirect way. I don't wanna preach. I know it's a lotta people out there going through the same struggles and the same thing I've been through. 'You're not a Martian, you're not an unusual person. I understand your struggle, I've been through the same thing.' And that's what I think is happening right now. There's a lotta people relatin' to my story. I don't hide it. I don't avoid it, I don't send my publicists out with "Don't ask me these questions." Nothin' to hide.

Q: *Is it true that you had a sexual relationship with Foxy Brown while she was underage?*

A: Oh, no. It's a total untruth.

Q: *But you had a relationship with her?*

A: A working relationship.

Q: *Only a working relationship?*

A: Yeah. A working relationship. I know at times people hinted at . . .

Q: *Because she is young. She's been in the public eye since she was underage.*

A: Even if she wasn't young, we just not there, you know what I mean? And I know people gonna say that, especially if you get the kind of reputation I have. But it just never happened.

Q: *How much do you value the wealth and fame? If it all ended tomorrow, if you woke up and were . . .*

A: As long as I was comfortable. Money is just . . .

Q: *Suppose you weren't comfortable?*

A: Then I'd have to do something to be comfortable.

Q: *What would you do?*

A: I don't know.

Q: *Would you go back to the drug game?*

A: If I was put in a situation of hopelessness . . .

Q: *Tomorrow. You're not in Miami, you're not at the hotel, and nobody's around, and you're just like, Where am I? And you have to get out of this . . .*

A: I'm the type of person, I'm liable to do anything. If I'm in a hopeless and desperate situation, I'm gonna do anything I can to get outta that situation. I just won't accept it.

Q: *What do you consider the ultimate good?*

A: To create a comfortable position for me and everybody around me. Like we doin' with Roc-A-Fella. 'Cause, like, blacks, when we come up, we don't normally inherit businesses. That's not a common thing for us to have old money, like three and four generations, inheriting our parents' businesses. That's what we workin' on right now. A legacy.

Q: *What is it that you learned from selling drugs that you use every day, in terms of doing business?*

A: This is the funny thing: You gotta abide by certain rules when you in the street. It's a certain code you have to operate on to have a good run, where not everybody wanna kill you. And the music business is totally opposite. I was operatin' with that [street] code and that loyalty and that honor and that whole ethic. And they wasn't operatin' that way. So I had to change my ways.

Q: *How were they operating?*

A: Like, with Priority, I had a messed-up contract. And everyone knew. But *we* didn't know. We was like, "Why were we . . ."? But they was like, "Why you so offended? It's just business." To them it's good business; to us it was deceit.

Q: *Transport it to the street. What would happen?*

A: A person wouldn't try you like that. Because either you would have to kill them, or they would kill you. When you make that kinda move, you gotta know that either you prepared to go to war or you prepared to die.

Q: *Or both.*

A: Yeah. You can go to war and die.

Q: *I was speaking to Clark Kent. I said, "Jay's the kind of person that if you confronted him a certain way, or you looked into his eyes, you wouldn't see hate, fear, or anger. You would just see nothing."*

A: I lost a lotta girls like that.

Q: *I'm glad you brought that up [laughter].*

A: It's real, man.

Q: *Do you have a wife, children?*

A: No wife, no kids. I'm a private person [as far as] the female I deal with. I don't wanna put that type of pressure on them. [People] mark women once you do that.

Q: *Some say celebrities do that because in every city, there's somebody thinking, I'm that [celeb's] one and only.*

A: Nah. I mean, it would be much better for a celebrity to have a significant other. Because everyone else—they know their place. It's not like a girl's not gonna date you 'cause she knows you're married. I hope the public don't believe *that.* It really doesn't make a difference. It actually makes everything fall in line better. You know, like, This is my *wife,* and me and you, we have relations. It simplifies.

Q: *You say you lost a lot of girls that way.*

A: They can't read me. They don't know, in their words, "whether I care or not."

Q: *Do you express anger with heat or with cold?*

A: More calm. Outta anger you make foolish moves. I made one foolish move when I was younger.

Q: *Which was?*

A: When I, uh, shot my brother.

Q: *Tell me about that.*

A: It was a very stupid thing. He was messed up at that time. He'd took a ring of mine. It was very, very foolish, you know, like a two-finger ring, but way back then . . . and it was like a certain thing leading up to these events. I acted outta anger. Since that incident, I've never lost it like that.

Q: *Where did you hit him with the bullet?*

A: In his shoulder.

Q: What *kind of gun did you use?*

A: A little gun, like a Dillinger. [*Laughs*].

Q: *Was that the only time you ever shot anybody?*

A: Yeah.

Q: *You've said you've never killed anybody. But you also said that if you had, you wouldn't say.*

A: Yeah. Nah, I wouldn't tell you.

Q: *Which means you could say no, but mean, ultimately, yes.*

A: [*Laughs*] It could mean that, but I'm just being a realist. I wouldn't just say no and leave it like that.

Q: *Did you sell crack to your mother?*

A: When *I* said that, I meant [it as a] a metaphor for, like, the mothers of our nation.

Q: *But did you or did you not?*

A: Nah.

Q: *What's your relationship like with your mom?*

A: Beautiful. Like brother and sister.

Q: *What does she do?*

A: Like, investment banking.

Q: *Is she an investment banker, or does she work in an investment banking office?*

A: She works in the office. She's a supervising clerk.

Q: How about your father?

A: He works odd jobs. After I was 12, I never knew where he was workin'. I never kept up with him, so . . .

Q: Have you seen him in your adult life at all?

A: I haven't seen him for maybe four to five years.

Q: Do you have any sisters?

A: Two sisters, one brother. I'm the youngest.

Q: What do your siblings do for a living?

A: My brother lives in upstate New York. He always cut hair, so he's trying to get a barbershop. My sisters, they got different jobs.

Q: Are you close to them?

A: Yeah. [One of my sister's names is Andrea], but we call her Annie. That's how the *Annie* sample came about. When I seen that on TV, I was like, *Annie*? And then I watched the movie.

Q: So that's how it became a part of your childhood.

A: Right. That's why we root for villains—the Scarfaces of the world—anybody placed in a situation of underdog, and they have some type of success, be it short-lived. We never pay attention to the ending, just the good parts. Anybody that comes from that situation and rises above that, we're with them. Think about that. From Marcy Projects to owning your own company? Any person that goes from ashy to classy or, you know, is from the orphanage or the projects—it's pretty similar. Instead of treated we get tricked, instead of kisses we get kicked—that's how every ghetto person feels. Like nothing good is gonna ever happen to you.

Q: People talk about your lyrics being, at first glance, very simple, but having a lot of stuff underneath.

A: Yeah, it's like double meanings. I hide those all over, like Easter eggs.

Q: What was your relationship with Biggie?

A: We knew each other since Westinghouse High School. We'd see each other, and we'd nod. Then we both was in the music business, and we always said, "We gotta hook up and do something together." Finally we did "Brooklyn's Finest." That's when we clicked. I sat there, he sat there. I was like, "Yo, you need a pen?" No pen. That's how I make my music, too. It was crazy, it was ill for me.

Q: *You don't write lyrics down?*
A: No, not at all.

Q: *There's no rhyme book anywhere?*
A: There was one green notebook from when I was young. I don't know where it's at. It's a shame.

Q: *All that stuff is in your head? How do you do that?*
A: I just *do* it. Like, right now I got a couple of verses in my head. Just verses.

Q: *So at some point you're going to have a whole album sitting in your head. And then you have to download it, as such?*
A: Yeah. But it never gets that far. I'll get three songs, the most, and then I'll do 'em, and then I'll get three songs again. But about the relationship: That night Big and I went to Bernie Mac, and ever since it's been, like, all the time on the phone.

Q: *Until he was killed.*
A: Yeah.

Q: *I know you gotta get on the plane.*
A: Interviews can be the same monotonous bullshit. Or they can ask interesting questions and make you wanna talk. As long as it's like this, a conversation between two people, I could talk for five hours.

Q: *We should do that, man.*
A: I could yap.

Q: *Alright, yo, beautiful. Respect, man. Safe flight.*

QUINCY JONES

By Emil Wilbekin
November 2001

THE DUDE

*He has spent his entire life creating music. Now Quincy
Jones wants to educate urban America about the history of
black music. Listen up!*

Statuesque, energetic, yet composed, Quincy Delight Jones Jr.,
68, is sitting behind a sleek, wooden desk in his New York
City hotel suite, and, as usual, he is multitasking. Peering over
his reading glasses, he scans some recent faxes while returning telephone calls. He's also holding a side conversation about *Blast!*,
a Broadway musical he saw last night. It inspired him so much that
he's going to see it again tonight. "Incredible sounds man, incredible."

After wrapping up his chores, VIBE's founder turns his attention
to discussing the three most important projects currently on his plate.
This month, VH1 will present *Say It Loud: Black Music in America*, a
five-part documentary chronicling the history of soul music, from sex-
uality to spirituality. In addition to contemporary stars like Puffy, T-Boz,
Babyface, Wyclef, Aretha Franklin, and James Brown, the series features footage of artistic giants like Louis Armstrong, Billie Holiday,

Charlie Parker, and John Coltrane. Jones is also releasing, with Rhino Records, an accompanying boxed set, which includes the jazz, blues, gospel, R&B, soul, and hip hop works on the documentary's sound-track. And finally, Doubleday is publishing *Q: The Autobiography of Quincy Jones*—382 pages of illuminating, keeping-it-real stories about a poor, African-American boy from Chicago who grows up in Seattle, follows his own beat, and becomes a legend, working with Count Basie, Ray Charles, Dinah Washington, Frank Sinatra, Miles Davis, Dizzy Gillespie, Michael Jackson, and countless other musical geniuses. A dream come true complete with 26 Grammys.

Jones walks across the room—past the Steinway baby grand, the treadmill, the five stacked copies of the book *Men of Color: Fashion, History, Fundamentals* by Lloyd Boston (for which he wrote the fore-word), the coffee table covered with handwritten musical compositions, a bag of Ricola cough drops, and the *Playbill* for *Blast!*—then eases himself onto a plush sofa decorated with brightly colored silk pillows. As he speaks, his legs wiggle and tap to the beat of his voice, and his eyes flash with excitement. His flow is interrupted only once, when his friend Bill Clinton rings. Plans to meet Bubba for drinks after the play are set, and Jones is focused again. The master is at work, con-ducting a conversation as if it were a symphony.

Q: *How did your documentary* Say It Loud: Black Music in America *come about?*

A: People have been on my case a long time to get involved in these things, and I have to say no because I'm too busy. But I said yes to *Say It Loud* because it was something that was real close to me, and I've been circling the field with this for a long time. After 50 years in the business, I said I want to go see what we're talk-ing about here. By the time I started work on this, I had been all over the world. I had been to see the School of the Samba in Brazil, the *santeria* in Cuba. And I wanted to pull the cover off of all this stuff and find the roots of our music, which is harder than you may think. So I went to hundreds of musicology books. It wasn't really there. Except for the work of Alan Lomax, there was very little documentation, and that frustrated me. A lot of the scholarly things didn't convey what really happened. Now I've got boxes and boxes of research, and my gift to myself is to do five different configurations on the history of soul. I want to do children's books and everything else to let people know what they're missing and why they are ignoring the greatest heritage in the world.

Q: *Do you believe young people are unaware of their own culture?*

A: Yes. Kids are just tossing it off and not paying attention to it, just trying to get the latest hip hop, and anything from three hours ago is old school. Everything is just in and out—*boom!*—and thrown away. It can't happen like that, and that's what this show is about. What's happening is that the world is taking all of our aura, and distilling it and taking it to the moon. They're rummaging our garbage cans, metaphorically speaking, taking stuff out and polishing it up. In 10 to 20 years, you could see all of the great jazz coming out of Europe. We have to find a way to get young people to realize what they're throwing away and what they're giving up. The VH1 special is about seeing this whole tapestry, the quilt—all of these colors. Because it is one of the few musics based on folklore. Soul is a voice of a whole people. My autobiography is like that. It is the voice of many. The voice is expressed by one or two, but it's millions of people's life experiences behind that sound. Whether it's a field holler, a John Coltrane wail, Aretha Franklin, Luther Vandross, Whitney Houston, or whatever it is. It's a lot of people behind that sound. It's as sociological as it is aesthetic.

Q: *Considering the broad topic of your documentary, how did you decide what to include and what to leave out?*

A: It's the most amazing saga ever, ever, ever, and we'll never get it all in here. It is huge. Huge! The music of Ella Fitzgerald, Billie Holiday, Dinah Washington, Bessie Smith, Duke Ellington, and this one, that one, and then the blues bands and all the Delta blues people, and Robert Johnson—people that black folks don't even know. They have a totally white audience now, just like B.B. King. I understand how we would have a tendency to try to cast off our past because it's so painful. But you can't throw the baby out with the bathwater. And that's what's happening. This documentary seeks to just pull it back in, and every single giant we've seen peak through each era. Stevie Wonder, Maurice White, Herbie Hancock, Donny Hathaway, Marvin Gaye, Michael Jackson, Aretha Franklin, all reached back into the jazz repository. They looked back to where they came from, and it took them forward. And it's an advantage—it makes you stronger. It's important to go back and emulate. I don't care whether it's Johnny Hodges, T-Bone Walker, or whoever. All of that needs to become a part of today's language. I mean, that's what happens with music.

Q: *In your book, you said you want to dedicate the rest of your career to educating children.*

A: Right. I just know that, before I go, I would like to see books all over homes in America talking about our musical history. Short books that explain who did this, and did that, you know, like "See Jane run, see Spot jump"—that kind of stuff. It is imperative for African-American kids to find out about all of their music, man. It's about the defining moments like Grandmaster Flash, Louis Armstrong. Louis defined this whole genre. We are the only people in the world whose music reflects and defines who we are as a people. It reflects our history. It's the voice of our political and social situation. It's the same with jazz and rap.

Q: *How do you feel about sampling? A lot of times, kids are exposed to older music, but aren't aware of its origins.*

A: I think it's a fusion, so I don't knock sampling. I remember my son used to sample, and I'd hear him downstairs with *The Dude.* I mean . . . they don't care, you know? They just go out, and they rummage through everything, and that's fine. It'll make them dig. As long as the people they sample are getting paid and nobody's getting hurt, then go for it. I get 36 sample requests a week for the

Brothers Johnson and all that stuff. One of Tupac's biggest hits, "How Do U Want It," features my samples of "Body Heat," and the remix of "Right Here" by SWV samples "Human Nature." It's just been amazing; it never stops.

Q: *What's the difference between sampling and what you do as a producer—taking layers of sounds and putting them together?*

A: It's that we *create* our music. All of it. We create the layers that we put together. I know how to use sampling, and I think there's a place for it, but I just wonder what they're going to sample 20 years from now. Samples of samples? And I cannot believe there won't be musicians coming out of this decade, just like Donny Hathaway and Stevie Wonder to do this. Stevie took it to a whole other level. He got into our history because he knew our history. So he became a teacher, a subliminal teacher.

Q: *You don't think a rapper has or will come along who has that same effect on this generation?*

A: It's gonna happen later on with hip hop. It's going to happen with somebody that comes and has that same *musical* genius as Stevie in them. And he will have been indoctrinated by hip hop, and so that's how his genius will come out. It's going to have to come from a conceptual thing, you know. It could be anybody, it could be anything. It could be something we've never heard before. A jazz musician that gets into hip hop. A rapper who gets into jazz. It will definitely be a crosspollination. It could be national, cultural, or genre pollination.

Q: *What do you think about the whole neo-soul movement with artists like Jill Scott, Musiq Soulchild, D'Angelo, Erykah Badu, and Bilal?*

A: Jill Scott's wonderful. I love her and her band. They've got a little Earth, Wind & Fire vibe, you know? I saw Jill at the L.A. House of Blues, and she was great, man. She talks to the audience, she communicates and identifies with the people. And that's absolutely great, because that's what music is, a part of the people.

Q: *And the others?*

A: Now, I came up with some bad people, man, some awesome people. Earth-shattering, innovative individuals, and I'm never going to settle for less, because once you know what the highest is you can experience, something else has got to be higher to get your attention. God bless all the girl singers today, man. But you got to really sing your ass off to get me to forget about Sarah Vaughan, Ella Fitzgerald, and Dinah Washington. You really do. You got to really give it up in terms of individualism. Whitney sings her ass off, there's no doubt about it. Sings her ass off.

But all these singers have Louis Armstrong to thank. I don't want to hear anyone calling him an Uncle Tom. Armstrong invented this music, man. He didn't have nobody to listen to. Every major singer in America wouldn't have happened if it hadn't been for Louis Armstrong, who sang like he played. Frank Sinatra sang like a jazz horn player, and Louis started all that. Nat "King" Cole and stuff like that? That quality is so high it's ridiculous. That's as high as it gets. Do you know a singer today that can mess Nat up? We've had an amazing past in America with black musicians, the most incredible on the planet.

Q: *Then what do you think about groups like 'N Sync that borrow from black music?*

A: So what else is new? Please, just don't forget about Fats Domino and Pat Boone, or Georgia Gibbs and Lavern Baker. How about Count Basie and Benny Goodman? Please, that tradition goes way back to the 1920s.

Q: *You produced both* Off The Wall *and* Thriller, *and 21 years later, you see Michael Jackson's influence everywhere. What do you think about Alien Ant Farm, Destiny's Child, Usher, Roberto Cavalli, and Dolce & Gabbana all referencing the King of Pop?*

A: The music represents itself pretty well. It holds up against anything that's out there. That makes me feel good, because we worked hard on that stuff. *Thriller* is 18 years old now, and Michael is 43. We're releasing interviews about *Thriller* soon on DVD and putting out the demo of "Don't Stop Till You Get Enough." We were working day and night.

Q: *Michael is releasing his eleventh album,* **Invincible,** *and it's been four years since his last album,* **Blood on the Dance Floor.** *With all the scrutiny and scandal, do you think the public will accept him now?*

A: Well, I don't know. Whatever happens, they're not going to write Michael out of history. You can't write Michael out of history. Never! That's why it's called *HIStory*. It's really up to Michael. I pray he has everything he needs and it all works. The objectivity is going to be all about the power of the record.

Q: *What do you want people to know about Michael?*

A: Michael can go out and perform before 90,000 people but if I ask him to sing a song for me, I have to sit on the couch with my hands over my eyes and he goes behind the couch. He is amazingly shy. What people forget about him is that for the first time, probably in the history of music, a black artist is embraced on a global level by everyone from eight to 80 years old. People all over the world, especially young people, have a black man as an idol.

Q: *What did you go through emotionally for your autobiography?*

A: Well, when I looked back on my life, I saw all this stuff. The first part sounded like somebody else's life, and I said, Who the hell is this? Because it was so rich and layered. It was as high as you can get and as low as you can get. And just being in all of these different places on the planet, man. To have Dizzy Gillespie call me at 23 years old. I just wanted to jump through the roof! I was supposed to be doing arrangements for a jazz album for Johnny Mathis. At the time, he was just a 17-year-old trade jumper from San Francisco. You saw in the book, man, I turned Johnny down for Dizzy. I didn't know who Johnny Mathis was then, you know? And I wanted to be with Dizzy, man. That's like going to heaven. There's a hundred other guys he could have called.

Q: *Your life was very rough in the beginning. How do you feel about all the ghetto posturing that takes place in hip hop, even by kids who aren't from the ghetto?*

A: Wanna-bes.

Q: *Does that upset you, especially considering your background?*

A: I think it's bullshit. They know it's bullshit, too. The romance of this era is violence and danger and jeopardy. And everybody is feeding into it, and it's cost a lot of people their lives. Big time. I first got attracted to what the notion of hip hop was about back with the Last Poets, who were real gangsters—revolutionary.

Q: *A lot of jazz artists slam hip hop, or at least dismiss it. Did hip hop have to grow on you?*

A: I constantly thank God for leaving my mind open. I can be attracted to something that just turns me on, instead of saying it's not my cup of tea. When I talk to the hip hop dudes, I tell them the same thing. I try to tell them don't be hung up on the bands now, man. Like even Russell Simmons doesn't act like this is the only music. I ain't having it. Black music is too powerful.

Q: *Let's talk about Tupac. There's a great story in your book about how he came to meet you in the Hotel Bel-Air, but first changed into a suit because he wanted to show you respect. A lot of people don't realize that Tupac wasn't a thug 24/7.*

A: Exactly. And we started out having trouble because he dissed my family in *The Source*. Rashida [Quincy's daughter], who just went to Harvard, wrote a letter—75 percent of it was in Harvardese, but the last part was stone ghetto [*laughs*]. Well, I forgot about that. And Tupac apologized. He was a sweet guy inside, man. I saw that side through my other daughter [Kidada, Tupac's fiancee]. His letters to her read like Lord Byron. *Please!* It's a shame that, because of a syndrome, he was forced to dumb down. I despise it. You have to repress your intelligence to be hip. It's absolute bullshit. And a lot of young kids think that, too. You have to act like you don't know how to speak English.

Q: *Who do you blame for that?*

A: It's nobody's fault, really. It's just a question of going into the future—let's try to ease from mind pollution to mind solution. Hip hop could still be hard, because it's one of the most powerful genres black music has been involved with. Bebop artists were actually some angry muthafuckers too, man! But they expressed it in a different way. They said they didn't want to entertain anymore, didn't want to shuffle around and dance with people, roll their eyes. They wanted to be artists, like Stravinsky. And the price was severe, because they were alienated, and so they had to withdraw. Charlie Parker died with a needle in his arm at 34 years old. But I think there's a space between saying it's all about the Benjamins and mutilation and self-hatred. There's something between that that could be just as powerful, that's going to elevate people. And I'm not talking anything corny now. It doesn't have to be soft. Stay hard, I come from that. Stay there, but you can still lay some things down that will enlighten people.

Q: *When you started VIBE 10 years ago, how did you know that urban music would become the force that it is today? You sensed where hip hop and R&B were headed.*

A: I don't know what it is. I feel it's a gift from God, to be able to see things before they happen. Once you play on that instinct, and you're right, you take the giant step the next time. It's not about knowing what anybody else is going to like, but rather knowing when it's something you love yourself. That's the greatest way to make records—when you make records that turn you on. When you get goose bumps, that's the factor. Those goose bumps really hit you hard, and you know some people are going to be right behind those goose bumps. That's as good as it gets.

MICHAEL JACKSON 21

By Regina Jones
March 2002

UNBREAKABLE

After more than 30 years as one of the biggest stars in the world, Michael Jackson remains an enigma. When the mysterious legend appeared on VIBE's cover for the second time, he agreed to a rare interview. Asking the questions was Regina Jones, who had covered Michael as a child star for Soul magazine, the black music journal she founded with her husband in the 1970s. The King of Pop felt safe enough with Jones to open up about hip hop, life as a single parent, and the mysterious joys of an all-out water-balloon fight.

I first met Michael Jackson some 33 years ago when Diana Ross introduced the Jackson 5—then a brand-new Motown act—to 350 music and media folk at the Daisy Club in Beverly Hills. My husband, Ken, and I were then publishing *Soul*, one of the first national black entertainment magazines.

Ten-year-old Michael already knew how to charm a crowd. Acknowledging Diana's support, he said, "After singing for four years and not becoming a star, I thought I would never be discovered—that is, until Miss Ross came along to save my career."

Just four months later, the Jackson 5's first single, "I Want You Back," soared to the top of the *Billboard* Hot 100 charts, followed two months later by "ABC." Thousands of letters from across the country poured into our mailbox. Responding to the Jacksons' first tour, one reader wrote: "Those youngsters performed in a manner that could be harmful to one's health. The heart can only stand so much soul, and their performance was definitely an overdose."

Over the next decade, *Soul* kept up with the Jackson family as a guest at parties, weddings, and concerts. We were also regular visitors to the family home, where Michael—soft-spoken, polite, curious, and quiet—was usually off by himself, drawing or playing with his snakes and other pets, while his older brothers, cousins, and visitors played basketball. But when *Soul* stopped publishing in 1980, I lost touch with the family.

And then Michael became a pop-culture superstar, changing the face of music, dance, fashion, and music video with hit after hit. He was idolized and chased by fans and media wherever he went. He took an art form, refined and packaged it, and became an international icon. The American Music Awards recently named him the Artist of the Century. When it comes to the King of Pop, the world is insatiable.

When we sat down for this VIBE cover story, Michael reminded me of the last time I'd interviewed him—long before the barrage of negative publicity he has received in recent years. He was 13 or 14 at the time and he had his younger sister Janet sitting with him and doing much of the talking. "I felt afraid," he explained. "I felt that if my sister was there to give me the questions they would go easier with me."

Q: *How does it feel to be re-entering the market and competing in sales with likes of 'N Sync and Britney, kids who were being born at the height of your fame?*

A: It's a rarity I think. I had No. 1 records in 1969 and '70 and still entered the charts in 2001 at No. 1. I don't think any other artist has that range. It's a great honor. I'm happy, I don't what else to say. I'm glad people accept what I do.

Q: *What are your thoughts on the current state of R&B?*

A: I don't categorize music. Music is music. They change the word R&B to rock and roll. It's always been, from Fats Domino to Little Richard, to Chuck Berry. How can we discriminate? It is what it is—it's great music, you know.

Q: *What are your feelings about hip hop?*

A: I like a lot of it, a *lot* of it. I like the music. I don't like the dancing that much. It looks like you're doing aerobics.

Q: *What made you put Biggie on your album* Invincible*?*

A: It wasn't my idea, actually it was Rodney Jerkins, one of the writer/producers working on the album. It was my idea to put a rap part on the song. And he said, I know just the perfect one— Biggie Smalls. He put it in and it worked perfectly. It was a rap that was never heard before.

Q: *Why did you choose Jay-Z on the remix of the first single "You Rock My World"?*

A: Because he's the new thing. He's hip, he's with kids today. They like his work. He tapped into the nerve of popular culture. It just made good sense.

Q: *What was it like for you to appear at New York's hip hop concert Summer Jam as Jay-Z's guest?*

A: I just showed up and gave him a hug. It was a tumultuous explosion of applause and stomping. It was a lovely, lovely welcome and I was happy about that. It was a great feeling—the love, the love.

Q: *Does it bother you to see people who emulate you, such as Usher, Sisqo, Ginuwine, and even Destiny's Child?*

A: I don't mind at all. Because, these are artists who grew up on my music. When you grow up listening to somebody you admire you tend to become them. You emulate them, to look like them, to dress like them. When I was little I was James Brown, I was Sammy Davis Jr., so I understand it, it's a compliment.

Q: *Did you know that you were creating classics while recording* Thriller *and* Off The Wall, *both classics that hold up today?*

A: Yes, not to be arrogant, but yes. Because I knew great material when I hear it and it just melodically and sonically and musically is so moving. It keeps the promise.

Q: *Do you feel that there is a larger acceptance of black artists these days?*

A: Of course, I think people have always admired black music since the beginning of time if you want to go back to singing Negro spirituals. Today the market is just accepting the fact that that's the sound, international, from Britney to 'N Sync, they are all doing the R&B thing. Even Barry Gibb of the Bee Gees, he'd always tell me, [*imitating a British accent*] "Man, we do R&B." I said Barry, I don't categorize it but it's great music. I understand where he's coming from. I love great music, it has no color, it has no boundaries; it's all wonderful music. I love from the Beatles to the Bee Gee's to the Mamas and the Papas to the Temptations, to Diana Ross and the Supremes, I love all of it. I love Queen, "Bohemian Rhapsody." It's a killer, I love it.

Q: *What's life like as a single parent?*

A: I never had so much fun in all my life. That's the truth. Because I'm this big kid and now I get to see the world from the eyes of the really young ones. I learn more from them then they learn from me. I'm constantly trying things and testing things on them to see what works and what doesn't work. Children are always the best judges to monitor something, especially in my field or any other field. If you can get the kids, you've got it. That's why *Harry Potter* is so successful, it's just a family-oriented movie. You can't go wrong there, you just can't. That's why I write lyrics when I write a song I try not to say things that offend parents because we want a wide demographic. I don't want to be like that. We weren't raised to be like that. No way, you know [my parents] Mother and Joseph wouldn't say stuff like that.

Q: *Do the pressures of your celebrity status affect your children?*

A: Yes, absolutely, from the day that they were born.

Q: *What music do Prince and Paris listen to?*

A: They listen to all my music and they love classical that plays all around the ranch. They like any good dance music.

Q: *How would you feel about your children becoming pop icons at 13 and 14 based upon your experience?*

A: I don't know how they would handle that. It would be tough. I really don't know. It's hard because most celebrity children end up becoming self-destructive because they can't live up to the talent of the parent. It's hard. Fred Astaire Jr., people used to say to him all the time, "Can you dance?" And he couldn't dance. He didn't have any rhythm. But his father was this genius dancer. It doesn't mean that it has to be passed on. The competition is hard, it's hard. I always tell my children, you don't have to sing, you don't have to dance, be who you want to be as long as you are not hurting anybody. That's the main thing. Don't you think?

Q: *How involved were you in selecting the artists to perform in your 30ᵗʰ special?*

A: I wasn't involved at all.

Q: *How were you able to let go of something so big and so special?*

A: Trust.

Q: *What was your experience on September 11?*

A: I was in New York [after performing at Madison Square Garden on September 10] and I got a call from friends in Saudi Arabia that America was being attacked. I said no way. I turned on the news and saw the twin towers coming down and I said, "Oh my God." I screamed down the hallway to all our people. "Everybody get out, let's leave now. Marlon Brando was on one end, our security was on the other end, we were all up there but Elizabeth [Taylor] was at another hotel. We all got out of there as quickly as we could. We didn't know if our building was next. We jumped in the car, but there were these girls that had been at the show the night before, and they were banging on the windows, running down the street screaming. Fans are so loyal. We hid in New Jersey. It was unbelievable—I was scared to death.

Q: *What artists past and present inspire you?*

A: Stevie Wonder is a musical prophet. All of the early Motown. All the Beatles, I'm crazy about Sammy Davis Jr., Charlie Chaplain, Fred Astaire, Gene Kelly, Bill Bojangles Robinson. The real entertainers, the real thing, not just gimmicks. Show stoppers. When James Brown was with the Famous Flames he was unbelievable. There are so many wonderful singers. Whitney Houston, Barbara Streisand, to Johnny Mathis, real stylists, you hear one line and know who it is. Nat King Cole, great stuff. Marvin Gaye, Sam Cooke, they are all ridiculous.

Q: *What do you do for fun, for recreation?*

A: I like water balloon fights. We have a water balloon fort here, there's the red team and the blue team. We have slings and cannons and you are drenched by the time the game is over. There is a timer and whoever gets the most points in is the winner. I don't do anything like basketball or golf. If I'm going to do some kind of sport, if you want to call that a sport, you have to laugh. I want to laugh. Basketball you get very competitive and so is tennis, makes you angry. I'm not into that I like to laugh, have fun, laugh with it. That's what it should be, fun, therapeutic. I love that. I also like to go to amusement parks, animals, things like that.

Q: *Is there still a fantasy that you maintain of something that you'd like to do in your career?*

A: I'd like to see an international children's holiday when we honor our children, because the family bond has been broken. There's a Mother's Day and a Father's Day but there's no children's day. I really would. It would mean a lot. It really would. World peace, I hope that our next generation will get to see a peaceful world, not the way it's going now.

Q: *At what point in your life did you realize that you were different, a visionary?*

A: I never thought about it, I just always accepted it from the heavens and said on my knees, "Thank you." Whenever I write a song and I know that it is musically correct, there are no laws to music, but when it feels right, I get on my knees and I say, "Thank you." I really do, I mean it. Because it drops into your lap just easy and magical with no effort.

Q: *Did singing ever stop being fun and become work?*

A: It's always been fun, unless I get physically sick, it's always fun. I still love it.

Q: *What is your financial status?*

A: I'm taken care of fine.

Q: *Michael, don't be embarrassed, but you are an innovator who has set a standard that still stands in music. Where does Michael Jackson go from here?*

A: Thank you, thank you. I have deep love for film, and I want to pioneer and innovate in the medium of film—to write and direct and produce movies, to bring incredible entertainment.

Q: *What kind of movies? Are you looking at scripts?*

A: Yes, but nothing has been finalized yet.

Q: *Are you ever lonely?*

A: Of course. If I'm on stage, I'm fine there. You can have a house full of people and still be lonely from within. I'm not complaining because I think it's a good thing for my work.

Q: *Tell me about the inspiration for your new song "Speechless." It's very loving.*

A: You'll be surprised. I had a big water balloon fight, I'm serious, in Germany. And what inspires me is fun. I was with these kids and we had big water balloon fight and I was so happy after the fight that I ran upstairs in their house and wrote "Speechless." That's what inspired the song. I hate to say that because it's such a romantic song. But, it was the fight that did it. I'd had fun, I was happy, and I wrote it in its entirety right there. I felt it would be good enough for the album. Out of this bliss comes magic, comes wonderment, comes creativity. It's about having fun, it really is.

Q: *Tell me about how you channel your creativity.*

A: You don't force it. Let nature take its course. I don't sit at the piano and think, "I'm going to write the greatest song of all time." It doesn't happen. It has to be given to you. I believe it's already up there before you are born and then it drops right into your lap. It really does. It's the most spiritual thing in the world. If people could witness what it feels like . . . When it comes it comes with all of the accompaniments, the strings, the bass, the drums, the lyrics and you're just the source through which it comes, the channel— really, honestly. Sometimes I feel guilty putting my name on the songs written by Michael Jackson because it's as if the heavens have done it already, I mean it. Like Michelangelo would have this huge piece of marble from the quarries of Italy and he'd say, "Inside is a sleeping form." And he takes hammer and chisel and he's just freeing it. It's already in there. It's already there.

Q: *What do you collect?*

A: I like anything Shirley Temple, babies, children, Shirley Temple, Shirley Temple, lots of Shirley Temple. Little Rascals, Three Stooges, a lot of Three Stooges. I love Curly, he kills me. My brothers, we love Curly. We just love him. I love Curly so much that I did a book on Curly. I got his daughter and she and I wrote a book on him. Women have a hard time with all the slapping and poking and stuff, guys love that stuff. My mother loved Abbott and Costello, but we would say, "We want the Three Stooges."

Q: *Tell me about your fashion selections.*

A: It isn't conscious, it happens that way.

Q: *Is there anything that you would like to say to VIBE readers?*

A: I love Quincy. I mean, I really do. I think he is wonderful soul and a beautiful person. And I think you should tell the readers, don't judge a person by what they hear or even what they read unless they heard from the person. There is so much tabloid, sensationalism going on that's totally false. Don't fall prey to it, it's ugly. I hate the tabloids. I'd like to take them all and burn them. I want you to print it, don't believe tabloid press, tell them that. Don't believe tabloid press. Some of them try to disguise themselves but they are still tabloid press.

Q: *They want to know about the plastic surgery that you've done.*

A: Who is they?

Q: *VIBE's editors.*

A: Tell VIBE, you know, that's a stupid question. Put it just like that. You should be embarrassed to ask that. That's why I don't do interviews for this very reason. That's why for years I didn't do them for that very reason.

50 CENT

By Noah Callahan-Bever
February 2004

22

ANGER MANAGEMENT

They say what goes up must come down, but if you ask 50 cent, or his devoted G-Unit crew, not even a hot head can stop their rise. Will he ultimately defy this simple law of physics, or die trying?

5O Cent is something like a phenomenon. In a little more than a year, the once marginal 27-year-old Queens, N.Y., rapper has gone from lukewarm to hot. Aside from selling more than 6 million records and rocking more than 400 shows in the past 18 months, he's inked deals for a record label, a movie, a Reebok shoe line, a clothing line, a book, and a video game.

But having saturated the market unlike any artist in recent memory, one can't help but wonder how 50 will maintain his celebrity in the face of a public that loves to build its heroes up, only to tear them down—and, if those heroes are lucky, build them up again. With 50's improbable rise, industry insiders wonder if a backlash awaits. "At first, I thought the same thing that made 50 Cent huge—his accessibility and willingness to do anything for press, radio, or TV—would be his downfall," says MTV News correspondent Sway Calloway.

"But after seeing him in action, I think that 50 has created a new relationship with the consumers, and all the other artists have to put themselves out there with the same frequency in order to remain relevant."

As it is, you can't get enough of 50 Cent. Even when his *Get Rich or Die Tryin'*—acclaimed in the 'hood and the talk of suburbia—was overlooked by the Grammys for Album of the Year, he still managed to stomp off with five nominations, including Best New Artist, Best Rap Album, and Best Rap Song ("In Da Club"). And that's why you care about his boys, the three other bullet-ridden fellas that make up GGGG Unit: Queens MCs Lloyd Banks and Tony Yayo, and Nashville-bred newcomer Young Buck. It's why 376,950 of you rushed to the store to fork over 15 bucks for their debut, *Beg for Mercy,* the week it was released. And when you brought said CD home, you probably noticed that, unlike most alpha-rapper's crews—who generally just suck—Banks, Buck, and Yayo are all unique and engaging. They add to 50's appeal rather than get in his way.

Tony Yayo, 25, whose prison term for a December '02 probation violation charge is set to end in January, is the crew's meathead maestro, bringing tough rhymes ripe with unlikely references and great adlibs ("I put the llama to ya mama and beat her like a piñata"). Banks, 21, is by far G-Unit's biggest gun—lyrically, that is. He's armed with a distinctive deep voice that's perfect for 50's sing-along choruses. His sense of humor will leave tears in your eyes ("Fuck if your favorite rapper dies, to me that's my spot / I celebrate his burial and eat at I-HOP"). And then there's Young Buck, 26, formerly down with Juvenile's UTP crew, whose Southern-fried drawl masks surprising East Coast–style punch lines ("Got the wrist of a chemist and the heart of a hustler / Plus, I prob'ly done robbed more artists than Russell").

Yes, believe it or not, G-Unit is something like a phenomenon as well. Unfortunately, as Hammer and Sisqo have taught us, phenomenons burn hot and bright, yet often quickly extinguish—something 50 and company say they have no intention of doing. But let's be real, despite their considerable contributions, it's not a secret that, for the time being at least, G-Unit's success hinges on 50 Cent. "He's been calling the shots since day one," says Banks, "and look where it's gotten us. So there's no question that what he says goes for G-Unit."

Seated in The Plaza Hotel's Palm Court restaurant in Manhattan during a busy day promoting the group's LP, 50 is not a worried man. He swears adamantly that he's strapped with a backlash-proof vest. "As long as you maintain good material people are going to buy," he says. "Why? Because you leave no room for other people to generate new interest as long as your consistency is there. Look at R. Kelly. People who don't like R. Kelly bought *Chocolate Factory!* Niggas had a perfect lane to take R. Kelly's spot, but the bottom line is that he's the best."

However, Curtis Jackson's future is not quite as simple as banging out hot records. While his aggressive approach is premeditated, it's also his instinct—the result of living with his back against the wall, where he stood one wrong decision away from jail or a funeral home. So with seemingly one shot at success, 50 employed a familiar strategy—the same one he'd been using all his life: He put it all out there, detailing his life in the street with real names and real stories. He verbally attacked rappers, knowing that—like the dealers on Guy R. Brewer Boulevard—nine out of 10 MCs would move out of the way of an assault.

No longer stuck in a corner, it's unclear how the aggressive tendencies that helped propel him to the top will impact his success in the long term. Dodging his own Incredible Hulk-like temper may be trickier than navigating the overexposure possibilities. Anyone who's watched TV or picked up a magazine in the last year knows the gist of 50's story (a drug dealer mother who was murdered, sold drugs himself, shot nine times, stabbed, down with Eminem and Dr. Dre, beef with Ja Rule, blah, blah, blah . . .). But this is much more than just his selling point or tipping point—it's *the* point. It's his beginning, his middle, and if he's not careful, it could be his end.

Today at The Plaza, 50 is frank about his precarious situation.

Q: *Your critics say you've used beef to fuel your success, starting with "How to Rob." Did you plan it that way?*

A: You know why I did "How to Rob"? I didn't have a choice. I was on Columbia Records. My album release date was coming. I had no buzz. It didn't matter if it turned into beef with everybody. I took that shot because it was my only shot. If it didn't work I was going back to the 'hood. I provide for myself by any means—I mean, *any* means—if I'm starving.

Q: *It's also been said that your beefs are being exploited by Shady and Interscope for their financial gain. How do you see it?*

A: They're not helping me promote the beef. They're allowing me to be me. Some things are inevitable, and they don't want to alter their relationship with me by saying, "Aw, 50, don't say that." Or else I'll say to myself, Why am I in business with them? Then at the first opportunity, I'd leave because I'd be uncomfortable.

Q: *So it's you that's exploiting your own situation?*

A: I'm not exploiting it. If you don't write about your true experiences then what do you have to write about? You're a fraud. "Keep it real" should never be said in music. If you're not already doing that, what are you writing about?

Q: *You've come under attack for violating the code of the streets with songs like "Ghetto Qu'ran" where you mention names. Is that a fair criticism?*

A: Everything that's in "Ghetto Qu'ran" is in *Cop Shot*—a book in the fucking library. Everything in that song was in the newspapers at the time that it went on. The shit that these niggas is talking don't make fucking sense—and that's why they're getting booed. You think I paid people to go boo them?

We all know the booed rapper 50 is speaking of. And on November 3, 2003, the eve of the release of Ja Rule's *Blood in My Eye* LP, which is filled with anti-50 sentiments, Ja sat down with Minister Louis Farrakhan on MTV in an apparent attempt to squash the beef between he and 50. "I'd sit down and talk to Farrakhan and see what he's talking about," said 50 at The Plaza, weeks before the special aired, "but they're not gonna alter me as an artist." 50 later declined to appear, saying that it was a "promotional stunt." The meeting went on without 50 and yielded no tangible results. Ja blamed 50's jealousy and the public's blood lust for their beef. All while Farrakhan focused on the personal rift between the two, rather than addressing the larger issues between the camps as well as their violent history.

Their opposition stems from either 50 being snubbed at a Ja video shoot or Ja catching feelings over a chain lost to an associate of 50's, depending on who's telling the story. Since then, Ja's been punched in the face in Atlanta, and 50 was stabbed at the Hit Factory recording studio in New York City, after which an order of protection was issued on 50's behalf against members of Murder Inc. (the label recently dropped Murder from their name) without, according to 50, his knowledge or consent. But even worse, there are questions about The Inc.'s involvement in the 2000 shooting of 50 Cent.

An IRS affidavit presented in the feds' ongoing case against The Inc. alleges that label associate Kenneth "Supreme" McGriff was involved in the shooting. And though it wouldn't stand in a court of law, a lyric from 50's "Many Men (Wish Death)" seems to beg the question of The Inc.'s possible involvement—at least in 50's mind. "Slim switched sides on me / Let niggas ride on me / I thought we was cool, why you want me to die, homie?" According to Irv Gotti, Slim, aka Chaz, whom he says used to be 50's manager, had tried unsuccessfully to broker a peace agreement between the two camps. Soon after Farrakhan's "intervention," 50 appeared on Angie Martinez's radio show on New York's Hot 97FM, remarking that, while he is also tired of the beef and has moved on mentally, formally addressing it at this point only helps Ja's situation, something he's not interested in doing. Later, while reflecting on that interview, he's more forthcoming about their feud.

Q: *How have you used the beef with Ja Rule to your advantage?*

A: When you try to destroy a career that doesn't exist, you create one. Their attacks at my credibility made my opportunity even greater. In the fall of '02, Ja had a fan base, but he was so bothered by my coming that he panicked. Every place he went on the radio to talk about the order of protection, I phoned in the next day to respond. There's a difference in our characters that's so visible you'd have to be blind not to see it. While Ja doesn't understand any portion of business, I own G Unit Records. I own G Unit Clothing. I have a sneaker deal with Reebok. I have a video game deal. I have a book deal. These are my deals that I made happen with the people I put in place place. He owns nothing. He wasn't smart enough to make these things happen for himself, even when he was in this position.

He's suffering and can't think straight because he's never been in a *real* situation. Whatever obstacles that are in front of me are put there on purpose. Every situation I've been through has enhanced my character, and when I get past it all, I'll become what God wants me to be.

Q: *What do you think that is?*

A: I don't totally know. When I figure it out, though, everyone will know.

Q: *Do you look at the world differently than you did a year ago?*

A: Absolutely. Now I can actually help some people. I'm going to start a nonprofit organization and do things for the community. Even the shoe, it'll be priced at $80.50, the 50 cents goes to charity. I'm going to donate that to programs in low-income housing. And I'm going to do a certain number of free performances to generate a few million dollars for charity. To do free performances is nothing. I did so many things for free to get in this situation that it's not a big deal.

❖

Riding up Sixth Avenue in a black SUV, 50 lounges in the back seat rocking a bulletproof vest; his bodyguard sits shotgun. 50 peeps a brown van that has been following for at least 10 blocks. A bit annoyed that security didn't catch it quicker, he alerts the driver to the van's presence. Evasive maneuvering manages to shake their pursuers momentarily. He barks at security, letting them know he's not pleased. But he's not really worried, after all, the truck is bulletproof. At a red light near 35th Street, the van catches up, pulling up to the left side of 50's truck. Much to everyone's relief, the van is filled with female teens desperate to catch a photo of their favorite rapper.

Relieved, but still cautious, 50 surveys the scene and notices a black GMC SUV with two middle-aged, mustached white men in the front seat. "Everyone wave to the hip hop police!" he says through a big smile. Laughter erupts, and 50's security guard seconds that the truck in question is most likely carrying members of the NYPD's so-called hip hop task force. It's funny, because these days, 50 very consciously obeys the law. But he's got a pretty good idea why they constantly follow him. "They figure, even if I don't commit the violent act, that I'm a magnet for that stuff anyway," he says.

It sounds like profiling, but the task force's tactic isn't the stupidest strategy ever conceived. On September 10, 2003, the news reported a shooting at a Jersey City, N.J., hotel that appeared to be directed at 50 Cent, who police believed was staying at the hotel. Reports surfaced that 50 had been subpoenaed in relation to the shooting, demanding that he turn himself in for questioning within five days. But the G Unit disappeared for the European leg of their tour in the days that followed. Rumors circulated that Ja Rule, who was shooting a movie within walking distance of the hotel, may have been involved. But it was later reported that the suspected shooter had connections to Lil' Kim, who 50 may have offended the previous evening during another interview on Hot 97. Either way, 50's name was the major news peg.

Q: *What was the Jersey City shooting about?*

A: I wasn't even physically present! I wasn't in the place they said the shooting took place, but the newspaper needs to put me on the scene to make it news. You had the police from Jersey saying I got five days before they put out a warrant. What is that? I still haven't seen the police about that incident. Why is there no warrant out?

Q: *Do you think the element of danger associated with you might keep you from the type of success you want?*

A: I haven't had any incidents in public situations. Not one. I sat in customs for four hours in London because of the things they put in the newspaper about me over here.

Q: *Do you feed off of the negativity?*

A: Yes, I use it for energy. I haven't missed a magazine interview. I haven't missed a radio interview. I think I missed one show, and I've been touring the entire time. It doesn't stop.

Q: *On "Stunt 101" you call yourself a psycho. Do you really believe that?*

A: I don't think I'm crazy—but crazy people don't ever think they're crazy.

Q: *Do you have a conscience?*

A: A little bit, but it goes away.

Q: What makes it go away?

A: Situations.

Q: And you're aware of that?

A: Yeah, it might not really make sense at first, but anger is my most comfortable emotion. You can use that energy for positive if you put it into your next move. So if you hurt my feelings, instead of crying, I get angry.

Q: What put you in the place where anger is your most comfortable emotion?

A: My upbringing, period. When you come from my neighborhood, you don't walk around crying. When you see me acting, in a scene, crying—and it looks real—then you know I'm getting good. I spent my childhood learning not to cry. I've adjusted to situations because I don't want to get killed. Most people just get uptight about a situation and get mad. But for some people, it could be something from last week that's a reason someone gets punched in the eye today. It's still affecting you because you didn't deal with the feelings in the right way.

Q: When was the last time you cried?

A: It's been a while. [*Long pause*] I guess after I got shot.

Q: From the pain?

A: Nah, it was the confusion. Getting shot wasn't the most confusing thing. In my neighborhood, when you're shot, you get up and keep moving. The most confusing thing was being dropped from Columbia Records. I had decided that I was going to write music for a living, and if that's taken away from me then what was I going to do? When you send a nigga back to the 'hood with no direction, you sentence him to die, whether he knows it or not. It's like a prison term, sentencing him to kill somebody or get killed. And the people around me were like, "Goddamnit kid, you almost had it." Like it ain't gonna happen. You have to tune those people out and say, It's gonna happen because I say it is. Then you start doing it on your own.

Q: Do you think anger could be your undoing?

A: I don't know. I do get mad faster now, but I don't worry about it. I do need to deal with my anger. I got to be able to look at situations and take them for what they really are. I get angry at the idea, like, Why would you think you could say what you say? Niggas need to get shot down in the street to remind everyone of what can happen. I get angry at situations now, but I don't act on them.

Not every piece of gossip about 50 Cent that makes the paper is fabricated. In what appeared to be 50's attempt to capitalize on the nation's current fixation with celebrity couples, he invited actress Vivica A. Fox to be his date to the 2003 MTV Video Music Awards. Between his ice and her cleavage, the two turned heads. But after a couple of weeks of romance, during which Fox spoke on the relationship in the press, things soured. Following the World Music Awards in Monaco, 50 said it was over. According to reports, Fox was upset over the attention 50 was receiving from other females at the show.

Q: What prompted you to invite Vivica to the VMAs?

A: I just wanted to hang out. You know what's weird? In entertainment they got rules, like rules of engagement. You gotta keep it secret until you're ready to be engaged, because everything gets altered, and there are rumors, stories, and situations that start to brew early when you're not even sure about that person. It makes things harder.

Q: What was the nature of your relationship?

A: It was cool—friends. We were headed in the direction of possibly a relationship. I don't know how to explain it without being disrespectful.

Q: Why's that?

A: Because of the way I feel about the situation. [*Long pause*] If someone is your friend, there are limits to what you can say about that person.

Q: *You mean in the press or in a personal relationship?*

A: Both. I was saying we're just friends and that's it. She did press for *Kill Bill* and just took that shit to the next level. I think her people did it. They knew that *Today's Black Woman* was going to have us on the cover together. But I ain't ready to be on the cover of a magazine with you. So you're making decisions without me. At that point it makes me feel like it's too much.

I had problems with my son's mother because Vivica mentioned my son. She had a conversation on the radio about me and said something about him—and his moms ain't feeling that shit. It's bad enough that she's a little awkward because I'm not with her at this point. And then it causes problems between me and my son, and he's the most important thing to me.

Vivica's a sweet person. I can't honestly say she's foul or anything bad about her. It's the other things that happened that bothered me so much that I'm not comfortable with it.

Back in the SUV, en route to Interscope's midtown offices, Jay-Z's new song, "What More Can I Say," pushes its way through the track's speakers. The song is new to radio, and 50 immediately asks everyone to be quiet and turn up the music. He listens, seeming to enjoy the record, until it gets to the line "No, I ain't got shot up a bunch of times / Or make up shit in a whole bunch of lines / And I ain't animated like, say, a Busta Rhymes." 50's eyes reveal something between confusion and anger. "Did you hear what he just said!?" he questions, to no one in particular. It's quickly explained that, while certainly a reference to 50, it's not necessarily a dis, and that Jay actually bigged him up on the radio before debuting the song. 50 sinks into his seat thinking, brooding, his fingers folded together. Surprisingly, he soon returns to his more amiable demeanor, whatever concerns he had appearing to roll off his back.

A month from now, he'll take a swing at founding Onyx member Fredro Starr—who's been publicly badmouthing him—during rehearsal for the VIBE Awards. He's a work in progress—not quite out of the woods, but not the same man seen laughing at Summer Jam saying he loved beef. Though he doesn't want to speak about the Jay-Z song on the record, it's clear from his body language that he's not really sweating the line, whatever its intended meaning.

Finally, he has the room to breathe, the room to think. And time to plan for the future of Banks, Buck, and Yayo as well. With a level-headed general in command, their success seems that much more certain. It's hard to imagine the 180-degree turn that 50's life has taken in the last year, but his changing outlook suggests that he may be just as hot, and just as far from where he is now, in another 365 days.

Q: *Now that you have the success and finances, are you happy?*
A: I'm doing things now to get where I want to be. I'm going to do everything an artist could do to elevate himself: be more lyrical, do storytelling, all that. But I'm happy with my progress.

Q: *Where is that place you want to be?*
A: I don't know. I believe when I'm fucked up I can do some shit where you'll be like, "Damn why did he do that?" Because I'm fucked up! But I'm moving towards a cool space where I don't have to do that.

Q: *How is your story going to end?*
A: You never know, unless you're psychic. Nobody anticipates death. Smart people prepare because it's a given, but humans are habit-driven, and we always keep thinking about the future.

SEAN COMBS 23

By Danyel Smith
December 2006

... AND STILL CHAMPION

*Oh, it's a comeback all right. Thirteen roller coaster years in
the game, and Sean "Puffy" Combs still won't stop.*

Google "Diddy" and among a zillion other details, you'll
find that Sean John Combs is a Scorpio. Born in 1969—
the Year of the Rooster. Catholic schoolboy, with a gor-
geous mom, a Baptist grandmother, and a father who was
murdered when Sean was 3. Eventually acquired the nickname Puffy.
Attended Howard University—promoted dance parties there, ran his
own shuttle service—until the pull of N.Y.C. and hip hop yanked him
to Uptown Records, where he was promoted to A&R director. Put
together a streak of hits, including platinum debuts for Jodeci (1991's
Forever My Lady) and Mary J. Blige (1992's *What's the 411?*). He got
fired, then negotiated an Arista Records bankroll with which he started
Bad Boy Records. There was, of course, the Notorious B.I.G. And J.Lo.
And the trial for which he was acquitted of felony gun possession and
bribing a witness. That's the bare bones.

Hang out with the guy, though, and you get the muscle, a little
heart, and a sliver of his Gordian soul. His crew still calls him "Puff."

He rents hotel penthouses for meetings and dips through New York City in his bullet-gray Rolls-Royce Phantom (with driver). One of his Manhattan residences—a chic, arbitrarily furnished crash pad with two assistants, racks and racks of clothes, and fresh fruit in the kitchen— overlooks the lush south end of Central Park. Diddy sweats through his clothes when he performs, even when it's just a taping for a Wal-Mart promo video. When the Rolls rests, Diddy's in his silver Maybach (with driver). He stood before it one recent afternoon, on a corner in New York's Hell's Kitchen, teasing round-the-way kids and signing basketballs with borrowed ballpoints. In slacks, a white tee, and black-on-black shell toes, Diddy could've been one of the hustlers gathered around the subdued spectacle of Diddy's ride—one such in a Lincoln Navigator (with driver!) with front doors tricked out Lamborghini style. From Puff, there was almost an imperceptible nod, then a similar nod in response—a clear case of game recognizing game.

It comes down to the fact that a boy from Harlem and Mt. Vernon, New York, has been making phenomenal impact on hip hop, on music, on fashion, and on the culture for thirteen years. His parties remain bacchanalian. His ego remains gargantuan. He is a charmer; he is profane. He talks so fast, he seems almost to stutter. People say he is wicked. They say his personality is beautiful. From different eras and areas of his life, folks call him an ass, a terror of a negotiator, a grudge-holder, a gem—plus horrifyingly manipulative, the most fun, richer than he's supposed to be, a genius.

Q: *Right now, with Danity Kane, Joc, Cassie—it's all about Bad Boy. But you guys have had some lean years.*

A: Before, I'd say, Yeah, we're back. People would say, "You ain't back, you ain't never went nowhere." You know what? I did go somewhere. I did lose focus. It wasn't like I was twiddling my thumbs. I was doing so much work as a producer. I ran a marathon. I starred on Broadway. I spread myself really thin, and my music suffered. But it was a blessing . . . because when I came back to music, I had clarity. Even for this new album [*Press Play*], the sounds and the melodies and the musicality of it is the perfect combination of sophistication and gutter. It's feel-good music. We had our two and a half years where [Bad Boy Records] fell off a little bit. I'll take that one. But I'm focused now and I'm better than ever.

Q: Did Puff put a bow tie on hip hop?

A: I was trying to show that hip hop can be true to its roots, but that doesn't mean every day you gotta wear a do-rag and white T-shirt [*laughs because he's wearing a do-rag and a T-shirt*]. I wear it every other day. But you gotta make a more gutter album before you can test my gutter. You can't even question my gutter until you do something more gutter. That lane's locked down. I put my stamp on that. At one o'clock in the morning, they're gonna throw on "It's All About The Benjamins," and you're gonna remember. I wanted to bring diversity to the game, and the idea we could do anything. Hip hop is supposed to be all voices. You're supposed to be able to say exactly what's on your mind.

Q: The recent beef with you and 50 Cent, was it real?

A: It was surprising to me, because we never had any bad energy. One of the things about being successful for a long time . . . Bad Boy Records was the first to go through the beefs [*chuckles*]. At Bad Boy we specialize in that.

Q: Do you feel like—?

A: Let me finish. Whenever people do come at me . . . it doesn't really upset me right away. Because I know that I'm a man, and I know that once I see another man, we'll have a man-to-man discussion. And ain't nothing really that deep. So it never really got to the point where it upset me, it got to the point where I was like, I'm going to see him, and we're going to have a conversation man-to-man. I don't think I pose a threat to anybody—because I'm in such a unique lane. To be honest, it's not a lane a lot of hip hop artists want to be in. My lane is celebration. My lane is entertainment.

In hip hop you're going to get tested. That's a part of the game. I'm not immune to it. But I've seen the results of playing that little game—playing with the name-callers—and then you get male egos involved, and crews, . . . so with me, if it ain't a win-win, it ain't really happening. I'm saying, in general, as long as a nigga ain't putting his muthafuckin' hands on me, we're good. He can say whatever he fucking wants to say. I'm out here getting money. Making history. Having me on your mind? If I'm not inspiring you, you're not receiving it the right way. 'Cause that's all it's meant to be—to inspire.

Q: _You won't let Mase record for G-Unit?_

A: I don't have a problem with Mase going to G Unit. I mean, we got some unfinished business we need to take care of. I'd love for him to go off to G Unit or whomever he wants to record for—once our business is straight. I'd never hate on him living his life and doing the deal, but I can't just erase that checks [have been written]. Everybody's adults and professionals, and we need to handle our business. The 50 shit—it wasn't even that big. When we talked, it was like a five-minute conversation, and we moved on.

Q: _Are you in love right now?_

A: I've always been in love.

Q: _Kim Porter?_

A: She's the type of person I'll fall in love with every day.

Q: _When you were involved with Jennifer—_

A: When I was with Jennifer, I got caught up. She was fine. I had my little problems or complaints as far as Kim.

Q: _People thought you and Jennifer were going to get married._

A: I couldn't marry Jennifer. I was in love with Kim that whole time. I'd never stopped being in love with her—you can't fall out of love with somebody who's your friend like that. I definitely left home. I admit I left home. The thing with Jennifer and me was we were so alike. Kim and I are opposite.

Q: Jennifer was somebody who 'got it'?

A: Somebody who got it. But after that runs out, you realize you're really just friends, and you went out, and it's all good.

Q: But you two went through it.

A: The hype can pull you in. Y'all are lookin' good together, and it's feelin' good, and the relationship is genuine . . . but I couldn't commit to her the way she wanted me to. Everybody who ever meets the girl winds up marrying or wanting to marry her. I couldn't be like Cris [Judd] and Ben [Affleck] and Marc [Anthony] and all. A lot of times . . . you think you can leave home—Oh yeah, I'ma leave home, I'm running away, I'm out—I talked that shit. Sometimes you think if people aren't paying attention to you the way you want, or things aren't going the way you want, you can go.

Q: How long have you and Kim been together?

A: Twelve years. She'll say it's eight. Kim never really sweated Jennifer. She was, "Ah, you're playin' yourself . . . you're running around with your little Puerto Rican girlfriend. You'll be back." Kim—just always cool, calm, collected—she knew I was gonna come back, and she was right. Some people just got your number like that. I ain't gonna lie: I'm hard to love. My hat goes off to her or anybody else who's dealt with me, because a lot of your time and attention is really not on that person. A woman deserves to be nurtured and taken care of. Kim taught me that. She . . . taught me how to love. Somebody gave me multiple choices early on—having a smooth working relationship, having a personal life, or being in the music industry. I chose the music industry.

Q: Why?

A: It was such an in-love thing. Like love can make you blind, you know. Some people fall in love with something, and they don't see anything else.

Q: They don't see the bad parts. . . .

A: I wasn't listenin' to nobody. I love so much what I do so . . . that was the choice I made. I knew that if I was gonna be great in this,

I wasn't gonna be great in any of the other things. I had to give my all. I didn't understand balance.

Q: *What would Kim say? You're Kim right now.*

A: Kim would say, That nigga's hard to love, but I love him. She'd say beautiful things. There are a couple of songs on the album about my relationship with Kim: "Partners for Life," a story about how I met her, and this other song called "After Love." I'll be in the studio playing that song for her, like, Baby, I made this song for you. She's like, Yeah. Check this out: You don't have to make no more songs for me. What you could do for me is start being the best man you can be.

Q: *So you're happy for Jennifer and Marc, and Jennifer and Marc are happy for you and Kim.*

A: I'm happy for her. I mean, I wasn't going to marry her, so I never had a problem with it. There was love there, but it just wasn't this type of love. It was two ships passing in the night.

Q: *What is a girl who's had sex with you going to say?*

A: I'm nasty [laughs]. I ain't gonna lie.

Q: *Let's say, mid-'90s? How was it then?*

A: I was buck-fuckin' wild. Beyond ménage a trois. Crazy—you're twenty-something and renting the presidential suite at the Hotel Nikko [now Le Méridien] in Beverly Hills. You got the bathtub filled with champagne and chocolate-covered strawberries. You're renting every Benz from the African guy who rented the cars in L.A. That was a wild time. Then sex became dangerous. You got to remember everything that happened with Eazy-E. Once it happened to Eazy, it was time to slow your ass down. And then all that energy you were spreading becomes a one-on-one thing. And, yeah, my girl right now is very happy. As meticulous as I am with my work, I'm even more meticulous with my lovemaking. I take much more time, and I like to do it for a long time. I like to look my woman in her eyes and kiss her deeply. Sometimes I'm making love and she's like, You gonna save some for the honeymoon?

Q: *Has fatherhood changed you?*

A: Totally changed my life. And I'm having twin girls.

Q: *You look as if you're about to cry right now.*

A: People say, to a so-called a ladies' man or whatever, that when you have girls it changes you. So I was like, What's God trying to tell me by giving me two girls? When I pray every morning, I thank God for showing me what He showed me while I still have a chance to enjoy myself.

The rented islands, the yachts, the private jets. People would say that's pure enjoyment. You can take your family out on a yacht, but if daddy's on the top deck pacing and yelling on the phone and closing deals . . . I'm trying to focus on the things that are price-less, the things I should really be successful at, like being a great boyfriend.

Q: *Are you going to get married?*

A: I would love to get married.

Q: *What's Kim say to that?*

A: I don't want to make that pledge in front of God and not be able to see it all the way out. I didn't grow up around a married family, so it's taking me a bit longer. A lot of guys out there get married, and they still do their thing. I don't want to get married and fail.

Q: *After dealing with acts like Heavy D—who was a kind of light-skinned, more pop version of B.I.G.—what made you look at Christopher Wallace?*

A: When I heard B.I.G., I heard an incredible artist. B.I.G.'s stuff, though it was gutter, wasn't a stretch for me because those were the things going on around me, around all of us. What drew me to him was his artistry, his genius as a writer, the sound of his voice, his uniqueness as far as his approach to records. It was his spirit. He wasn't a man of many words, but when he was on that mic, it was like listening to a miracle.

Q: *Tupac Shakur. First thing that comes to your head.*

A: Genius, that's all.

Q: *The most meaningful moment to pass between you as men—*

A: When he came to my birthday party at [N.Y.C. nightclub] Roseland Ballroom. It became more of a meaningful moment after he passed. People don't know we all used to hang out. Suge [Knight] used to pick me up from the airport when I'd go to L.A. You know how you have that person who comes to pick you up from the airport? Suge was the person. [We didn't] have no car service—we'd just started getting money. And with me and Tupac, it was always a respect thing.

Q: *One of the labels you've been most associated with competitively is Death Row Records, and recently the founder/president Suge Knight was in bankruptcy court. What do you think about that?*

A: I have no thoughts about it . . . don't have any emotion when it comes to him. It's really none of my business. We've got our own lives, our own lanes. People ask a lot, because of everything that's gone on, but he's not someone I think or know about as far as what's going on in his personal or business life.

Q: *You always say you don't hate on anyone—*

A: On nobody. Hate is when you don't give a cat his just due. We're all cut from the same hip hop cloth . . . all represent each other . . . protect each other . . . because there are so many people intimidated by us now politically, economically, socially. This hip hop thing is a threat, beyond a phenomenon. If [hip hop] ever got focused . . . when it does get focused . . . it's the movement that can change the world. We're the bomb ass generation—but for real, we got guns and shit! You see how we can scare a muthafucker. We got tempers and we got guns and we got passion. Our passion is crazy.

Q: *Bad Boy Records is back?*

A: We're the last label standing. A lot of people came and gone.

Q: *Who's come and gone?*

A: Everybody! No disrespect, but to have a label go over ten years? You can go and sell your label—but it ain't your label no more. To have your label exist, and you own it? Def Jam Recordings sold their label. LaFace Records sold their label. It's hard to keep a label going. We get offers every day to buy Bad Boy; I'm not stuck on this thing, like, I'm never going to sell it. But this is still hip hop—you're able to pop shit: We've been here the longest. It's what I'm most proud of. Through all the wars, the ups and downs, the cold times, the hot times, the rumors, the shiny suit shit, whatever—all that—we're still standing. I'm like that old G on your block, and he still getting money. That nigga was getting money back in '68, and he still riding round in a Rolls-Royce. And you wondering, like, How in the hell is he still doin' it? I'm the truest definition of the new Negro—rich, black, intelligent, and powerful. I'm America's worst nightmare.

MARY J. BLIGE 24

By Keith Murphy
March 2007

LOVE NO LIMIT

For 15 years we've been in love with Mary J. Blige. She was featured in the very first issue of VIBE, and there's no way we'd celebrate our 150th issue without her. She's making some of the best music of her career and earning long overdue recognition from the Grammys. In short, Mary is finally taking it to the limit.

Just two years after Mary J. Blige's landmark 1992 debut, *What's the 411?*, the Uptown/MCA publicity machine was presenting her as a changed woman. The soaring track "Be Happy," which anchored her definitive statement album, 1994's *My Life*, said as much: "How can I love somebody else / When I can't love myself enough to know / When it's time to let go?" Even her first VIBE cover read Mary J. Blige . . . Back From the Brink.

Who was she fooling? Many did know, though, about the mythology of Mary: the battles with alcohol and drugs, the abusive relationships, the rampant unprofessionalism, the canceled concerts, the "fuck you" attitude she took towards journalists and even some fans. Hell, the consensus among those in the know was that the Yonkers, N.Y., project chick with the big voice might not make it to see 30. Which is why today a 35-year-old Mary is genuinely taken aback by the news that she's been chosen to grace the cover of VIBE's commemorative 150th issue.

This is vintage Mary J. Blige: fabulous enough to post up in an elegant suite at Los Angeles' posh Beverly Hills Hotel on a windy January evening, but still unashamedly 'hood—to the point where she can stroll into an interview wearing an oversized gray turtleneck, form-fitting black jeans, and flip-flops. You gotta love her.

Q: *What were your thoughts when you heard that you were chosen to grace the cover of VIBE's 150ᵗʰ issue?*

A: Just the fact that I'm still around—to me that's a blessing. I'm really humbled by the whole situation because VIBE has been there for me for many years in my career.

Q: *Okay, so let's go back to the your first VIBE cover in February of 1995. [Pulls out a copy of the now iconic headshot of Mary—in a red hat with red hoodie and red lipstick—looking out from the page somberly with those signature Bambi eyes]. What are your memories of that New York photo shoot?*

A: Mary: [*She takes a look at the cover and goes into an animated burst*] You ready for this?! That day I had been up for about three days just getting high. My nose was running constantly. And I was doing more drugs just trying to stay up until I could get home. I was just angry at the world. My sole thought back then was, I wish a motherfucker *would*.

In '95, I was on a rampage. I just wanted to do anything that would keep my mind off of how ugly I thought I was. I thought everything was my fault. I was just burying my head in alcohol and drugs because I was afraid of success. I was afraid of this thing that was bigger than me so I allowed people to be around me that would lie, steal and cheat right in my face. I was allowing all of this. I was just scared.

Q: *You once described your battles with drugs as fighting through a room filled with shit. How so?*

A: Think about that analogy. Imagine a pile of shit the size of this whole room is piled on you and you have to fight your way up. Now you may be on the mountain of that shit, but you haven't even taken a shower yet . . . You are still dirty. And people can see that. People saw that I was in trouble and I didn't even realize it. You thinking that you can wear a mask and hide everything that you are going through. You can wear the makeup, get your hair done, and wear the long nails, but people can really see through all that.

Q: *How did you even get through it all?*

A: You just have to love and accept yourself. [But back then] I was just thinking, "I hope no one knows that I'm high." It was that simple. The VIBE folks made me feel so comfortable about the whole thing. But it was a very uncomfortable situation.

Q: *What made Mary J. Blige tick back in those days?*

A: All of my insecurities. Nothing really looked good to me. I didn't know how big that period was. It was always like "Okay, this is work. Okay, the cover of VIBE . . ." I just kept my head buried in negativity. And that came through in my music as well.

Q: *But I'm sure not even you would have guessed that 15 years into your career you would be enjoying your most successful year with The Breakthrough. I mean being nominated for 8 Grammys is just crazy, right?*

A: That's the word . . . crazy. I was getting over the insanity of winning nine Billboard Awards [*Laughs*]. My heart was still racing. And then when they were reading the Grammy nominations off, I didn't realize how many nominations I got. All I was hearing was, "Mary J. Blige, Mary J. Blige . . ."

Q: *That must have been a great feeling considering the marginal success of your 2005 album* Love & Life.

A: I mean, I could have accepted all the talk of, "Oh, she's finished, she's washed up, she's 35." But when I did *The Breakthrough* album I went into it like, 'Uh, uh, I ain't finished yet.' My people are not finished with me and I could feel it in my heart. But you have to learn to stop accepting what people expect of you and expect what God expects of you. I was blown away by the first week sales [of *The Breakthrough*]. I didn't know where God was going to lead me, but I knew a greatest hits album was not going to finish my career.

Q: *What were some of the comments that were being made specifically by your label?*

A: It was just strange. The record company was like, "Just put the greatest hits album out" as if I was finished. I remember how people were laughing at me during the *Love & Life* album. I know it wasn't a very good record for me, but wait a minute. I put out one bad album out and I'm done? How disrespectful. That's why someone like Prince is very inspirational.

Q: *In what way?*

A: Prince is an artist that knows he has a following. He doesn't even think about demographics. He just makes music. This man is doing it big. He proves that you don't have to stay an urban artist or an urban AC where they stamp you after you turn 40. When your thought pattern falls into what they expect of you, then you are finished. And that's just it. My thought pattern was way above what the record company was planning for me.

Q: *Plus, it's hard to argue with over 700,000 albums sold in the first week, isn't it?*

A: I'm coming off an amazing album so now I'm like, "Here's your greatest hits." I'm about to go back in the studio and make another album by the grace of God. I don't know if it will do what *The Breakthrough* did. But how about this: It will penetrate who it needs to penetrate. The success of The Breakthrough really solidified me. I feel like right now in my career I don't have to be aggressive because I'm already a leader in who I am. I'm not a yes woman or a follower, but I don't have to stick my chest out. There's a certain power in just being a woman . . . being cool, calm and always in control. You have to command respect. You don't have to try so hard.

Q: *Still some of your longtime fans that have been with you since* **What's The 411?** *and* **My Life** *have said that the new kindler, gentler Mary does not exude the same gritty, emotional feel of your past work. What do you say to them?*

A: Well, there are probably a million fans that said, "Oh, I'm mad at Mary. She's on all this happy girl shit now." I had to risk losing those fans in order to save myself. And when I saved myself, I ended up picking up probably 3 million more new fans. But the some people say, 'Oh, she's not keeping it real—fuck her.' It's like I'm damned if I do and I'm damned if I don't. What those same fans don't know is that people like me suffer the most because we want the best. We suffer because people tear us down because we are trying to get somewhere. They are like, "Come back down to us" and I tell them all the time that music artists are not in the music business to save you. We are in this to go somewhere and if we touch some souls along the way, that's a plus.

Q: *But you do realize that fans take their music idols very seriously?*
A: And that's a problem.

Q: *Are we talking about some of your more overzealous fans who live and die with your songs?*
A: Yes. People get so deep into you that it turns into a cult. So right now, the whole "my man left me and I'm so sad" thing may not be what they need because we all have to grow. I'm still going to give them the old Mary, but I'm trying to wean them off of the pain and suffering. I want to give them a balance. But the most important thing is to make you think. "Good Woman Down," "Take Me

As I Am," and "Baggage" are songs that make you think. You can make them party, but you have to bring something else to the table. My relationship with my fans is very different. They gave me everything. I love them. I'm so thankful in what they've done for me. They've saved my life and they don't even know it.

Q: *Well, on behalf of all the men around the world, I would like to thank you for taking it easy on us.*

A: Of course not all men are bad. My husband [producer Kendu Issacs] is a good man and I didn't know they existed [*laughs*]. I'm not going to beat up our man while the system beats him up. Now, I'll tell him off and let him know that he can't keep hurting my sisters like that. But at the end of the day, I'm not going to beat you down. I want to build you up.

Q: *How much has your marriage influenced the change in your lyrics?*

A: My husband is a good man. We have our problems. But the thing is, you can't depend on one person to save you. In marriage, you learn quickly that he's not going to compliment you all the time and he's not always going to be there. I can't constantly depend on him to make me feel smart or special. I have to feel that about myself first and believe it. Marriage has challenged me to find out my own strength, my own self worth. And that's a lot of work because the truth is devastating. It more than hurts.

Q: *What would the old Mary have done in December of 2006 when you was invited (along with Sidney Poitier, Chris Rock, Tina Turner, and Spike Lee) to travel to South Africa with Oprah Winfrey in celebration of the opening of her all-girls charter school?*

A: The old Mary J. Blige wouldn't have come. The old Mary J. Blige would have hid and would have been scared. She would have caved in to the voices of the people saying, "Oh, she's not keeping it real. She's on the Oprah show." But the new Mary is like, "You know what? Oprah Winfrey is damn near the blueprint for what we all strive to be." We all strive to give back to the community whether it's in Africa or in the 'hood. You don't want to give to a bunch of people that don't really want help. You want to use you influence and power wisely. And I think that's what Oprah does. I mean she gave $40 million to start this school. She did it herself. She's done no wrong to anyone, yet she suffers just as much as we all have. But look at how she is standing today.

Q: *The way you are talking, the same could be said for you.*

A: Well, thank you. Truthfully, early on, I didn't know how much of an influence I was. But what I've done is educate myself. I'm able to stand up straight and say, "I am a proud black woman." And this is coming from someone that's always been told that they were a dumb, nigga bitch. That's what they pegged me as. But right now, I'm a black, educated woman that wants more out of life, and you can hear it in my music.

Q: *The one thing that has stayed the same is your hip hop swagger. Do you still feel like the same young girl that was given the title Queen Of Hip Hop Soul in 1993?*

A: Every day. Hip Hop is in me [she says in a stoic tone]. I would never deny that. Hip hop gave my generation a reason to want to go on and better ourselves. The lyrics in certain hip hop records like KRS-One's "You Must Learn," the impact of a MC Lyte just being a female MC, the impact of Rakim being a 5 Percenter.

Q: *Mary J. Blige, the hardcore hip hop head . . .*

A: *What?!!* [*Laughs*] That's when Special Ed and Biz Markie was making it fun to go to the clubs and dance. EPMD, Run DMC . . . I can go on and on. All that I am comes from hip hop culture. It's imbedded in my being, my walk, my style. I could sit with my legs crossed and you could still see hip hop in me. This is not an act.

Q: *In that same VIBE article you basically called out all of the female acts of that time like SWV, Jade, and Xscape "copycat singers." Do you look back and cringe at comments like that?*

A: That was one of my "oops" moments. Maybe somebody did that interview for me [*laughs*]. But look at the state of mind I was in. Everybody was a threat to me because I didn't love myself. I love all those girls. People like Faith Evans and SWV, they could really sing. Looking back, that was a great time for music.

Q: *It's easy to take that period for granted, but how do you feel when music critics say that the early '90s was one of the last great eras of R&B?*

A: I'm glad that those artists are getting their due. There was an incredible amount of fresh talent at that time. I mean Jodeci was like . . . [*pauses*] There will never be another group like them. They touched you and your pores opened when you watched their shows. Janet Jackson was the truth at what she was doing. She inspired all the girls.

Q: *You were getting your* Rhythm Nation *on?*

A: [*Laughs*] Of course! Janet had every chick dancing. She inspired me like, "I'm going to get the six pack one day." [*Laughs*] But I think that's why I've survived. I grew to have respect for people.

Q: *You've even been called your generation's Aretha Franklin. Are you comfortable with such a lofty compliment?*

A: I'm flattered that they would compare me to such a powerful force. But I always say I can't say that. Aretha is alive and well and still the queen. I'm Mary J., a whole other element. But I'm starting to understand that people hold me dear.

Q: *Even the great Aretha Franklin dealt with critics early in her career who said she didn't always hit the right notes. You've gone through some of the same criticism.*

A: I just feel like when a voice is technically the best, there's nothing in it that you can relate to. People love a technically great singer like a Whitney Houston, who is beyond great. You may even get a standing ovation. But a person with that imperfection like Aretha can emotionally deliver a song that will hit your heart. You are showing people that we are all not so perfect.

Q: *What's your take when you see your influence on vocalists like Keyshia Cole and Fantasia?*

A: All of that just lets me know that when I was running around being insecure about myself vocally, I was really affecting people. I wasn't where I am right now, but that time was where all the young girls got their influence. To me that's a blessing. I knew that, as far as my clothing style and my whole swagger, that that would be an influence. I saw this happening earlier in my career. The female [singers] were starting to wear the sports jerseys and the Timbaland boots just like me.

Q: *It's ironic because a lot of the R&B chicks today look up to you in the same reverence you did for Chaka Khan. They see you as their R&B deity. Are you surprised by all of this?*

A: It's weird, but in a good way. All the stuff that Chaka Khan has been through, I've been through a lot of it too. Aretha's been through a lot as well. They are the reason I exist in a business like this. They suffered and went through everything for us to even have a shot. I tell those girls like Fantasia all the time, "I'm you. I'm that little kid that grew up with a lot of problems. But right now I'm a woman that's still trying to get my life together."

Q: *Of course, those early imperfections were not always embraced. There's one legendary incident in the early '90s where you got booed off the stage during a concert in England. Do you recall that moment?*

A: [*Laughs*] Yeah. Again, that was the old Mary J. Blige. If I had the chance to give her some advice back then, you know what I would say? "You are not professional." The old Mary didn't know how to make decisions, so she didn't hire professional people. She wasn't punctual. I would have told the old Mary to make sure that knew what was the hot songs in London so the DJ could warm them up. I would have said, "Mary, pay attention to detail."

Q: *How ugly did it get?*

A: It was a disaster. When people started shouting negative things at me, I was shouting negative things back at them. They were like, "You bitch!" And I'm going crazy like, "You are not going to call me a bitch and get away with it!" [*She goes back to old-school Mary from Yonkers*].

Q: *The fans had no idea what you were going through.*

A: People didn't understand what was happening behind the scenes. When I was miserable and in abusive relationships with men, I was dying and damn near ready to kill myself. And I had access to money and fame. But then I began to wake up. It was like, "Oh my God, I almost missed all of this!"

Q: *That reminds me of an April 1997 VIBE interview you gave in which you said, "the reason Phyllis Hyman and Billie Holiday are dead is 'cause they thought they could turn to a man or drugs for the love they needed." You were headed down that same road. How did you avoid the tragic ending?*

A: Being a survivor of that, I found that there is no man or drug that can make me feel better than the love God makes you feel. I've depended on drugs and men myself, so I know that for a fact. And God doesn't hold you down like a drug. He helps you to love yourself and take all of that makeup off and say, 'Hey, I like who I am.'"

Q: *Was there a particular moment that brought you closer to God?*

A: It was in 2001. My friend Aaliyah had just died on August 25 and then the World Trade Center was hit on September 11th. I gave my world to Christ. I needed to have a relationship with God. I just saw a young girl die that I just spoke to three weeks ago, a girl that was a beautiful human being and she's dead in a plane crash.

Q: *That will pretty much make you see things differently.*

A: But it's bigger than that. When I was miserable and dying and damn near ready to kill myself. I had access to money and fame. But it didn't make me happy. I was always challenged in my mind and that's the hardest part about trying to get free.

Having a relationship with God is not some fairy tale. You

have to do the work. You have to forgive. For me it's not about using God to judge people. I can't save the world because I'm too busy trying to save myself. I can't fix anything if I'm not fixed. I'm trying to be an example for my people as well, but I want them to understand that Mary J. Blige is still trying to get it together.

CONTRIBUTING
WRITERS

HARRY ALLEN, Hip-Hop Activist & Media Assassin, writes about race, politics, and culture for *VIBE*, *The Source*, *The Village Voice*, and other publications, and has been doing so for over twenty years. As an expert covering hip hop culture, he has been quoted in *The Wall Street Journal*, *The New York Times*, on *National Public Radio*, MTV, VH-1, CNN, the BBC, and other information channels, and is also well known for his association with the seminal band Public Enemy. Allen serves as an adviser to the Archives of African-American Music and Culture at Indiana University, and as the volunteer host/producer of the weekly WBAI NY 99.5 FM radio show, *Nonfiction*. Presently, he is working on a book about architectural design in computer and video games; research which has already been recognized by the Graham Foundation, the Smithsonian Institution's Lemelson Center for the Study of Invention and Innovation, the New York State Council on the Arts, the Architectural League of New York, and the MacDowell Colony. Harry Allen lives in Harlem, NY.

NOAH CALLAHAN-BEVER writes (about) rhymes like he comes from New York City, which he does. This 28-year-old got his start as a teenaged apprentice of the *ego trip* in 1997. VIBE insiders, themselves ego trippers, helped Callahan-Bever conceal his age and secure a job fact-checking at the house that Quincy built. He met 50 Cent during the summer of 1999 when he profiled the rapper for *VIBE*'s spin-off *BLAZE*. Since then, he's interviewed artists innumerable times and climbed VIBE's ladder of success, becoming senior editor and penning several cover stories. Noah still resides in the city, where he's the editor in chief of *Complex* magazine and is coauthoring *50 X 50*, a coffee-table autobiography of 50 Cent.

FARAI CHIDEYA's mother was once offered 30 camels if she gave Farai's hand in marriage. Despite the generous offer, Chideya remains single, is the host of National Public Radio's "News and Notes," founded Popand-Politics.com, and is the author of four books—three published nonfiction titles and one forthcoming novel. *Don't Believe the Hype: Fighting Cultural Misinformation About African Americans* is now in its eighth printing. *The Color of Our Future* explores the changing racial identities of America's teens, and was named one of the best books for teens by the New York Public Library. *Trust: Reaching the 100 Million Missing Voters* shows why half of Americans are cut out of the political system—and what we can do about it. Chideya serves on the Journalism Advisory Committee of the Knight Foundation, which disburses over $20 million in journalism-related grants each year. She has also been a correspondent for ABC News, anchored the prime-time program *Pure Oxygen* on the Oxygen women's channel, and has contributed commentaries to CNN, Fox, MSNBC, and BET.

KAREN R. GOOD was raised in the college town of Prairie View, Texas. After obtaining a B.A. in Print Journalism at Howard University, Karen went on to work full time editorial gigs at *People*, *Seventeen* and *VIBE* where she was Associate Music Editor. In 1997, she quit her day job to become a Writer-At-Large for *VIBE*; wrote the liner notes for Erykah Badu's 1998 live release of her debut album *Baduizm*; and joined the start-up team of *Honey*, an entertainment, fashion and lifestyle magazine for women. Karen has freelanced for publications such as *New York*, *ego trip*, *Details*, *The New York Times Magazine*, *Interview* and *The Village Voice*. Her *VIBE* feature about hip hop groupies ("The Show, The Afterparty, The Hotel") was included in the anthology *And It Don't Stop: The Best Hip Hop Journalism of the Past Twenty-five Years* (Faber & Faber). At the turn of the century, Karen accompanied Mary J. Blige on the singer's first tour of South Africa, and later traveled as a photojournalist to Madras and Mumbai, India. Karen is now working on her first book.

REGINA JONES is a founder of *Soul* magazine, one of the first national black-entertainment magazines. She is currently at work on a biography of Marvin Gaye's widow, Jan Gaye.

JAMES LEDBETTER is deputy managing editor at CNNMoney.com. Prior to that, he was a senior editor at *Time*, working for the magazine's European edition. He is the author of *Starving to Death on $200 Million: The Short, Absurd Life of The Industry Standard* one of the most widely reviewed business books of 2003. Ledbetter is also the author of *Made Possible By . . . : The Death of Public Broadcasting in the United States* and the editor of *Dispatches for* The New York Tribune: *Selected Journalism of Karl Marx*. A former editor-in-chief of *The Industry Standard Europe* and a former staff writer for *The Village Voice*, Ledbetter has written about politics and media for *Slate*, *GQ*, *The American Prospect*, *The Washington Post*, *The Nation*, *The New York Times*, *Mother Jones*, and *VIBE*.

"CHAIRMAN" JEFFERSON MAO (government name: Jeff Mao) began writing about rap music in the early '90s in order to get free promo vinyl from record companies. He's since contributed to such publications as *Rolling Stone*, *Spin*, *Entertainment Weekly*, and *Wax Poetics*, and has written cover features for *Blender*, *The Source*, *Vibe* (where he was a staff "writer-at-large" for three years), and *XXL* (for whom he is currently a senior writer and columnist). Mao is also the one of the "furious five" scribes behind beloved underground humor/hip-hop 'zine, *ego trip* (1994–1998). He is co-author of the Gleason Award–nominated *ego trip's Book of Rap Lists* , and *ego trip's Big Book of Racism!* and a co-executive producer of the acclaimed 2007 VH-1 television series *ego trip's The (White) Rapper Show*. When not plotting further world domination with his *ego trip* cohorts, Mao may be found every other Saturday evening at the controls of his longtime DJ residency: downtown Manhattan watering hole APT (no requests, please). His Internet radio show, "Across 135th Street," may be heard monthly on *www.redbullmusicacademy.com*. He resides in Harlem with his wife, their cats, and his record collection.

KRISTINE MCKENNA is a widely published critic and journalist who wrote for *The Los Angeles Times* from 1977 through 1998. Her profiles and criticism have appeared in *Artforum, The New York Times, Artnews, Vanity Fair, The Washington Post*, and *Rolling Stone;* and she was the recipient of a National Endowment for the Arts administration grant in 1976. In 1991 she received a Critics Fellowship from the National Gallery of Art, and she co-curated the 1998 exhibition *Forming: The Early Days of L.A. Punk* for Track 16 Gallery. In 2001, a collection of her interviews, *Book of Changes*, was published and a second volume *Talk to Her*, followed in 2004. She is archivist for the Charles Brittin Collection of Photography, which was recently acquired by the Getty Research Institute, and is co-editing a monograph on Brittin's photography to be published by Greybull Press in 2006. She was co-curator of *Semina Culture: Wallace Berman & His Circle*, a group exhibition that opened at The Santa Monica Museum of Art in 2005, traveled to five U.S. museums, and was accompanied by a comprehensive catalogue published by D.A.P. She is co-producer and co-writer of *The Cool School*, a documentary directed by Morgan Neville about L.A.'s first avant-garde gallery, and is editing a book about Ferus that will be published by Steidl in the spring of 2008. She is presently writing the first authorized biography of Wallace Berman. Her monograph on the photography of Berman has been published, and she is presently organizing an exhibition of Ann Summa's photographs of the early L.A. punk-rock scene for exhibition at Los Angeles gallery Track 16 in November 2007.

A Brooklyn native, **ROBERT MORALES** has written more than he cares to remember. With artist Kyle Baker, he created Isaiah Bradley, the black Captain America, for Marvel Comics' *Truth: Red, White & Black*. Gratuities are welcome.

JOAN MORGAN, Jamaican-born and South Bronx-bred, is an award-winning journalist, author, and provocative cultural critic. A pioneering hip-hop journalist and entertainment writer, she began her professional writing career freelancing for *The Village Voice* before having her work published by *VIBE, Interview, Ms., More, Spin, Giant* and numerous other publications. Formerly the executive editor of *Essence* and one of the original staff writers at *VIBE*, Joan Morgan is the author of *When Chickenheads Come Home to Roost*—a fresh, witty, and irreverent book that marks the literary debut of one of the most original, perceptive, and engaging young social commentators in America today. Her work appears in numerous college texts, as well as books on feminism, music and African-American culture. She currently teaches "The History of Hip-Hop Journalism" at Duke University.

KEITH MURPHY is *VIBE*'s senior associate editor, a native of Southside Chicago, and a lover of Brandy Alexanders. Prior to joining the staff of *VIBE*, he served as editor-at-large of *King* magazine for five years. Mr. Murphy's work has been published in such publications as *Complex, The Source, XXL,* and the men's lifestyle book *Manifest X.O.* He has appeared as a guest on FOX's *The O'Reilly Factor* as well as BET. Over his ten-year career, Mr. Murphy has interviewed iconic sinners (Rick James) and saints (Sugar Ray Leonard); controversial leaders (Minister Louis Farrakhan); maverick film makers (Quentin Tarantino); hip hop power brokers (Jay-Z); great white hopes (Eminem) and of course hip hop soul royalty (Mary J. Blige). He's still chasing his ultimate story.

KEVIN POWELL is widely considered one of America's most important contemporary voices. Legendary feminist Gloria Steinem proclaims that "as a charismatic speaker, leader, and a very good writer, Kevin Powell has the courage . . . to be fully human, and this will bring the deepest revolution of all." Powell is a political activist, poet, journalist, essayist, hip-hop historian, public speaker, and entrepreneur. A product of extreme poverty, welfare, fatherlessness, and a single mother-led household, he is a native of Jersey City, New Jersey, and was educated at New Jersey's Rutgers University. Powell is a longtime resident of Brooklyn, New York, and it is from his base in New York City that he has published seven books. Powell is presently at work on a new collection of essays, *Letters to Young America* (2008); his second volume of poetry, *No Sleep 'Til Brooklyn* (2008); and his childhood memoir, *homeboy alone*, slated for 2009. Additionally, Powell is compiling *The Kevin Powell Anthology* (2010), which will highlight the first two decades of his literary career. Powell has written essays, articles, and reviews for publications such as *Esquire*, *Newsweek*, *The Washington Post*, *Essence*, *Rolling Stone*, *Ebony*, *The Amsterdam News*, and *VIBE*, where he was a founding staff member and served as a senior writer, interviewing and profiling—among many others—the late Tupac Shakur on numerous occasions. Today, Powell is pursuing a Masters of Fine Arts degree in creative writing at Queens University of Charlotte, and is planning to run for the United States Congress in Brooklyn, New York.

ISHMAEL REED is the author of novels, essays, plays, and one libretto. He has won prizes in every medium, including a John D. MacArthur award, an Otto Award for Political Theater, a Robert Kirsch lifetime-achievement award from *The Los Angeles Times*, and a Langston Hughes medal. In 2007 he received the Gold Medal from the Commonwealth Club of San Francisco for his book of poetry *New And Collected Poems, 1964–2006*.

A novel and a book of poetry of his have been nominated for National Book Awards. He is also a songwriter whose songs have been recorded and/or performed by Little Jimmy Scott, Taj Mahal, Eddie Harris, Bobby Womack, Cream's Jack Bruce, and Mary Wilson, formerly of The Supremes. In June 2007, Cassandra Wilson recorded two of his songs on the album *Sacred Ground*, featuring David Murray. On the CD *For All We Know*, by the Ishmael Reed Quintet (featuring David Murray), Ishmael Reed made his debut as a jazz pianist.

VERNON REID is perhaps best known as the founder and primary songwriter of the rock group Living Colour. He was named #66 on Rolling Stone's "100 Greatest Guitarists of All Time." In 1985, Reid co-founded the Black Rock Coalition with journalist Greg Tate and producer Konda Mason. Through the BRC, Reid hoped to counter the pigeonholing and marginalization of black musicians. He released *Mistaken Identity*, his first solo album, in 1996; and has collaborated with the choreographers Bill T. Jones on "Still/Here" and Donald Byrd on "Jazztrain." He performed "Party 'Til The End of Time" at the Brooklyn Academy of Music (BAM) with The Roots, an end-of-the-millennium tribute featuring the music of Prince's album *1999*. He also composed and performed "Bring Your Beats," a children's program for BAM. Reid has also produced records by Resort (a Mexican hard-rock group) and two Grammy-nominated albums: *Papa* by the great African singer Salif Keita, and *Memphis Blood: The Sun Studio Sessions* by James "Blood" Ulmer. Reid composed the score for the celebrated documentary *Ghosts of Attica* (directed by Brad Lichtenstein), which aired on Court TV in the fall of 2001 and has been featured at several film festivals. Reid composed the score for the film *Paid In Full*, directed by Charles Stone III and released by Miramax in the fall of 2002. Reid and DJ Logic, calling themselves "The Yohimbe Brothers," released an album in September 2002 called *Front End Lifter*. Vernon is also the music supervisor for the film *Mr. 3000* starring Bernie Mac and directed by Charles Stone III; *Mr. 3000* was released in the fall of 2004. Vernon's record with Masque (Leon Gruenbaum—keyboards, Hank Schroy—bass and Marlon Browden—drums), an instrumental album entitled *Known Unknown*, was released in April 2004 on Favored Nations Records. The Grammy Award–winning guitarist and his band Masque recently recorded a collection of 13 new songs. *Other True Self*, a sonic kaleidoscope, a tumble of colors, and a whirl of astonishing visions that exposes a vivid personal landscape and illuminates all sides of Vernon Reid, was released on April 18, 2006.

CHRIS ROCK is an award-winning comedian, actor, and director. Born in South Carolina and raised in Brooklyn, Rock first appeared on *Saturday Night Live* in 1990. In 1991, he portrayed the crack addict Pookie in *New Jack City.* His 1996 HBO special *Bring the Pain* established him as one of the world's sharpest comedians. He is the writer and director of the film *I Think I Love My Wife* and executive producer of the UPN TV series *Everybody Hates Chris.*

A former editor-at-large for Time, Inc., **DANYEL SMITH** joined *VIBE* in 1993 and was appointed Music Editor a year later. In 1996, she was awarded a National Arts Journalism Program fellowship and was appointed Editor-In-Chief upon her return, serving until 1999. She rejoined *VIBE* in 2006 where she is still Editor-in-Chief of VIBE and VIBE Vixen. Smith has written for *Elle, Time, Cosmopolitan, Essence, The Village Voice, The New Yorker, Entertainment Weekly, Rolling Stone, Spin, The San Francisco Bay Guardian,* Condé Nast Media Group, and *The New York Times.* Smith is the author of the *San Francisco Chronicle*–bestselling novel *More Like Wrestling,* and she wrote the introduction for the *New York Times*–bestseller *Tupac Shakur.* Her second novel, *Bliss,* was published in 2005. Smith comments regularly on pop culture for VH-1, WNYC, and CNN. She holds a Master of Fine Arts in creative writing from the New School University.

GREG TATE was a staff writer at *The Village Voice* from 1987–2004. His writings on culture and politics have been published in *The New York Times, The Washington Post, The Nation, Artforum, Rolling Stone, Premiere, Essence, Suede, The Wire, One World, Downbeat, JazzTimes,* and *VIBE.* He was recently acknowledged by *The Source* magazine as one of the "Godfathers of Hip-hop Journalism." Tate has also written for The Museum of Modern Art, The Whitney Museum, ICA Boston, ICA London, Museum of Contemporary Art Houston, The Studio Museum In Harlem, The Gagosian Gallery, and Deitch Projects. His books include *Everything but the Burden: What White People Are Taking from Black Culture* (Harlem Moon/Random House, 2003); *Midnight Lightning: Jimi Hendrix and The*

Black Experience (Acapella/Lawrence Hill, 2003); and *Flyboy in the Buttermilk; Essays on American Culture* (Simon & Schuster, 1993). Next year Duke University Press will publish *Flyboy 2: The Greg Tate Reader*. For Penguin Books, Tate is currently completing *The 100 Best Hip-Hop Lyrics* for a fall '07 release. Tate is also musical director for the 20-plus-member conducted-improvisation ensemble Burnt Sugar: The Arkestra Chamber, who regularly perform in Europe, Canada, and the United States. The band has released 12 albums on their own TruGROID imprint since 1999. Their recordings and live performances have won them enthusiastic acclaim from *Rolling Stone*, *Downbeat*, *The Wire*, *The Village Voice*, *Straight No Chaser*, and *The New York Times*. They can be reached via www.burntsugarindex.com

EMIL WILBEKIN is a renaissance man. Best known for his twelve years of work at *VIBE* magazine, where he exposed the diversity of urban music and culture to the masses, defined hip-hop lifestyle, and helped build the franchise from publishing into multi-media. As editor-in-chief of *VIBE*, Wilbekin garnered the 2002 National Magazine Award for General Excellence, helped build the magazine's circulation to 825,000, and executive-produced the first annual *VIBE Awards* on UPN (one of the highest-rated programs in the network's history). Aside from his publishing background, Wilbekin also worked as Vice President of Brand Development at Marc Ecko Enterprises, consulting on media and creative projects; oversaw the Marc Ecko Cut & Sew collection; served as style guru for *Complex* magazine; and executed "Style & Sound," a collaboration with Ecko and the CFDA's Fashion Target's Breast Cancer initiative. He has also done consulting work for Sean John, AXE, and the Estabrook Group; and styled music videos for Mary J. Blige. He frequently appears on VH-1, BET, CNN, and the BBC commenting on hip-hop and youth culture. He's contributed to the following books: VIBE's *Hip-Hop Divas*, Ben Watts' *Big Up*, and Jamel Shabazz's *Last Sunday in June*. A graduate of Hampton University (where he was inducted into the Mass Media Arts Hall of Fame) and Columbia University's Graduate School of Journalism, Wilbekin is currently a freelance writer and consultant who is also working on a screenplay and a book. His writing has appeared in *The New York Times*, *The Chicago Tribune*, *Essence*, *Rolling Stone*, *Teen Vogue*, *Paper*, *Inked*, *Out*, and *Bleu*. He's a blogger/reporter for Lebron.msn.com, a Microsoft website devoted to LeBron James. He serves as a contributing editor at *Paper*, has a column in Complex entitled "Style Guru," contributes to AOL Black Voices, and is editorial director of *Bleu*. He also serves on the Board of Directors for Lifebeat: The Music Industry Fights AIDS.

JOE WOOD was a young writer and editor of extraordinary accomplishment and promise who was last seen hiking on Mt. Rainier in July 1999. His disappearance at age 34 sent shockwaves through the communities to which he belonged. He had already edited one stellar anthology, *Malcolm X: In Our Own Image*, and in his work as an editor at The New Press (one of only two black male editors then working at a major New York publishing house), he had acquired and edited such important works as *The Race to Incarcerate* by Marc Mauer (with The Sentencing Project), about America's crazed prison system, and the novel *Another Way to Dance* by Martha Southgate, which won the Coretta Scott King Genesis Award for best first novel for young adults in 1996. Wood had also written reams of dazzling essays and reportage for publications like *The Village Voice*, *The New York Times Magazine*, *Transition*, and *VIBE*. In an effort to honor Joe's memory, to perpetuate his legacy, and to keep alive his work as an author, editor, and supporter of other writers, his family, friends, and colleagues came together to memorialize him with the Joe Wood, Jr. Fund.